The Paradox of Intellectual Property in Capitalism

João Romeiro Hermeto

The Paradox of Intellectual Property in Capitalism

palgrave
macmillan

João Romeiro Hermeto
Dipartimento di Studi Umanistici
Università degli Studi di Pavia
Pavia, Italy

ISBN 978-3-031-49966-1 ISBN 978-3-031-49967-8 (eBook)
https://doi.org/10.1007/978-3-031-49967-8

This Palgrave Macmillan imprint is published by the registered company Springer Nature Switzerland AG.
The registered company address is: Gewerbestrasse 11, 6330 Cham, Switzerland

Paper in this product is recyclable.

Preface

In 2013, while researching capitalist relations, the topic of private appropriation of human knowledge in the form of intellectual property seemed to me a secondary topic. During my MA and PhD in Germany, the question of epistemology increasingly seemed to be umbilically connected to the question of the production of human life. As labour and particular forms of appropriation—not only of nature but also of products from labour activities—could not be detached from the issue of production and appropriation of knowledge, investigating their relationship under contemporary capitalist relations of social production and reproduction became unavoidable.

The first manuscript of this book was conceived in German and was profoundly more philosophically laden, rendering it relatively inaccessible to a broader audience. Changing it to English was thus the obvious decision. However, at the time, what was not evident to me was the need to change both the content and mode of presentation. It goes without saying that this is not a short literary book but rather one that deals with practical social matters from a scientific point of view, based on the method of immanent critique; therefore, it demands a more in-depth involvement from the reader. The subjects presented are nevertheless mundane and very topical, which should help connect with anyone who is slightly familiar with some of the struggles of present-day societies, such as digital surveillance, immense political-economic power of technological and pharmaceutical companies, changes and pressures in the labour market due to mechanisation and digitalisation, etc.

Palgrave Macmillan's acceptance of publishing this book was based on the agreed condition that I change the first section of the original manuscript, which provided a philosophical discussion of property of some of the greatest philosophers and schools of thought. The new version ought to present, instead, the contemporary debate on intellectual property. This change opened a Pandora's box. The topics and scope treated by intellectual property theorists are so vast that after I had provided my analysis, an entire new book emerged. The problem was that it did not fit with the rest of my analysis. Hence, I rewrote the entire second part of the book to match both the style and the contemporary discussion of intellectual property. It became much more complex and topical. The problem I was then faced with was that I had two books, and the first should be contained in the second, but in its entirety, and combining both would render it far too extensive.

As each book contains three main sections (Chaps. 2, 3, and 4), I decided to introduce these sections of the present book with a summary of the corresponding sections of the other manuscript. For instance, the historical analysis of the genesis of intellectual property, which constitutes a considerable part of the third chapter of the unpublished manuscript, briefly introduces the present book; the second chapter of the former, dealing with contemporary intellectual property theory, concisely establishes a basis for the third chapter of the latter; and chapter four of the former, dealing with the fraught intellectual property relations, briefly familiarises the reader with some crucial dynamics depicted in the fourth chapter of latter.

In this fashion, the present book combines the entire content of both books while abiding by the condition agreed upon of presenting crucial elements of contemporary intellectual property theories before diving deeper into a more critical assessment under Marxist immanent critique.

Having performed the bulk of the research in Germany and Italy and not having full access to English translations (in some cases non-existent), I have chosen, in the case of some literature, to refer to the works in the original language and translate them myself. For instance, I have studied and accessed both Hegel's and Marx and Engels' writings in German with publications that compile the totality of their works. Even if MEW (Karl Marx Friedrich Engels Werke) does not contain all the writings, the continuation of the remaining publications was done by MEGA (Karl Marx Friedrich Engels Gesamtausgabe), which was undertaken by the same publishing house, namely, Dietz Verlag Berlin; however, the work of MEGA was left unfinished and failed to include all the works; only after resuming with MEGA^2 under the responsibility of IISG (Internationaal Instituut voor Sociale Geschiedenis) in Amsterdam, which is still an ongoing project and (as of today) not yet finished (Rojahn, 2001), was it continued. In this sense, by proving a cohesion of totality, such compendiums enable a more nuanced work for both myself as a researcher and the reader who might want to refer back to the original publications. Another element that enhances the need to refer back to the originals is that translations are always interpretations that sometimes (unintentionally) deflect from the original meanings. A classic example is Marx's use of the term *Klassenkampf.* While in English it is commonly translated as class struggles, in German struggle is singular while classes in plural, that is, *struggle of classes*. In the foreword of the fourth Italian edition of his work *The Society of the Spectacle*, Guy Debord explicitly criticises the translations of his work and the problems they bring (Debord, 1997, p. 145). Because they may significantly change the meaning of terms, I have opted, wherever I could, to refer to the originals, at the risk of committing deviations myself.

An additional remark concerning some reference literature involves works researched and referred to directly from eBooks. While some digitalised books, usually PDFs, perfectly mirror their corresponding physical copies, others are offered in formats such as .epub, .mobi, .azw, or .iba, which digitally adapt to the reading device to fit the screen, making it challenging to include quotes and provide consistent references. In these cases, I have opted to merely allude to the content of the book, referring to its title and author but avoiding quotations altogether. Some examples of works I have only accessed in these types of files were Vandana Shiva's *Biopiracy*, Mariana Mazzucato's *The Value of Everything*, and William I. Robinson's *Global Civil War*.

Finally, I would like to thank all the people who supported this project. Special thanks to my family, who always support me emotionally and psychologically with their care and love. To my German "family" also for all their love and support during my nine years living in Germany. To all my friends who give me more strength and encouragement than they might know. To Maria Rita Guedes, who helped with proofreading, improving the entire manuscript with a very meticulous, professional, and thorough work. To all the labourers—farmers, nurses, garbage collectors, teachers, bureaucrats, etc.—whose work builds the material and social basis not only for this work but for all our lives. To Prof. Dr. Birger Priddat and Prof. Dr. Matthias Kettner for endorsing my philosophy studies and PhD research at the Universität Witten/Herdecke. To Prof. Dr. Anne Eusterschulte, who warmly welcomed me as a postdoctoral candidate at the Freie Universität Berlin. To Prof. Dr. Luca Vanzago and Prof. Dr. Giuseppe Cospito for hosting me as a visiting scholar at Pavia University and supporting the endeavour of writing this book. Additionally, to the whole library staff of Pavia University and the state library, which have become my second home while I was writing this book. Finally, I want to thank my book editor Brendan George and his colleagues for supporting and believing in this project and the anonymous peer reviewer whose critiques and suggestions conferred upon this book a much richer and more complex analysis, culminating in the present book, as well as a still unpublished manuscript.

It goes without saying that any possible errors and shortcomings in this book are my sole responsibility. However, I hope I have managed—albeit in the slightest—to contribute not only to the scientific community but most importantly to society, in helping build a tomorrow in which human exploitation and domination may become a thing of the past.

Pavia, Italy João Romeiro Hermeto

References

Debord, G. (1997). *A Sociedade do Espetáculo*. Contraponto.

Rojahn, J. (2001). Publishing Marx and Engels after 1989: The Fate of the Mega. *Journal of Socialist Theory, 29*(1), 196–207. https://doi.org/10.1080/03017600308413467

Contents

Acronyms

AI	Artificial Intelligence
AOSP	Android Open Source Project
BRR	Book Rights Registry
CALO	Cognitive Assistant that Learns and Organises
CIA	[US-American] Central Intelligence Agency
DARPA	[US-American] Defense Advanced Research Projects Agency
DNA	Deoxyribonucleic Acid
DOS	Disk Operation System
EPO	European Patent Office
GATT	General Agreement on Tariffs and Trade
GDP	Gross Domestic Product
GPS	Global Positioning System
IMF	International Monetary Fund
IPC	[US-American] Intellectual Property Committee
KBE	Knowledge-Based Economy
MPS	Mont Pèlerin Society
NATO	North Atlantic Treaty Organization
NIH	[US-American] National Institutes of Health
NSA	[US-American] National Security Agency
OS	Operating System
PR	Public Relations
USPTO	United States Patent and Trademark Office
R&D	Research and Development

RNA	Ribonucleic Acid
SRI	Stanford Research Institute
TNC	Transnational Corporation
TNS	Transnational State
TRIPS	Trade-Related Aspects of Intellectual Property Rights Agreement
WEF	World Economic Forum
WIPO	World Intellectual Property Organization
WTO	World Trade Organization

1

Introduction: Breaking Free from Private Control over Knowledge

1.1 Introduction: Breaking Free from Private Control over Knowledge

At the end of his book on *Piracy*, Adrian Johns draws attention to the now almost 20-year-old project, which was then announced by Google, called the Library Project. This episode gives a remarkable representation of the contemporary phase of the constant transformation of social property relations. With the advent of the Digital, creating a universal library became a much more palpable dream. However, from the outset, it was not free from contradictions and challenges. For one, copyright was a not inconsiderable issue that had to be addressed. Second, some of the very institutions involved—namely, some university libraries—had been caught up and promoted the logic of the privatisation of knowledge. This is antithetical to such a project, aimed at the universalisation of knowledge, not to mention Google, whose very *raison d'être* contains the most significant contradiction of capitalism—social production and private appropriation—and elevates it to new heights.

In appearance, this was a project to liberate and universalise knowledge; in practice, it represented a battle to assert control over it, enabling the extraction of surplus-value as well as immense power over social

J. Romeiro Hermeto, *The Paradox of Intellectual Property in Capitalism*,
https://doi.org/10.1007/978-3-031-49967-8_1

relations. On the one hand, the existing system of "copyright could remain inviolate only at the expense of its own purpose of enhancing the public good" (Johns, 2009, p. 512); on the other, the Library Project was developing a workaround which "left intact the problems that had led to its formulation" (Johns, 2009, p. 514). An institution called the *Book Rights Registry* (BRR) was announced to stand up for copyright holders, a combination of the old registry system (see *infra*) with digital antipiracy tactics. This change in social property relations was not a move away from the privatisation of knowledge but, instead, epitomised a battle and, simultaneously, a shift of and within private power.

Presented as the new freedom, extreme dependency on a single private entity—namely, Google—had been created. A vast array of copyrighted but out-of-print books as well as orphan works (Boyle, 2008, p. 287)—whose copyright owners are unknown—were subjected to this singular and monolithic control. Uncountable hours of socially produced knowledge were now under private control. The immanent capitalist contradiction, which is expressed by the fact that it constantly privately appropriates past and present social labour, gains a new inflexion with the dawn of the Digital. Google not only benefits from socially conceived knowledge in general, but its foundational infrastructure was shaped by public funds and social effort; furthermore, its everyday activities vastly depend not only on collective work coordinated within its boundaries but also, not less importantly, on the prosumer labour performed by the billions of unpaid labour activities engendered by users.

Google's privatisation of knowledge contains different layers. First and foremost, it is dependent on private ownership of the means of production; second, despite its technological apparatus, it also relies on wage labour, which transforms and produces Google's value; third, it remains contingent on the extraction of surplus-value, which now overflows from its immediate wage labour-force to also an unpaid workforce; fourth, not only does its foundational dimension need the capitalist state, but the relationship between Google and the state remains closely intertwined (for instance, state institutions such as the CIA or the Pentagon); fifth, it is deeply reliant on the advertisement propaganda apparatus; sixth, sustaining this process, in which knowledge is expropriated from individuals and societies and appropriated for profits, requires a constant change of perception and behaviour—for many people, "Google is steadily *becoming* the internet" (Assange, 2016, p. 46); finally, the very promotion of knowledge as something ubiquitous in order to secure profit simultaneously destroys the value of the production of knowledge (see *infra*).

According to the United States Patent and Trademark Office (USPTO), a not inconsiderable portion of the US-American economy revolves around *intellectual property*$_{(private)}$, representing 7.8 trillion dollars of the 2019 GDP (Toole et al., 2022, p. 3). According to the study, US-American industries accounted for 41% of the economic endeavours and comprised 63 million or 44% labour positions. "Output in the IP-intensive industries grew at roughly the same rate as the entire domestic economy during the previous five years, with the exception of the copyright-intensive industries, where output grew at a faster rate than the domestic economy" (Toole et al., 2022, p. iii). The report also shows a distribution of industrial sectors which are *intellectual property*$_{(private)}$-intensive: manufacturing; wholesale and retail trade; information; finance, insurance, real estate, and leasing; technical, management and administrative professional services; education and health care services; and arts, entertainment and recreation (Toole et al., 2022, p. 6). Still from the USPTO, a 2022 economic note states: "In 2019, of the 103 industries identified as commodity-exporting industries, 76 were IP-intensive. These 76 industries accounted for $1.31 trillion or 79% of all U.S. commodity exports in 2019. In fact, 18 of the 20 top exporting industries were found to intensively use intellectual property" ('Exports and Imports by U.S. IP-Intensive Industries', 2022). Therefore, it is fundamental to recognise that societies are undergoing at least a phenomenological change in social property relations. However, how much and in which ways does this transformation impact social relations? Which existential conditions remain the same, which are metamorphosing, and which are being dissolved?

The ongoing artificial intelligence (AI) "revolution" is catalysing this process, and these questions can no longer be avoided. With AI making many wage labour positions redundant, with science being generally applied to production, social relations based on private property attain a qualitative new paradoxical paradigm.[1] Private appropriation constantly denotes an anachronic social condition, and power relations lose their ontological determinations. The contradiction between social production and private appropriation becomes so accentuated that complementary power and coercion systems must be implemented to sustain the capitalist mode of production. Going beyond such social arrangements based on domination is hence not only a utopia but also a necessary condition. Forcing old structures with no ontological basis upon collective social life produces enormous social tensions, which emerge in different forms. While knowledge and material productions in the twenty-first century epitomise previously unimaginable degrees of development, which could render starvation, poverty, most diseases, conflicts and wars over resources, economic competition, and social control all things of the past, capitalism not only sustains but intensifies the plethora of existing tensions.

To name a few phenomena: a significant portion of the world's population is becoming surplus humanity and managed by the logic of slums which are no longer a by-product, but produced and reproduced by design (Davis, 2006); precarity and inequality have invaded the core of capitalism and countries like the Unites States and Germany are increasingly suffering its consequences (Alvaredo et al., 2018; Chancel et al., 2022; Nachtway, 2018; Pfeffer, 2018); the most powerful capitalist society is falling apart not only economically but also socially, as its social values are obliterated behind mass problems of opioid and gambling addictions, sadism, hate, suicide, corruption, evictions, and the debacle of social bonds (Hedges, 2018); besides vast amount of social and economic resources being redirected towards bottomless military outwards expansion, militarism is also expanding inwards to be part not only of culture but also whole police apparatuses (Robinson, 2020; Vitale, 2018), while the economic crisis of 2008 has unveiled the outstretches of financialisation in the world economy, its grips are even broader than most people imagined, for financialisation has become so intertwined with the real capitalist economy, that currently one cannot be decoupled from the other without their mutual ruin (Hudson, 2015); and finally, a

[1] An interesting example is Achim Szepanski's book *Financial Capital in the 21st Century*, which was translated from German to English by the digital machine engine *Deepl* (Szepanski, 2022).

phenomenon that has become part of every person who owns a computer, tablet, or smartphone with Internet connection is the overarching surveillance being imposed to guarantee social control and economic profits (Zuboff, 2019).

Being one of the most crucial tools for contemporary social control, as it should become clear throughout the analysis of this book, *intellectual property*$_{(private)}$ is commonly regarded as something abstract. Sharing this perception, Peter Drahos sees it as "a fragile form of power, for it relies on the acceptance of legal norms and on the efficacy of the enforcement mechanisms that support those norms" (Drahos, 2016, p. 195). He conceives this power as a form of threat power because it relies on the law. "Threat power which is so inextricably linked to law is perhaps the most dangerous kind of power for a society to contemplate creating and facilitating because it derives legitimacy from the law itself" (Drahos, 2016, p. 195). Moreover, this danger often goes unnoticed because the cult of private property in liberal ideologies primarily conceives it as a form of liberty and a prerequisite for freedom. However, describing this does not suffice; it is crucial to explain its existence from the point of its determinations; that is, why has *intellectual property*$_{(private)}$ been needed in reality?

Intellectual property theorists have thus far broadly failed to relate *intellectual property*$_{(private)}$ to capitalism. Mistaking cause and effect across the board, these thinkers assume the legal system as if it were the originator of *intellectual property*$_{(private)}$. This analytical failure is the product of not only limitations imposed by ideological constraints but also theoretical shortcomings that play a major role in limiting the apprehension of social property relations. For example, the lack of differentiation between personal and production property; property and private property; social from privatised appropriation; and the list goes on, as briefly presented below still in this introductory section, before it can be thoroughly discussed along the broader discussion of this book. All this hinders a critical assessment of intellectual appropriation which is merely assumed as a feature established by legal relations, that is, when the legal system is not itself hypostasised and presented as a thing-in-itself, also deprived of ontological dimensions. In most cases, not only intellectual property but also any legal dimension are presented as something merely abstract.

This book neither merely repeats the theoretical assessments of intellectual property theories nor is it constricted within the walls of a singular school of thought. It is evident that the present book is based on immanent critique; however, it seeks to learn from multiple theories and approaches, presenting a rich and multifaceted understanding of the production, appropriation and reproduction of knowledge. Knowledge is consequently not regarded as merely the phenomenological forms of copyright, patent, and trademark. Instead, it gains a twofold representation: a general condition in which humanity has made use of knowledge throughout history to guarantee and assert its own existence, and a particular condition under the capitalist mode of production. The latter, however, is neither homogenous nor fixed. As capitalist relations mutate and evolve, so do property relations and, accordingly, intellectual appropriation.

Contemporary intellectual property will only be thoroughly understood when it achieves full maturity, or rather, only after it has been superseded by a distinguished new form of intellectual property. Leaning on Marx and Marxism to apprehend capitalist legalities neither exhausts the understanding of capitalism nor capitalist categories. Nevertheless, they certainly provide a crucial methodological basis for analysing capitalist relations. On the other hand, the existing literature seems colossal, yet hardly any contains a critique basis of capitalism. Needless to say, critique here means revealing the hidden essence behind the phenomena; furthermore, it means unveiling the limits of the theory and the possibilities of a concrete reality or determined social relations. The choice of being receptive to interdisciplinarity encompasses both merits and demerits. On the one hand, its virtue lies in the fact that it brings more connections, more nuances, more perspectives, and more complexity to the analytical body; therefore, it fosters the establishment of the notion of totality; on the other, it has the disadvantage of not addressing each point thoroughly, leaving flanks opened to critique and even criticism. Nonetheless, it cannot be accused of lacking depth.

This book does not aim to perform a moral critique. If the reader understands the ongoing analysis in moral terms, either I have failed in my task of representing the immanent critique, or the reader is limitedly interpreting the coming lines through his or her own moral lenses. By the same token, it is essential to distinguish between critique and criticism. While the latter has a negative connotation, or at least the intention of passing judgement, the former intends to provide an examination, an analysis from the standpoint of a dialectical relationship between the dynamic of internal contradictions presented by the object under investigation as well as between the object of analysis and its relationship with its external spheres of mutual influence. For instance, the immanent critique of intellectual property is not based on a juxtaposition of several theories of law or, conversely, economic theories on the topic. On the contrary, it demands the investigation of its existential conditions. Insofar as the concept of intellectual property does not exhaust an understanding of the matter, intellectual property must be investigated as a social relation that not only emerges historically but also constantly changes its essence, for here, essence is not understood as an intrinsic metaphysical quality but rather as the expression of real social movements. Accordingly, the present immanent critique of intellectual property depicts the existing action of intellectual property in its complexity, nonetheless maintaining the awareness of the limitation, better still, of the ontological impossibility of providing a complete and exhaustive understanding of intellectual property. The reason is twofold: first, intellectual property as a movement, a social relation, is constantly changing; therefore, the current effort is to reveal its tendency within contemporary reality; and second, any theoretical analysis can never exhaust or obtain a comprehensive understanding of objective reality; if reality and its grasp were to collapse into a single synthesis, then theory would become obsolete, for theory would become reality, and reality would be identical to theory.

As mentioned, intellectual property theories have thus far neglected differentiating between property and appropriation; private and non-private property; property and intellectual property; the totality and isolated parts of property; the tangible and intangible; first and second paradox; general human and capitalist particular dimensions; science before and after capitalism; the abstract right as originator and legitimator; appreciation and destruction of the value of knowledge; premise and result; among other elements. Some of these elements are analysed in isolation in some intellectual property theories; nevertheless, the necessary scrutiny that understands these elements and their contradictions as interdependent parts of a totality is nowhere to be found.

This book concretises one general and another particular research. On the one hand, it is part of broad research on capitalist relations, which entails multiple interdependent dimensions; on the other, it gives representation to one particular aspect of social relations, namely, intellectual appropriation. Gaining an understanding of something is always simultaneously an individual and social endeavour. One cannot occur without the other. Isolated individuals, if not embedded in the scope of social knowledge, would merely react by means of genetic response to the environment, but even this is too abstract. This because many living beings are not simply conditioned by genetic reactions but also learn from their peers through a process of proto-mimesis. Therefore, assuming isolated, abstract individuals as creators of knowledge is necessarily an ahistorical undertaking. On the other hand, it is equally absurd to consider social knowledge as deprived of individual inputs, transformative actions, and transmission acts. Knowledge arises when individuals, relating to each other, find common ground and establish mutual recognitions of specific things and relations, which consequently become facts or simply objective knowledge.

The capitalist drive to privately appropriate everything in order to extract surplus-value by subjecting each particular privately appropriated thing to economic imperatives creates an immanent conflicting existence between the capitalist mode of production and the production and reproduction of human knowledge. The more complex capitalism becomes, the greater this contradiction. Most intellectual property theorists have thus far tried to address this problem, which I call the *first paradox of intellectual property*, by advocating for a balanced relationship between them through regulation. It goes without saying that this is an illusion that must ignore capitalist legalities. As I claim, when capitalist relations reached a certain degree of development, in which the most advanced capitalist nations had to physically divest their mass of capital, then the contradictory relationship between intellectual appropriation and capitalist production underwent a crucial change. The subsumption of knowledge by capital suffers a profound metamorphosis. It went from a condition of real subsumption to one of formal subsumption only to reach an even greater degree of real subsumption from the 1990s onwards. Detailed below, this process is what I call the *second paradox of intellectual property*. For now, it is sufficient to understand that a vital transformation took place, mirroring the changes in social property relations, in which property of the means of production that had already been split into two, marking the advent of capitalism when private property became a dominant social relation, underwent a new fissure, bestowing *intellectual property*$_{\textit{(private)}}$ actuality as a dominant relation in-itself.

The present book is divided into five chapters. In addition to this introduction and the last chapter summarising some of the findings, each of the other three main chapters is introduced by a brief analysis of each of the respective three main chapters from an unpublished manuscript on the same topic. Following this introductory chapter, the second chapter addresses capitalist appropriation and how this process relates to intellectual appropriation. *First*, a discussion on how property relates to appropriation and power moves the analytical understanding to a closer understanding of private property and the necessary social control to sustain it. *Second*, examining the abstract right reveals a significant difference between theoretical claims praising its neutral character and its real practice that closely relates to arbitrary power, hindering any possibility of positive freedom. *Third*, revolving around the notion of value, an analysis of both its historical apprehension and concrete form is performed, which clearly reveals the political character of science, epitomising two major streams in the context of capitalist relations: one that provides the legitimation of capitalism by suppressing the awareness of its ills and shortcomings and a second that divulges its legality, including that of exploitation. *Fourth*, with the gained awareness of production, appropriation, and accumulation of surplus-value, the notion of productive and unproductive labour is then addressed, which is crucial for the discussion of the so-called digital capitalism further ahead. *Fifth*, the understanding of intellectual appropriation in capitalism requires further apprehending both what mainstream science means by the so-called primitive accumulation when equating it with enclosure movements and its alternative interpretation, providing a historical character that debunks the rigid temporal stipulation that postulates the terms "primitive" or "original". *Sixth*, what is here called the first paradox of intellectual property is presented, meaning the unresolved contradiction between the social character of the production of knowledge and the necessary private character of capitalist appropriation. Subsequently, *seventh*, the notion of gift economy is introduced and contested in relation to the Digital; although for most of the history of humanity gift economies have existed in multiple forms, any gift economy under the capitalist mode of production must revolve around capitalist logic and obey its legality until private property relations of the means of production cease to be the dominant social relation. *Eighth*, Hegel's and Marx's notions of result and premise provide a vital methodological dimension to the perception of intellectual property, which throughout the analysis is regarded within a totality and fosters the understanding of multiple aspects of human social dynamic both in general and in particular terms—that is, under capitalism. *Ninth*, before conducting an investigation of the genesis of capitalism in the upcoming section, in this chapter, the existential (ontological) condition of capital is examined, revealing the qualitative transformation in economic relations, which attained a dominant dimension within social relations. Social relations, instead of making use of the economy to develop themselves, under the capitalist logic become the means to economic development in-itself, as an end. As when religion attains a socially dominant character over society itself, the logic of exchange-value (or simply value) imposes self-valorisation as the main driver of social relations. Rhetorically asserted as a means of freedom, value asserts and unfolds a qualitative new practice of exploitation. *Tenth*, such an understanding opens up the possibility of discussing the forms of capitalist subsumption conceived by Karl Marx, namely, formal and real subsumption. This comprehension is pivotal when distinguishing between the existence of capital as an epiphenomenon or a dominant social force. *Finally*, as mentioned, the introduction of this entire chapter is based on the third chapter of a currently unpublished manuscript. That chapter encapsulates a historical analysis of the development of intellectual property, considering some of its chief aspects. It also includes a brief taxonomy of the main categories of *intellectual property*$_{(private)}$: copyright, patent, and trademark.

The second chapter of the unpublished manuscript presents theoretical frameworks dealing with contemporary intellectual property and epistemology. A condensed assessment of these bridges the third chapter of this book. Accordingly, the role of intellectual property theory starts to reveal itself, in particular, its justificatory commitment to validate capitalist relations, thus accommodating and dampening capitalist contradictions. These perspectives offer a necessary contrast to the following analysis presented in this chapter. *First*, instead of conceiving a transcendental epistemology, an investigation on the historical development of human cognition is performed, enabling the twofold perception: unveiling the knowledge apparatus of human beings in contrast to other living beings, therefore revealing its peculiar character but also outlining human knowledge in a broader sense, capturing the mode of thinking from an ontological perspective and not merely amending it to fit the logic of capitalism. In short, thinking, as a particular endeavour of human beings, contains two dimensions, one particular dimension associated with each specific mode of production and, therefore, the historical moment, and one universal form, which is constantly evolving and being shaped and found in each of its particular forms. *Second*, building upon human knowledge, human consciousness is differentiated, for it is not, as many thinkers have conceived, a unique feature of human development. *Third*, the notion of teleology, introduced in the second chapter, is examined within the context of cognitive development. *Fourth*, cultural and genetic development are explained in their mutual interdependence throughout the development of human beings. *Fifth*, the connection between vital human activity and the new qualitative transformation that teleology introduces, which is further developed later. *Sixth*, it is impossible to understand the general and individual historical human development without understanding the evolutionary role of cooperation and socialisation; therefore, analysing this aspect becomes crucial. However, *seventh*, for this mode of transformation to arise, a very highly developed form of communication had to simultaneously emerge. In this sense, grasping the protagonist role of communication through conceptualisation is vital. *Eighth*, after presenting these evolutionary moments relating to human cognition in general, the analysis of the particular form it takes under the capitalist mode of production begins with an enquiry into the origins of capitalism. Understanding capitalism is imperative, as it determines both the limits of theoretical apprehension and the real capacity to change objective reality when it is based on theory. Needless to say, transformations can be complete products of causal—namely, unintentional—relations; however, the more complex something is, the greater the need for theory to enable a conscious transformation of reality, therefore imprinting, at least to some extent, intentionality on causal relations. *Ninth*, understanding human life must necessarily recognise the part played by property in its shaping. Property relations must hence be apprehended as a totality, which reimposes on property its ontological dimension. *Tenth*, assessing the relationship between labour—vital human activity—and teleology is then resumed. Their totality expresses property's totality; this interdependency itself represents a totality, for both intellectual and non-intellectual appropriation can only gain concrete representation through a process of actualisation. *Eleventh*, this interplay imposes the need to differentiate among causality, teleology (as isolated categories), and "teleologised" causality (which cannot be mistaken for teleological causality). *Twelfth*, the partially intentional transformations imposed on objective reality also shape human beings themselves. The notion of value (in general and not exchange-value) emerges from labour relations. To produce and reproduce human life mediated by cooperative labour arrangements gives rise to trust and recognition, with the materialisation of regulatory instances to ensure the necessary mediation. A value thus necessarily represents an *Ought*, when mediated by a norm, namely, a determination of how one should behave. Simultaneously, collective production qualitatively reconfigures not only the perception but also the practice of time. Consequently, the development of the economy moulds nature, time and behaviour, further changing both subjective and objective human realities. *Thirteenth*, it then becomes clear that the development of the economy went pari passu with that of knowledge. Science is not a product of isolated geniuses but, throughout human history, of mostly anonymous and regular people. *Fourteenth*, as capitalism became dominant, it engulfed science. Not only did it become subjected to economic imperatives, but was completely appropriated, dominantly operating under capitalist logic. *Fifteenth*, the unfolding of knowledge subsumed to capital meant the need to control and restrict it. Thus, property was artificially split, contrasting with its ontological totality. *Sixteenth*, while in so-called liberal societies the capitalist state is often downplayed and its roles underestimated, the pivotal part it plays in enabling capitalism is blatant. Furthermore, the capitalist state not only provides the capitalist infrastructure—legal system, police, military, roads, bridges, etc.—but is fundamentally the capital's risk taker. Since the 2008 crisis, it has become apparent that the whole financial system would fail if the capitalist state did not transfer staggering amounts of social wealth upwards in order to sustain it. The risk that the state takes, which is now clear in this financial dimension, also occurs in other important spheres often associated with the so-called free market, entrepreneurs, venture capitalists, etc. The state has historically organised, financed, promoted, invested in, researched and developed both the technologies and infrastructure often associated with big tech and big pharma. These contradictions lead to, *finally*, the second paradox of intellectual property in which the conflictual character between knowledge and capitalism gains a second independent dimension as an internal conflict of intellectual appropriation, production and reproduction.

Beginning the fourth chapter, a last recapitulation of the unpublished manuscript summarises its fourth chapter, in which *intellectual property$_{(private)}$* is loaded with fraught. Monopolistic capitalism ceases to be a condition of capital in general and becomes embedded within the particular social relations of intellectual property. This tension is epitomised through the intellectual appropriation of life itself, culminating in the privatisation of genetics. In addition, such private control of capital over knowledge leads to a transformation of the knowledge about knowledge; in other words, how knowledge is perceived suffers a significant qualitative transformation under the dominium of universal capitalist appropriation. The dangers that erupt with the privatisation of intellectual appropriation reach a qualitatively higher dimension with the consolidation of the Digital. Therefore, this chapter focuses on aspects involving such relations, including propaganda, exploitation of digital labour, and surveillance. *First*, the notions of fictitious capital and fictitious commodity are examined, for despite appearing similar, they result in very different corollaries. The theoretical extrapolations that each of these categories permits are extremely dissimilar because they possess two ontological bases that rest on two opposite poles. One reflects an ontology more similar to Hegel's, namely, of the absolute spirit, which asserts a metaphysical reality, despite Hegel's own criticism of metaphysics; the other echoes a Marxian ontology of the social-being. *Second*, the fact that fictitious capital is not something merely abstract enables it to be used as economic weapons; this logic does not apply only to *intellectual property*$_{(private)}$, as financial instruments become more dependent on the intellectual property system, and finance and intellectual property start to compose a new totality in which economic weapons cannot be disassociated from private control over intellectual appropriation. *Third*, it is not only metaphysical considerations that render capitalist relations incomprehensible. Some capitalist critiques have reached the point in which the very critique represents an affirmation by negating the existence of capitalism in contemporary society, for it would have already been superseded by a return to feudal relations; these theories in fact legitimated capitalist relations because they deprived capitalism of the very relations that characterised it. Thus, both a transcendental reality and transcendental capitalism appear simultaneously. Capitalist reality is not capitalism, the reality is not real; capitalism is feudalism, and the idea determines objective reality. This hypostasis leads to, *fourth*, a de-ontologised apprehension of political economy. Context and historical determinations transcend themselves. Interpretation asserts itself and arbitrarily and abstractly determines social reality. In this sense, *fifth*, the society of the spectacle overarches to such a broad scope that objective reality ceases to exist. However, this colossal level of irrationalism, in which appearance seems to attain ontological priority over concrete reality, is not the cause of contemporary historical development but, *sixth*, rather a pivotal mechanism of social control and organisation. Propaganda, marketing, advertising, and public relations have become the necessary tools to guarantee capitalist domination to the detriment of the masses. Already at the end of the nineteenth century, Gustav Le Bon was theorising about social control and manipulation of the masses; with World Wars I and II, the development of propaganda was gaining pace, and not only the capitalist state but also the capitalist class itself were celebrating it. *Seventh*, this appeared to have culminated in the model of manufacturing consent, in which capitalist corporations, marketing companies, media giants, and the capitalist state act in unison to impose social control, behaviour shaping, and political-economic dominance. Research has determined a set of filters used by them to assert their ideological power. However, *eighth*, this model was based on a world pre-digitalisation. In contemporary capitalism, those relations in which ideological control occurred on an already broad scale gain a whole new quantitative and qualitative dimension. First of all, the audience ceases to work passively to begin actively working for this industry of behaviour control, albeit unwittingly. Needless to say, regardless of being passive or active labour, both are modes of production of surplus-value decoupled from wage labour relations. For this reason, some theorists claim that this leads to an infinite level of exploitation. *Ninth*, a whole new apparatus to appropriate, store, transform, and resell the digital data produced by users is created, which is by no means abstract; for instance, the so-called clouds are composed of enormous storehouses and servers' infrastructure. This process is further intensified, *tenth*, by what has become a ubiquitous state-private industry of mass surveillance, in which people are being monitored and tracked here and now to the point of being subjected to behavioural changes in real-time.

Finally, the concluding chapter summarises some of the key points in my book. The intention of this book has been to unveil some vital dimensions of a system in which knowledge is privatised by capitalist powers. While knowledge is crucial to enable both individual and social actions, its removal from the social sphere promotes a double destruction. First, the demolition of the very social tissue. This because knowledge is a precondition to recognise social reality, acknowledge its shortcomings, envision both necessary and desired changes, establish the intended goals, and set in motion transformative acts. Second, the devastation of the development of knowledge, which retreats and atrophies as its existential condition succumbs. It is obvious that these two elements operate interdependently and only analytically can be conceived as two separate moments. It is therefore no surprise that, as capitalism unfolds to determine private appropriation of everything as end-in-itself in order to promote its logic of infinite extraction and accumulation of surplus-value, knowledge becomes entangled in this process and crumbles as society crumbles. If the development of knowledge is a condition for human development, human development is, conversely, a condition for the development of knowledge; accordingly, the demise of one necessarily represents the demise of the other and vice versa.

References

Alvaredo, F., Chancel, L., Piketty, T., Saez, E., & Zucman, G. (2018). *World Inequality Report 2018*.

Assange, J. (2016). *When Google Met WikiLeaks*. OR Books.

Boyle, J. (2008). *The Public Domain: Enclosing the Commons of the Mind.* feek-books. https://doi.org/10.1177/0276146711416981

Chancel, L., Piketty, T., Saez, E., & Zucman, G. (2022). *World Inequality Report 2022*. https://dds.cepal.org/redesoc/publicacion?id=5585

Davis, M. (2006). *Planet of Slums*. Verso.

Drahos, P. (2016). *A Philosophy of Intellectual Property*. Australian National University. https://doi.org/10.22459/PIP.06.2016

Exports and Imports by U.S. IP-intensive Industries. (2022). In *Economic Note, No. 101, Office of the Chief Economist*. United States Patent and Trademark Office. https://www.uspto.gov/sites/default/files/documents/oce-ip-econ-note-101.pdf

Hedges, C. (2018). *America: The Farewell Tour*. Simon & Schuster.

Hudson, M. (2015). *Killing the Host: How Financial Parasites and Debt Bondage Destroy the Global Economy*. CounterPunch Books.

Johns, A. (2009). *Piracy: The Intellectual Property Wars from Gutenberg to Gates*. The University of Chicago Press.

Nachtway, O. (2018). *Germany's Hidden Crisis: Social Decline in the Heart of Europe*. Verso.

Pfeffer, J. (2018). *Dying for a Paycheck: How Modern Management Harms Employee Health and Company Performance-and What We Can Do About It*. Harper Business.

Robinson, W. I. (2020). *The Global Police State*. Pluto Press.

Szepanski, A. (2022). *Financial Capital in the 21st Century A New Theory of Speculative Capital.* Palgrave Macmillan. https://doi.org/10.1007/978-3-030-93151-3

Toole, A. A., Miller, R. D., & Rada, N. (2022). Intellectual Property and the U.S. Economy: Third edition. In *United States Patent and Trademark Office*. https://www.uspto.gov/sites/default/files/documents/uspto-ip-us-economy-third-edition.pdf

Vitale, A. S. (2018). *The End of Policing*. Verso.

Zuboff, S. (2019). *The Age of Surveillance Capitalism: The Fight for a Human Future at the New Frontier of Power*. Profile Books.

2

History and Dialectics of Intellectual Property

2.1 Prolegomena: A Brief History of Intellectual Property

2.1.1 Italy and England

Intellectual property has not only a history but also a prehistory. According to Daniel Stengel, signs were protected by moral rules and norms, performing a function of identification and differentiation. Most likely tribal signs were the first type and also unique, for the removal from their context simultaneously meant cancelling their meaning, "specific functions and therefore their defining characteristics" (Stengel, 2004, p. 20). Signs represent an essential element of mediation, enabling a social context to be objectively perceived. They are embedded within signal systems. According to György Lukács, there are at least three signal systems. The first belongs to conditioned reflexes; on the other pole, there is language with all its complexity; a third category which sits between both is art (Lukács, 1963). For the present discussion, what is important to consider is that signs and signal systems are products of human social activity which predate any commercial intellectual property. And even during the Roman Empire, forgery of "trademarks" already existed (Stengel, 2004,

J. Romeiro Hermeto, *The Paradox of Intellectual Property in Capitalism*,
https://doi.org/10.1007/978-3-031-49967-8_2

p. 21), providing more evidence for Adrian Johns' claim that piracy was indeed the condition of *intellectual property*$_{(private)}$ (Johns, 2009).

The genesis of modern commercial intellectual property first appeared in the Renaissance. Even before the *Decreto Veneziano 1474*, an industrial patent was first granted in 1444 to the French Antonius Marini for the technology of a mill that could grind wheat without water. Others followed, but the most significant occurred in 1469 when Johann von Speyer introduced Johannes Gutenberg's new printing method with mobile characters. Soon after, Speyer's death catapulted a new phenomenon: the newly introduced printing spread unrestrained since his patent was non-transferable and perished with him. *Venezia* became a colossus in the art of printing, casting a shadow over its competitors *Roma*, *Firenze*, *Milano*, and *Paris*. Therefore, the decree did not inaugurate a new system but simply legitimised an already ongoing practice (Schippel, 1989; Squassina, 2019). These privileges were economic instruments to enable the political power of the state (Foucault, 2004). The idea was not only to foster technical advancements but also to prevent the emigration of qualified labourers. Thus, *the very body appeared as intellectual property*, and a clause found in Tuscan privileges confirms this as part of immediate cultural development, for it "imposed the obligation to teach the procedures for the activities for which a patent was requested to the inhabitants of the Grand Duchy, to employ citizens as labourers, etc." (Ammannati, 2019, p. 28). This power cannot be seen through the lenses of today. While it also aimed for prestige and political domination, the economy was merely a tool. *Venezia*'s early commercial development did not translate into capitalist development, which supports Ellen Meiksins Wood's thesis that capitalism did not emerge from commercialisation (Wood, 2017). The *Concilio di Trento* solidified the subsumption of commercial activities under the feudal-religious social mode of production, hindering the unfolding of economic undertakings when the catholic church reacted to protestant dissemination in Europe.

While intellectual property can be said to be a historical product of these upheavals, it did not occur in Italy but rather in England with the advent of the *Stationers*. According to Johns, the Stationer's register—a book of recordkeeping—gave birth to piracy and, correspondingly, to intellectual property. It was neither the state nor official laws but, in their place, the stationer's parallel activity that enacted (a proto-)copyright. The Stationers controlled the publishing activity with the register, which provided protection against competing illegitimate printing-copying activity. This independent-from-the-state-power practice gave birth to the subsequent appearance of an official legal practice of recording. Because the new printing methods had rendered knowledge extremely mobile, an authoritative figure to provide credibility became fundamental. The Company of Stationers regulated book trade through a system of secrecy and punishment based on propriety rather than state law. "The register regime served the booksellers well, but it largely ignored authors and readers" (Johns, 2009, p. 27). Because the crown could issue privileges, a system of state patents was more suitable for authors. In this sense, proto-copyright (register system) and patents (state privileges) were two colliding systems. It was "intellectual purloining" that gave a new accent to the term piracy. From being until then related to creativity, it then becomes an outlaw-like practice. A complicated process of contradictory powers gave rise to literary property, becoming sedimented under the sanctification of private property.

The Statute of Monopolies 1624 did not protect inventors but granted "patents for new and newly introduced arts, declaring for the first time in English law that innovation warranted protection" (Johns, 2009, p. 71). Analogous to the Venetian system, it did not confer on someone a right but rather a privilege with limited duration (Johns, 2009, p. 126). The chief goal of the statute was to ban "the vast array of monopolies that were, for half a century or more, being handed out at will by the sovereigns of the land to the favoured few" (Nicol, 2021, p. 103). The notion of inherent patentability, in which "a broad principle, and not a piece of machinery as such", was being controlled, first emerged with the contestation of James Watt's steam engine condenser (Nicol, 2021, p. 103). This is still a major problem today, especially as genes and their use become privatised by means of *intellectual property*$_{(private)}$; the living being becomes privately controlled and enters a sphere of private biopower (Hull, 2019, p. 5). Back to the historical consideration. Peter Drahos and John Braithwaite claim that the contradiction between trade interests and monopolies, such as patent monopolies, expressed great tension. The Monopolies Act of 1624 intended to remedy this by abolishing monopolies "except for those in invention"; however, no actual change took place because it "swept away the monopolies of individuals, but not those of corporations" (Drahos & Braithwaite, 2002, p. 35).

The Statute of Anne 1710 (Patterson & Joyce, 2004, p. 918) represented the climate of printing opposing interests. The guilds sought to attain and preserve monopolistic power, on the one hand, while, on the other, the crown saw it as a supporting tool of state power. Replacing the system of privilege, it was, according to Peter Drahos, "a revolutionary statute because it heralded the arrival of a public interest dimension to copyright" (Drahos, 2016, p. 31). For Johns, this did not mean the official beginning of copyright, as the "term itself did not appear in it, and it left important questions unaddressed as to the nature of any such 'right'" (Johns, 2009, p. 111); it nonetheless established the basis upon which a copyright doctrine could develop. While common law endowed literary property with an eternal character, the statute relinquished it altogether, "literary property did not exist" anymore; it "had vanished" (Johns, 2009, p. 137). It is thus crucial to highlight the fact that "the foundation of such 'property' [literary property] had in any case been customary and practical rather than legal" (Johns, 2009, p. 138) because, when putting the genesis of capitalism in perspective (see *infra*), as with private property, *intellectual property$_{(private)}$*—often regarded as intellectual property—was not born by the power of the law but rather from social power relations; the law merely sanctioned and legitimised those relations a posteriori.

Taking a leap from the beginning of the eighteenth to the second half of the nineteenth century, among many international conventions—such as Madrid, Den Haag, Rome, etc. (Adewopo, 2016, p. 111)—the most important ones must be brought into light: the Paris and Berne Conventions. TRIPS, as shown below, did not appear out of thin air but was built upon a continuous internationalisation and consolidation of *intellectual property$_{(private)}$*. Together, multiple countries from Latin America and Europe formed the Paris Union, shielding "invention patents, industrial designs or models, trade marks and commercial names" (Convention de Paris Pour La Protection de La Propriété Industrielle, 1883, p. 3). Despite the 1979 amendment of Article 2, making it even broader in scope than its original form, the Berne Convention already had a remarkably extensive range, including:

> books, pamphlets or any other writings; dramatic or dramatico-musical works, musical compositions with or without words; works of drawing, painting, sculpture, engraving; lithographs, illustrations, geographical maps; plans, sketches and plastic works, relating to geography, topography, architecture or science in general; finally, any production of any kind in the literary, scientific or artistic field, which could be published by any means of printing or reproduction. (Convention de Berne Pour La Protection Des Œuvres Littéraires et Artistiques, 1886, p. 30)

As Alexandra George states, the more these doctrines were extended, the greater the political dimension intellectual property attained; correspondingly, institutions, such as the World Intellectual Property Organization (WIPO), were created to manage it (George, 2012, p. 48). In theory, the convention was established to protect the exclusive rights of authors; in reality, it was a system "run to suit the interests of copyright exporters. Each successive revision of Berne brought with it a higher set of copyright standards" (Drahos & Braithwaite, 2002, p. 76). These events, which initiated a process of international coordination of intellectual property that culminated during the 1990s in unprecedented concentration of power, started to gain pace during the "imperial expansion" (Johns, 2009, pp. 284, 325).

2.1.2 The Bayh-Dole Act and TRIPS

A crucial piece of legislation which helped pave the way towards (almost) total control of private capital over knowledge was the Bayh-Dole Act of 1980. US Senator Birch Bayh proposed the preposterous contention that a robust patent system was a prerequisite to secure US-American advantage over competitors by enabling private agents to appropriate "patents in inventions" which were "developed with federal funds" (Drahos & Braithwaite, 2002, p. 163). According to Peter Drahos and John Braithwaite, before this act, publicly funded patents in inventions would go "into the public domain by means of publication" (Drahos &

Braithwaite, 2002, p. 163). Bryn Williams-Jones and Vural Ozdemir suggest a rupture in which universities and researchers, on the one hand, and education and athletics, on the other, were constrained to entangle themselves with private capital (Williams-Jones & Ozdemir, 2007, p. 140). Niklas Bruun correctly asserts that this is based on a paradoxical relationship in which universities ought to simultaneously produce long-term open basic research and short-term knowledge to be commercialised and enclosed (Bruun, 2021, p. 9). Knowledge would then be subjected to rivalry (Pellizzoni & Ylönen, 2012, p. 55f), which on an abstract idealised level does not exist.

The culmination of this process, which still impacts most people on a worldwide scale, was the Trade-Related Aspects of Intellectual Property Rights Agreement (TRIPS). Gigantic blocs of capital—big pharma, big tech, and showbiz—not only strongly supported it but also played a vital role in its inception and transnational enforcement. Nevertheless, according to Luigi Pellizzoni and Marja Ylönen, "TRIPs [sic] extended the scope of patentability to all commercially exploitable products and processes, including genetically modified plants and animals" (Pellizzoni & Ylönen, 2012, p. 56). As every piece of written information became copyrighted, the expansion of digitalisation simultaneously meant making *intellectual property*$_{(private)}$ ubiquitous because all social interactions digitally mediated by writing were now part of the intellectual property system. A further paradox arose. While information could be accessed like never before without the then current constraints of space and time, the "proliferation of intellectual property rights inhibits access to such information in areas (basic research in general, the life sciences, software)", which were mostly part of the so-called public domain (David & Foray, 2002, p. 13). Accessible knowledge meant it would have to be situated outside capitalist markets, consequently constraining profit (Nelson, 2003, p. 1701). Knowledge expropriation was absolutely pivotal in changing this dynamic. The loss of capitalist dynamism after the so-called Golden Age (after World War II) accelerated the need to impose control over knowledge as a necessary condition of production (Sum & Jessop, 2013, p. 292).

The strategy to secure hegemonic control over knowledge did not fundamentally change; the novelty was the new tactics. While governments and universities were already vastly entangled with capital (Conner, 2005, p. 472f), the expansion and universalisation of intellectual property gave *capital* a tighter grip on knowledge which could endure a greater separation/autonomy within the productive process, enabling an even greater division of labour. “Designed in California, made in China” is one of the many examples in which knowledge production and industrial production have been separated. As such, it required an extension of the powerful protection thus far reserved for the immediate private property of the means of production. On the other hand, producing novel knowledge and technology is an uncertain practice. It is uncertain when it is going to be accomplished and whether it is going to be successful, and how many resources it is going to take before it can yield the expected results. This unpredictable character renders private capital an unsuitable candidate for this endeavour. Instead, resources are drawn from society—usually by the capitalist state—enabling the so-called basic research (Hull, 2019, p. 31f).

TRIPS was clearly not an organic development of the forces of the so-called free-market. Instead, it “came about after the chief executive officers of Bristol-Myers, CBS, DuPont, General Electric, General Motors, Hewlett-Packard, IBM, Johnson & Johnson, Merck, Monsanto and Pfizer joined forces to form the Intellectual Property Committee (IPC)” (George, 2012, p. 45). It consolidates intellectual property rights in an international system (Sonderholm, 2012, p. 110). Yet, its greatest advocates were those countries that violated previous intellectual property agreements (Chang, 2001, p. 10).

By the end of the nineteenth and beginning of the twentieth century, DuPont played a major role in integrating scientific endeavour into capital. Patents became so crucial that it gave rise to the so-called profession of Patent Locksmith. Patent bureaucracy did not fall short of importance to inventions themselves. Knowledge control was imposed not only by isolated patents but also by what Drahos and Braithwaite call a “web of patents”, thus enabling great power to block competition (Drahos & Braithwaite, 2002, p. 46). The cartelisation of economies was—probably inadvertently—legalised by means of the universalisation of the patent system.

Almost a century later, TRIPS came about and was integrated into the World Trade Organization (WTO). However, it emerged from the General Agreement on Tariffs and Trade (GATT). At first, it seemed an incongruity because the GATT "related to goods crossing borders, not knowledge" (Drahos & Braithwaite, 2002, p. 68); however, the private companies involved—see *supra*—, headed by Pfizer, promoted a plan to actualise TRIPS. Pfizer sponsored a crusade to behavioural-perception change, "linking the trade regime to investment" (Drahos & Braithwaite, 2002, p. 68). National strategies of investment were therefore encumbered. The strategy imposed over the world was relatively simple: if US-American conditions of intellectual property were not met, trade would be blocked. According to Drahos and Braithwaite, "less than 50 individuals had managed to globalise a set of regulatory norms for the conduct of all those doing business or aspiring to do business in the information age" (Drahos & Braithwaite, 2002, p. 73). This imposition was a spectacular feat and an impressive display of capitalist power. Only fifty people were responsible for how the entire world would come to terms with intellectual property under TRIPS.

2.1.3 Intellectual Property Mainstream Taxonomy

Before a different understanding of intellectual property can be presented in the sections below, for the reader unfamiliar with *intellectual property$_{(private)}$*, it may be important to comprehend how it is commonly referred to. A more extensive demonstration of theories encompassing *intellectual property$_{(private)}$* has been dealt with in more detail in the still unpublished manuscript on the same topic, while Chap. 3 of this book summarises some of those formulations. For now, instead of dealing with those theoretical formulations, the *intellectual property$_{(private)}$* taxonomy coined by the World Intellectual Property Organization (WIPO) is presented.

Intellectual property$_{(private)}$ is usually conceived as abstract things, referring "to creations of the mind, such as inventions; literary and artistic works; designs; and symbols, names and images used in commerce" (What Is Intellectual Property?, n.d.). Its main categories are *patents*, *copyrights* and *trademarks*. Anchored in law, they "enable people to earn recognition or financial benefit from what they invent or create", and it is justified as a means to nurture innovation and creativity (What Is Intellectual Property?, n.d.).

Still according to WIPO, "[a] patent is an exclusive right granted for an invention, which is a product or a process that provides, in general, a new way of doing something, or offers a new technical solution to a problem" (Patents, n.d.). Obtaining it also means disclosing the information. This protection provides a monopoly to the patent owner, that is, an "exclusive right to prevent or stop others from commercially exploiting the patented invention", and it must also abide by territorial rights with a 20-year protection period (Patents, n.d.).

Copyright refers to what is also known as an *author's rights*, and it characterises "the rights that creators have over their literary and artistic works" (Copyright, n.d.). At first, one might think this right is restricted to the area of arts, but its range—"from books, music, paintings, sculpture, and films, to computer programs, databases, advertisements, maps, and technical drawings" (Copyright, n.d.)—is very extensive and, especially because digitalisation plays a crucial role in contemporary life, copyright appears to have an omnipresent existence. As research shows, WIPO's claim that "[c]opyright protection extends only to expressions, and not to ideas, procedures, methods of operation or mathematical concepts as such" (Copyright, n.d.) misrepresents the power attained by copyright holders, for the growing intrinsicality between "expressions" and "methods" has blurred these arbitrary divisions. Another relevant remark is that there are economic and moral copyrights. While the latter secures non-economic interest—such as recognition—it is the former which enables an owner to extract an economic benefit from it. Finally, obtaining is not a matter of option but rather occurs "automatically without the need for registration or other formalities" (Copyright, n.d.).

Trademarks, on the other hand, are acquired through registration against payment. "In principle, a trademark registration will confer an exclusive right to the use of the registered trademark. This implies that the trademark can be exclusively used by its owner, or licenced to another party for use in return for payment" (Trademarks, n.d.). Although its protection expires after a certain period of time, it can be renewed open-endedly. The scope of trademarks is remarkably broad. Not only words, letters, numbers, drawings, symbols, and shapes but even "sounds or fragrances, or color shades used as distinguishing features" can be subjected to privatisation and, consequently, private control (Trademarks, n.d.).

2.2 Intellectual Property as Premise and Results

2.2.1 Property

At first sight, the understanding of property is clouded by its theoretical multitude, which portrays a remarkably heterogeneous character of property. Property theoreticians and theories cannot reduce the social understanding of property to a singular, general, common understanding, but precisely each particular claim conveys its own anathema because property ends up in each case being reduced to a specific theoretical set and definition. However, property entails an exceptionally relevant and foundational aspect. Its ontological dimension necessarily carries with it a question of the social means of life, that is, how humanity produces life according to given actual circumstances. For this reason, the question of property is often associated with the ethical question of a good life.

A summary of the anthology edited by Andreas Eckl and Bernd Ludwig provides a broad view on the topic (Eckl & Ludwig, 2005): *Plato* undertook an investigation of the distribution of goods (mainly land) and the avoidance of possessions in excess in order to promote the common good (Hoffmann, 2005). *Aristotle* puts forward a notion of (personal) private property, meaning the proper use of goods to achieve wealth and prosperity (Szaif, 2005). The *Roman* approach establishes the right of property, where property is a direct relation between the human-being and a thing—this relation is to be respected and thereby, a state of peace can be maintained (Chiusi, 2005). *Medieval* property theory brings forward the Christian doctrine, in which the question of claimable use cannot be separated from the question of the circumstances of use (Kaufmann, 2005). *John Locke's theory* is strongly directed towards contractualism, and coins appropriation by labour as the justification of property in clear contrast with the divine conception of property of his time (Ludwig, 2005). *David Hume* and *Adam Smith* assert a common good to be achieved through the state and the market by means of private property (Fricke, 2005). *Immanuel Kant* attempts to develop a justification of property purely from reason but, in doing so, distances himself from real conditions (Unruh, 2005). *G.W.F. Hegel*, on the other hand, steps back from pure reason and designs a theory of property that adapts well to bourgeois social conditions, developing the theory of property as the actualisation of freedom (Eckl, 2005).[1] In contrast, *Karl Marx* presents private property as something that, instead of promoting freedom, is a hurdle to any possibility of human emancipation—despite the fact that capitalist relations of production not only have had great historical importance but also been necessary (Zintl, 2005). *John Rawls*, on the one hand, argues that concerns about relations of production are not decisive but that the empowered state should preserve justice in order to promote the general good (Esser, 2005). *Robert Nozick*, on the other hand, maintains that property is an inviolable natural right and must not be touched by the state under any circumstances (Esser, 2005).

Despite seemingly endless understandings of property, Marx's consideration must be emphasised because, instead of providing a conceptualising definition, he perceives property in a unique fashion which enables explaining both property in general as well as its specific modes of existence. While for Hegel, thinking about an object means appropriating it, making it something immediate mine (Hegel, 2013, p. 47, Supplement §4), in reality, thinking does not exhaust, nor suffice to grasp, nor to make use of, nor to control a concrete object (*Gegenstand*). The notion of property is often defined *a priori*, but as stated elsewhere (Hermeto, 2020b), precisely because it is a social relation, it always has distinctive historical determinations and cultural aspects, preventing an aprioristic definition. Marx's interpretation can be grasped not only by his private property critique but also by the manner in which he interchangeably refers to property and property relations by using yet another concept. Despite noticing that this element appears in the *Grundrisse*, Peter Drahos

[1] The unpublished manuscript contains an extensive assessment of Hegel's theory.

curiously disregards its centrality because it is one among many interpretations of what property is (Drahos, 2016, p. 113). Already in the *Introduction* of the *Grundrisse*, Marx emphasises: "Every production is the appropriation of nature from the part of an individual within and by means of a determined society. In this sense, it is a tautology to say that property (appropriation) is a condition of production" (Marx, 1983a, p. 23). Thus, *Eigentum* and *Aneignung* appear to be synonymous. This intercalation opens a very relevant pathway to the understanding of property among the many interpretations because *property* as a concept expresses particular forms of *appropriation*. Whether common or private, physical or intellectual, analogously, being legitimated by fear, violence, common goals (cultural and social values), or by the abstract right, etc., the form of appropriation of the means of doing necessarily reflects the social property relations emerging from particular social relations of production. "The capitalist mode of appropriation arising from the capitalist mode of production" is "hence the capitalist private property" (Marx, 1962, p. 791). Therefore, *appropriation* perfectly encompasses these differences, and when Marx speaks of *property* relations, its historical and process character becomes clear and, therefore, cannot be aprioristically confined in a rigid definition (Marx, 1962, 1983b).

As pointed out by Drahos, Morris R. Cohen unveils the character of power of private property over others (Drahos, 2016). Nonetheless, a deeper understanding may be called for. Theory often merely justifies certain social relations instead of explaining them. It is no different with private property. Property acquires an arbitrary existence under theoretical veils, thus hiding its true social practice. Private property, "as opposed to social, collective property, exists only where the means of labour and the external conditions of labour belong to private individuals" (Marx, 1962, p. 789), representing, therefore, the divorce between the unity of labourer and the means of labour (Marx & Engels, 1962, p. 131); such property relations represent an estrangement among people (the producer/labourer and society), between the individual (worker) and his vital sensual activity (the act of production), between the worker and the product of his labour, and finally between the individual worker and himself (Marx, 1968, pp. 454, 515, 517f). Marxian estrangement is consequently not just an economic phenomenon, but it impacts the totality of the human self and social relations. It affects both body and psyche (mind), individual and family, society and nature. The social impact of the estrangement derived from private property relations culminates in social disintegration, powerfully synthesised in the concept of *anomy* (Durkheim, 1952, p. 350).

Maintaining this situation requires some counter-measures so that these social impacts and pains can be numbed in order to be sustained and reproduced. For now, it should suffice to highlight that commodity fetishism, irrationalism, and the spectacle are some fundamental enablers which are constantly weighted against the concrete struggles of people.[2] Thus, this process of reification, the commodification of the human being into the labour commodity, expresses the *imperium* of capital (social dominance of capitalist private property of the means of production) over workers; as this condition historically emerged, namely, capitalism (see *infra*), then the capitalist—as the "embodiment of capital" (Marx, 1962, p. 320)—extends his *dominium* over the labour commodity. Evoking the notions of imperium and dominium, of course, refers to Cohen's elucidation of property and sovereignty, which has the merit of understanding that "the primary effect of property on a large scale is to limit freedom" because, as it excludes people from guaranteeing their existential subsistence, "it rather compels people to part with their freedom" (Cohen, 1927, p. 18f).[3] Furthermore, what constitutes a socio-economic desire, with private property, becomes decoupled from what is privately strived to become a compulsion to obtain individual profits. Intellectual properties are used to exclude competition from entering capitalist markets; planned obsolescence becomes another mechanism to secure profits to the detriment of social productivity; and marketing changes, controls and imposes behaviour by convincing one to buy what one does not need—even if lacking money by debt creation (Hudson, 2015). Not only that, Cohen emphasises the "inherent sources of waste

---

[2] This is the object of the research of two other books I am developing and should be briefly unfolded in the last section of this book. For some crucial literature see: (Debord, 1992; Lukács, 1973, 1974a, 1974b; Marx, 1962, p. 85).

[3] To which he further adds: "The principle of freedom of personality certainly cannot justify a legal order wherein a few can, by virtue of their legal monopoly over necessities, compel others to work under degrading and brutalizing conditions" (Cohen, 1927, p. 19).

in a regime of private enterprise and free competition", in which eliminating competitors enriches the few but disenfranchises the many (Cohen, 1927, p. 20). However, Cohen's critique falls short in light of how he conceives property. Contrary to its historical forms, property is assumed as a right derived from the legal term property (Cohen, 1927, p. 11f). Its corollaries are twofold. First, the power of capital emanates not from particular social property relations but rather property rights (or legal relations), which "confer sovereign power on our captains of industry and even more so on our captains of finance" (Cohen, 1927, p. 29); second, assuming what needs to be explained has the "advantage" of building a solution as idealist, as the idealist genesis of the formulated problem.

Adam Smith plainly understood the necessary conflict emanating from private property relations. "Wherever there is a great property, there is great inequality. For one very rich man, there must be at least five hundred poor, and the affluence of the few supposes the indigence of the many. The affluence of the rich excites the indignation of the poor"; hence, only the existence of a government can prevent civil insubordination (Smith, 2012, p. 709). The capitalist needs the state's support to sustain his despotic rule. Smith, nevertheless, does not see a relation of exploitation but one of racial superiority within the process of natural subordination. Race virtue and the domination of the mind presuppose such superiority. "The first of those causes or circumstances, is the superiority of personal qualifications, of strength, beauty, and agility of body; of wisdom and virtue; of prudence, justice, fortitude, and moderation of mind" (Smith, 2012, p. 710). It is thus the relationship of a superior body and mind that enables the attainment of superiority and authority. In Cohen, nevertheless, the control capital has over the social capitalist political system is framed upside-down; hence, instead of capital using its power to influence politics and legislation, political and legal regulation also have the power to impose limits on capital—namely, social private property relations of the means of production (Cohen, 1927, p. 23ff).

2.2.2 Shaping Behaviour: The Abstract Right

The right (by the practical means of laws) is a normaliser of social behaviour—in the sense of standardising. As social relations, especially those involving domination, become more complex, there is a need to create equalising mechanisms for more fluid social intercourse while hindering the growth and flow of antithetical social actions. At the social level, there is ideology, which "is above all that form of mental processing of reality which serves to make people's social practice conscious and capable of action" (Lukács, 1986, p. 398). At the level of language, there is grammar, creating a whole body of normative categories, e.g., phonology, morphology, *accidence*, orthoepy, *orthography*, composition, semantics, *syntax*, etymology, the ones italicised, "as the bare essentials for writing & reading, represent for most of us the whole of grammar" (Fowler, 2009, p. 220). On the economic plane, means of exchange, currency exchange rates, contracts, interest rates, etc. On the political plane, sovereigns and hegemonic arrangements. On the plane of social control and regulation, the right—and, more recently, the media, communication, advertisement, and propaganda apparatuses. Cohen's hypostatisation regarding the abstract right is not his monopoly because most authors dealing with either property or intellectual property have the illusion that the abstract right creates property by virtue of law. We turn our attention to some of Hans Kelsen's insights to counterbalance this. Nevertheless, his extensive analysis and knowledge of norms and legal affairs can neither be fully discussed here, nor is there the pretension that they could be exhausted in some brief lines. However, it can give the current discussion an essential layer in deciphering the common hypostasis presented. Two points considered pivotal for this discussion are *arbitrariness* and *behaviour shaping*.

Usually, the concepts of right and law (or the rule of law) are used to convey the notions of neutrality, predictability, trustworthiness, justice, etc. (Thus, the intellectual property debates over the last decades have tried to figure out how to balance it, assuming it as part of a given framework of impartiality and fairness. Except for the critique of the political economy of the media (see *infra*), hitherto, most theories have neglected to analyse intellectual property within the scope of capitalism critique.)

As with the political economy and mainstream intellectual property theories, also this understanding of norms is laden with mystic and religious content. This has, of course, different historical roots, but central to it was the need for a higher form of deity to legitimate social power and, accordingly, its imposed rule. "The assumption that there must be norms which do not originate in arbitrary choice leads to the concept of a norm which is not the meaning of a human act of will", whereas in reality, "norms posited by human acts of will are arbitrary, in the genuine signification of the word: that is, they can decree any behaviour whatsoever to be obligatory" (Kelsen, 1991, p. 4). It is thus just a hypostasis to consider that an aggregate will in societies with dominating ruling classes, such as the capitalist mode of production, represents the will of all, as idealism's conception of non-arbitrary (impartial) justice anchored in the true being, which "is that of the Idea, of moral value hypostatised as a transcendent essence" (Kelsen, 1991, p. 64).

Moreover, the commandments of given norms, presented as expressions of true freedom, as *Is* (from the verb to be), as given conditions, are in fact *Oughts*. According to Kelsen, these norms are *hypothetical* (specific) or *categorical* (general). The categorical formulations of hypothetical norms are context-based and dependent; thus, they are always determined by social relations and historicity. This immanency imposes a double conditionality. "When a norm decrees that a certain behaviour is obligatory under a certain condition—when a conditional behaviour is obligatory—then it is also the Ought (i.e. the behaviour's being obligatory) which is conditional" (Kelsen, 1991, p. 21). It becomes clear that the overwhelming discussions and analyses of intellectual property operate within this sphere of Ought (*Sollen*) (see *infra*). The link between ethic imperatives culminating in a "general norm of morality" is intertwined with legal norms, for the latter, even though—theoretically—different because it departs from the "legal science", still expresses *Ought* and not *Must*. Kelsen states, "[i]t is a normative and not a causal necessity" (Kelsen, 1991, p. 22). The law is a coercive act; it not only imposes behaviour to submit, conform, and obey the norms but also sanctions behaviours that violate them. However, this requires another layer of mysticism, since imputation cannot be bestowed upon causal relations.

Conditioning behaviour by stipulating aprioristic consequences creates a "first cause" belief, "a *prima causa*", which becomes "the endpoint of imputation"; this, however, "is incompatible with the idea of causality expressed in the laws of classical physics", instead, it "plays an important part in religious metaphysics" (Kelsen, 1991, p. 25). Marx also noticed this metaphysical character of the right, especially the right to private property, which is abstractly evoked as a right to freedom, the freedom to dispose of private property, but in practice is the right to egoism, to "de-actualisation" (*Entwirklichung*) and estrangement (*Entfremdung*). "The human right of freedom is not based on the connection of human with human, but rather on the separation of human from human" (Marx, 1981a, p. 364). Intellectual private property gains a broad social dimension within this scope. However, and Marx is fulminating, "none of the so-called human rights, therefore, goes beyond the egoistic human being, beyond the human being as he is a member of bourgeois society, namely, as an individual withdrawn to himself, to his private interest and his private arbitrariness, and separated from the community" (Marx, 1981a, p. 366). This idealism is what Ludwig Feuerbach denounced as a form of *subject-predicate-inversion*: "Religion is human-being's *divisiveness* [*Entzweiung*] *with himself*: he confronts God as a being *opposed* to him" (Feuerbach, 2016, p. 54). By imputing legal and moral meaning to secure political-economic power and discarding, disregarding, and de-ontologising the true causal character of intellectual property, does *intellectual property$_{(private)}$* not attain a religious, metaphysical character? Created by social property relations, *intellectual property$_{(private)}$* must relinquish its ontological dimension (see *infra*), actualising its objective side, namely, acquiring self-independence (*Verselbständigung*); thus, it presupposes imposing and asserting itself as a power relation. Kelsen is unequivocal: "If the command is not empowered, then this is merely the *subjective meaning* of the act of commanding"; furthermore, "only an empowered command also has the *objective meaning* of Ought, that is, only an empowered command is a *norm* binding on the addressee, obligating him to act in the prescribed way" (Kelsen, 1991, p. 27).

2.2.3 "Positive" Alienation and the Negative Right

According to Axel Honneth, modern ethics is predominantly minted "under the spell of the idea of freedom" (Honneth, 2013, p. 36). Its ideological character is unequivocal. In the so-called liberal societies, atomised individuals regard themselves as independent persons, subjects who have and freely assert their free will "if they have subjective rights that grant them a state-protected leeway to explore their predilections, preferences and intentions" (Honneth, 2013, p. 129). This legal apparatus that intended to overcome feudal privilege authorised and shaped the capitalist state rules, enabling private autonomy at supposedly equal degrees. "On this path of establishing an egalitarian legal order, an independent sphere of action gradually emerges, characterised by a type of norms that neither demand moral consent nor depend on a moral agreement, but require mere intentional-rational [zweckrationale] acceptance" (Honneth, 2013, p. 130). Abstract rights grant individuals a space in a private sphere that enables being released from the necessary social interactions. Based on Hegel's *Elements of the Philosophy of Right*, Honneth explains the *raison d'être of legal freedom* (*Daseinsgrund der rechtlichen Freiheit*). First, he explains that for Hegel, abstract law seems to have a dual nature, granting the subject an *outwardly* "intentional-rational form of decision-making", thereby protecting *inwardly* the ethical "formation of his will" (Honneth, 2013, p. 132). On the one hand, persons act according to their arbitrariness; that is, they follow their individually determined preferences. On the other hand, however, law represents a "protective cloak" where personal arbitrariness is abandoned and thereby limited. "To the subjective rights, which from the beginning have formed a core element of the modern legal system, belongs above all the individual right to property, in addition to the right to freedom of contract" (Honneth, 2013, p. 133). With this, Honneth explains precisely the predominant character (within) the right to private property, constituting therefore the foundation of liberal ideology.

Thus, the so-called free will and abstract freedom are *subjected to economic imperatives*. Freedom derives from private property relations, that is, relations of private appropriation and exclusive dominium over external things. "Subjective rights, according to the conception of the first generation of liberal theorists of freedom, are negative rights that protect the scope of individual action by establishing enforceable claims to the injunction against unauthorised interference with liberty, life and property" (Honneth, 2013, p. 138). The state makes this possible and is the space of this freedom. However, Honneth suggests, this legal freedom has limits. The withdrawal from "all social obligations and ties" into private autonomy corresponds to a legal subject who has private freedom, albeit limited (Honneth, 2013, p. 147). That is, there is a protective space (shaped from the outside) that constantly determines and authorises individual boundaries. The subjective objectification of the individual or the transformation from an individual into a person is produced by its institutionalisation, namely, the right—this in Hegel is unambiguous (Hegel, 2013).

The person, the abstract right and property are the prerequisites of legal freedom. This freedom, however, is limited; it corresponds to an economic logic of action. Individual subjectivity, if not vanished, remains ineffective behind the veil of the abstract right. "What moves the other, what actually induces him to his actual action, is not relevant to communication here" (Honneth, 2013, p. 149). That is, what moves the other is of no one's concern. Indifference is not a product of individual autonomy but of constraints from economic imposition. It is *externally imposed to justify its opposite*; established rules negatively bind individuals not in acts of mutual affirmation but mutual self- and inter-negation. As legal persons, all are subjected to the same rules. Individual autonomy, freedom, and self-realisation are professed as high ethical values; in reality, conformity, abnegation, and indifference sway the individual's scope of action. "Such a subject must, on the one hand, have learned to abstract from his or her own moral or ethical convictions, if necessary, so as not to allow them to become actionable in the legally mediated interaction with others" (Honneth, 2013, p. 150). Honneth is emphatic when stating that legal freedom in no way corresponds to self-actualisation: "on the contrary, as long as a subject occupies the status of a legal entity, it cannot engage in precisely the kind of reflections or activities that constitute the precondition for an actualisation of aims in life" (Honneth, 2013, p. 154). In conclusion, legal freedom is a hypostasis because it precludes the very thing it postulates to generate and maintain: "it lives from the merely negative, interrupting reference to a moral context of practice that feeds on the social interaction of subjects who do not cooperate legally" (Honneth, 2013, p. 156).

2.2.4 Social Surplus-Value or Individual Subjective Utility?

Despite his groundbreaking discoveries and analyses, Adam Smith's understanding of capitalism was not free from errors and misconceptions. Contemporary to David Hume and forebear of David Ricardo, naturally, Smith could not have fully grasped capitalism—as no one ever will until it ceases to exist—for it was still in a very embryonic phase, and he could not have seen its legalities developed and matured. When addressing capital and the relations that enabled it, he places particular emphasis on some elements which are worth remembering. The notion of productive and unproductive labour—which until today is often miscomprehended—delineates labour that produces value and labour that does not. Moreover, unproductive labour is not something with a negative connotation. It simply relates to those activities which are "unproductive of any value" no matter "how honourable, how useful, or how necessary soever" they may be, yet "their service" "produces nothing" (Smith, 2012, p. 326). Unproductive labour is thus not a moral judgement but the activities which, on an ontological level, depend on productive labour for its existence, such as "the people who compose a numerous and splendid court, a great ecclesiastical establishment, great fleets and armies" (Smith, 2012, p. 337). Such a discussion is by no means anachronic, as it should become clear when discussing the critique of the political economy of the media (see *infra*). "The distinction between *productive* and *unproductive labour* is vital for accumulation since only the exchange for productive labour can satisfy one of the conditions for the reconversion of surplus-value into capital" (Marx, 1988, p. 116).

However, as capital is a social relation, one cannot simply accept the examples given by Marx or Smith as rigid, eternal truths if the intention is to contemplate productive and unproductive labour in the contemporary capitalist mode of production.

In another sense, Smith also places great emphasis on accumulation. "Parsimony, and not industry, is the immediate cause of the increase of capital"; thus, industry without accumulation has no potential for producing capital (Smith, 2012, p. 332). However, Smith conflates the meaning of capital with profit and is consequently unable to differentiate between capital, surplus-value, and profit. "It thus directly grasps surplus-value in the form of profit. Hence, the difficulties that are about to arise" (Marx, 1965, p. 61). Despite this not irrelevant mistake, Smith underlines that a person must employ his capital, which "puts into motion an additional quantity of industry" (Smith, 2012, p. 332), in this sense correctly representing an essential feature of capital, namely, its need to be in constant motion.

However, as capital represents a particular form of surplus labour accumulation, one must differentiate between its idiosyncrasies and other modes of production. While surplus labour characterises the social-labour that exceeds the immediate need for social production and reproduction—denoting surplus-use-value—, labour subsumption under capitalism subordinates all forms of value to surplus-value (surplus-exchange-value). From the labourer's perspective, surplus labour loses both its social and individual dimensions; appropriated by the capitalist, it appears as surplus-value. The neoclassic economics (the so-called marginal revolution) disregarded the notion of value, in which social relations are considered in totality, and instead presented models based on subjective apprehension of reality, namely, so-called marginal utility (Jevons, 2013; Menger, 2004; Walras, 1954). Its house of cards is based on endless assumptions, which presuppose leaving the most essential things, such as time, out of the model. Other unreal abstractions, such as perfect information, perfect competition, Pareto optimum, (stable) equilibrium of supply and demand, etc., are central in this made-up-economy. Its basis was contested by thinkers such as Ernest Mandel and Maurice Dobb. Piero Sraffa also reintroduced the issue of value in neo-Ricardian terms, deriving it from production instead of neoclassical (marginalist) theoretical assumptions. Building on Sraffa's critique, Samir Amin leaves no room for disputes: "The subjective theory of value has been shown to rest on a tautology—it does not even meet the criteria of formal logic" (Amin, 1977, p. 117; Sraffa, 1960).

Following Sraffa, Dobb demonstrates that prices are the result of "widely different proportions of labour and other inputs at different 'layers' in the vertical production-process" and not "independent" of social production relations, thus neoclassic expedient, abstractly regarding them as and in singular units emergent from timeless subjective perception of utility, must be considered "fallacious" (Dobb, 1973, pp. 254, 257, 243f). Mandel attacks it even further. It was political economy's failure to tackle the question of value posed by critics of capitalism, such as Marx, exposing political economy's intelligentsia to join the rows of socialist struggles, which made it necessary "to neutralise the 'socialist danger'", that is, "the entire structure based on the labour theory of value had to be demolished" (Mandel, 1968, p. 713). To achieve this, arguments concerning historical-ontological social relations exposing capitalists could not be confronted on their own merits. A whole new methodological set had to be founded *ex nihilo*. "The system is coherent, but it is divorced from reality, which it fails either to grasp statistically or *a fortiori,* to explain in its laws of development" (Mandel, 1968, p. 713). Therefore, marginalism abandoned not only the critique of political economy but political economy itself.

While Marx's critique managed to attain a notion of totality—namely, "a synthesis between micro-economic and macro-economic conceptions"—neoclassical economists abandoned this project altogether, becoming "a school of pure micro-economics, considering that value can and should be determined for each commodity taken separately" (Mandel, 1968, p. 713). Production was abandoned; exchange-value, which is completely different from use-value, was conflated together in a bizarre attempt to quantify utility. Residing on this dogmatic assertion based on subjectivism—for "its starting-point is purely arbitrary, subjective" (Mandel, 1968, p. 714)—the only possible explanation to sustain the absurdity that a diamond has greater utility than water or air, as it possesses greater exchange-value, was to postulate the concept of *marginal utility*. In this sense, "it is not the intensity of the need in itself, but the intensity of *the last fragment of need not satisfied* (of the *marginal* utility) that determines value" (Mandel, 1968, p. 714). The entire rigid and postulated apparatus, impervious to any dimension of reality, followed upon its own dogmas to forge layers of absurd corollaries, which, after the dogmas were either uncritically accepted or overlooked, could in-themselves resemble some validity. It is in this context that curves of demand and supply, those of indifference, of marginal costs, of utility, etc., presented a given structure, which was consecrated as the marginalist theory of general equilibrium. Its hollowness can be best summarised by the following: "In the end, the whole system is in perfect static equilibrium, 'profit' itself having disappeared, at least in Walras's work, since under conditions of total competition the value of the marginal product—which determines the value of all production—is dissolved into depreciated capital, wages, interest and ground-rent" (Mandel, 1968, p. 714). Already in Mandel's time, economists had little to no appreciation for the neoclassical model to explain or apprehend reality. It epitomises economic theory as pure ideology, apologetically rendering capitalism unreceptive to critique because it completely ignores the actual capitalist structure.

2.2.5 (Exchange-)Value Is Exploitation

This brief digression was necessary because—as neoclassical economics has become the foundation of mainstream economics—the understanding of real social property relations has become a tabu. Since the 2008 financial meltdown, capitalism critique has been developing, and even Marxist analysis appears once more to become acceptable. Nevertheless, generations of neoclassical (and neoliberal—see *infra*) economics have destroyed most of the cultural memory in which notions of value, surplus-value, and exploitation were virtually common sense. What is, then, the relationship among these three categories?

While use-value is the substance of value, exchange-value represents its dimension (size). The former refers to quality, the latter to quantity. The quality of a thing is independent of its quantity and, according to Marx, is actualised when it is being used. Dimensionality, on the other hand, exists only in relation to something else; it epitomises a proportion between two use-values. Unlike marginalist economists, this understanding renders both value categories irreducible to one another. "As use-values, commodities are above all of different quality; as exchange-values they can only be of different quantity, and thus contain no atom of use-value" (Marx, 1962, p. 50). Obtaining exchange-value of a thing presupposes abstracting, negating, and nullifying its use-value; that is, two different things cannot be equivalent. Only insofar as their differences are abstracted can they be regarded by a proportion in which a common denominator must be contemplated.

The only way to compare banana and train, popcorn and software, etc., is by reducing them to time—but not abstract time, rather abstract human labour-time. This abstraction enables the exchange-relationship to emerge, namely, a relationship which presupposes from the outset equality, a rapport between a mass of undifferentiated human labour. Self-negation or estrangement is, therefore, a precondition of exchange. Thus, in a society which "appears as an enormous accumulation of commodities", exchange-value becomes the supreme value, a value that reigns over all other forms of value; its ontological priority over other value forms is the reason why Marx can regard "value" as a synonym of exchange-value (Marx, 1962, pp. 49, 52).

In this relationship of equality and abstraction, value appears to be the measurement of all things and also the expression of concrete relationships of estrangement and alienation, in which all substance is abstracted, and the absence of the means of production imposes upon the labourer the necessity of selling himself as abstract labour-time through the act of alienation [*Entäußerung*]. Therefore, Marx explains, value is not determined by the dexterity of singular individuals but by the social mass of the labour-force, which appears as a singular labour-force. Insofar as individual labour is abstracted, value is represented by socially necessary labour-time, which "is labour-time demanded to represent any use-value with the existing, socially-normal conditions of production and [with] the social average degree of skill and intensity of labour" (Marx, 1962, p. 54). In this sense, value derives from labour, which, when bought, appears as labour-force, namely, the only "commodity" "to be the source of value" (Marx, 1962, p. 181). Labour transforms existing use-value and social relations; it confers upon them a new emphasis and objectifies its subjective-intentional character. Living labour becomes dead labour.

Logically speaking, it would be tautological to buy labour-force prior to the act of production and, after finishing using it, to have yielded the very same amount of its costs. Obviously, considering markets and acts of exchange, the very notion of equivalency is what enables those acts. Therefore, private property of the means of production and wage labour would be understandably tautological; socially, it would be an absurd relationship; why divest money in production to yield the same output of the value of the resources used during the act of production? If labour produces value, the only commodity which could yield surplus-value is labour itself. However, if labour power were being bought and sold within the legality of equivalency, no surplus-value could be created. Profit would have to be created not within production but rather in circulation, that is, not production-profit but profit on alienation (buying cheap and selling dear). Individually, this is possible in the sphere of distribution; however, capitalist production would yield zero profit and be pointless, socially representing a zero-sum relationship. Before capitalism emerged, it "was still a matter of recycling wealth or 'profit on alienation' in the process of circulation, rather than the creation of value in production, and the appropriation of surplus value, in the capitalist manner" (Wood, 2017, p. 79). Thus, capital creation and accumulation would be systemic impossibilities. Extra-economic measures would have to be implemented to enable vast amounts of wealth accumulation.

Private property relations, however, enabled profit to emerge within production; that is, money entering production as capital could be transformed into a commodity and realised in a larger sum of money than initially placed. "I call this increment or surplus over the original value—surplus-value" (Marx, 1962, p. 165). Capital thus represents a qualitatively different relationship in which profit is obtained. Instead of labour objectified as a commodity obtaining money to buy (necessary) commodities (C-M-C), from the perspective of the capitalist, money is the beginning and the result—but now augmented (M-C-M'). While objectified-labour constitutes the constant portion of capital, living labour represents its variable part, which must be reproduced. "All value originally arises from labour. All constant capital is originally as good a product of labour as variable capital. And here again, we seem to witness the direct emergence of capital from labour" (Marx, 1967, p. 486). As with any other commodity, its value arises from the socially necessary labour-time of its production. Thus, labour must be produced and reproduced not on an individual but rather on a social dimension.

It is neither about natural nor atomised individuals but social subsistence in which production and reproduction take place. Living labour thus requires a set of provisions for its reproduction. If working "X" number of hours enables the reproduction of labour, capital must simply either increase working hours of labour above "X" in order to obtain the necessary excess of working hours for its reproduction, namely, surplus-value, or the necessary "X" number of hours for labour reproduction must diminish, therefore sustaining the original "X" working hours after reproduction of labour value has decreased, that is, fewer than "X" hours; that is another form of obtaining surplus-value. The former, Marx calls absolute surplus-value, the latter, relative surplus-value; and he emphasises, in reality, that a mutual interplay takes place; one is accentuated and the other attenuated and vice versa depending on historical, social conditions (Marx, 1962, pp. 192ff, 331ff, 531ff). "What is reproduced and newly produced is not only the *existence* [*Dasein*] of these objective conditions of living labour, but *its existence as independent values*, i.e., *values belonging to a strange subject, in opposition to this living labour-capacity*" (Marx, 1983b, p. 374). It is obvious that Marx cannot be regarded as an economist, providing an affirmative theory of social reproduction; instead, what he unveils is capitalist exchange-value, or simply value, as relations of estrangement and alienation, which are not natural but rather socio-historically determined; capitalist surplus-value is based on human exploitation and presupposes private property of the means of production.

2.2.6 Productive and Unproductive Labour

Comprehending the production of surplus-value is essential to understand the issue of productive labour, which is paramount for intellectual property relations through digital transformations. As the value of the production of knowledge is virtually destroyed, can intellectual labour be considered productive [labour]? Relying on Marx, Christian Fuchs questions the consistency of this category, for, in Marx, productive labour is sometimes an activity which yields useful products, in others an activity that produces surplus labour, or even "Marx abstracts from the capitalist production process and argues [...] that all work is productive because it creates products that conditions and results of work" (Fuchs, 2012, p. 717f). Any attempt to seek a rigid definition must overlook a crucial element of Marxian methodology, namely, everything is in flow and motion; definitions can only be regarded relatively to certain determined relations; thus, the same substance can become something utterly different under different relations. "The same use-value that forms the product of this labour forms the means of production of that labour. Products are therefore not only the result, but at the same time the condition of the labour-process" (Marx, 1962, p. 196). Only in this fashion can he conceive the same thing as premise and result (see *infra*). Therefore, reducing productive labour to either this or that definition fails to understand its legality. From the capitalist perspective, Andreas Wittel correctly says, "productive labour is labour that is productive for capital" (Wittel, 2017, p. 80).

If wage labour was a condition for productive labour during the nineteenth century, in the twenty-first century, wage-less-labour has become an increasingly important source of the production of surplus labour (see *infra*). As in contemporary capitalism, reproduction of living labour depends not only on the aggregate value of rent, water, and food (as a gross simplification of nineteenth-century conditions) but also on a greater level of social relations among economic and extra-economic activities, resulting in a more heterogeneous labour-value to be reproduced. Examples of this are the consumption level of mass-consumer goods, entertainment, and drugs, the constant replacement of planned-obsolescent goods, the necessary access to social digital relations with friends, family, work, and the state, etc., by means of combined hardware-software commodities. Therefore, as social subsistence becomes more complex, many vital activities which are imposed occur outside wage labour relations; nevertheless, they remain subsumed under the economic imperatives of capitalism. The socially necessary labour-time, which is essential for the reproduction of the labour-force, is now divided among many contractual relationships. While the first appears to be the one imposed by wage labour, all access to the digital world entails contractual relations that the user—now a prosumer, a creator of surplus-value in the digital realm (see *infra*)—must subdue to participate in the digital social life.

While the notion of the social contract represents an idealist theoretical notion, in the digital sphere, one-sided contracts are imposed as an existential condition for the individual's digital actualisation. "And the development of this material wealth therefore in opposition to, and at the expense of, the human individual. *Productivity of labour* in general = *maximum of product* with *minimum of labour*, therefore as much as possible the improvement of commodities" (Marx, 1988, p. 107). Digital commodification and productive labour thus appear as the summit of productive labour, namely, labour which produces surplus-value. The purpose of the capitalist mode of production is that "the individual product, etc., *contain as much unpaid labour* as possible, and that this is only achieved by *production for the sake of production*" (Marx, 1988, p. 107). Marx leaves no room for doubt. The capitalist mode of production presupposes the production of surplus-value because it is its primary and highest goal; productive labour is subordinated to the production of surplus-value, "thus only the labour which *is* directly *consumed* in the process of production for the utilisation of capital" (Marx, 1988, p. 108).

It is therefore also absurd to attest to what productive labour ought to be in-itself. Thus, not only prosumers but also knowledge production by intellectual labourers, when subordinated to the economic imperative, become productive labourers. Amazingly, already in the 1860s, Marx realised this, removing from isolated individuals the character of being productive or not. "*Productive* labour is only an abbreviated expression for the whole relation and manner in which the labour assets and labour figure in the capitalist process of production", that is, it is its social character that endows it with legality, "*productive labour*" is "*socially determined labour*, labour which involves a quite definite relation between the buyer and seller of labour" (Marx, 1988, p. 111). And even when labour cannot be regarded as productive labour, under capitalist relations, it is still subdued and exploited. "The capitalist process of production is not merely the production of commodities. It is a process which absorbs unpaid labour, which makes the means of production the means of absorbing unpaid labour" (Marx, 1988, p. 113). Intellectual labourers and prosumers should thus be regarded in Marxian terms as productive labourers because the money involved in this process does not reside in a monetary form but metamorphoses into capital through the mechanism of surplus labour relations.

2.2.7 Debunking the Primitive Accumulation Myth

Although the notion of primitive accumulation became widely known with Karl Marx, he merely borrows and gives a critical accent to the concept initially used by political economy. For instance, in Adam Smith, it is called "previous accumulation" (Smith, 2012). As sagaciously explained by Ellen Meiksins Wood, claims that regarding capitalist development as the development of the division of labour, conversely, as the mere unfolding from exchange and specialisation, in fact, are ahistorical conceptions which naturalised capitalism (Wood, 2017). Capitalism appears as an inherent human feature which blossoms into maturity when the time is right. Adam Smith does not shy away from contributing to this mythologisation. "As the accumulation of stock must, in the nature of things, be previous to the division of labour, so labour can be more and more subdivided in proportion only as stock is previously more and more accumulated" (Smith, 2012, p. 267f). Marx ironically regards this reckoning "like the original sin in theology" (Marx, 1962, p. 741). It is not an exaggeration to consider it in a religious, mystical fashion because it derives from a fanatic defence of [the private] property as if it were sanctified, to which Marx underscores: "In real history, as is well known, conquest, subjugation, robbery-murder, in short, violence, play the major role" (Marx, 1962, p. 742). By doing so, he stresses the historical character of property and its concrete existence as a product of constant human struggle over appropriation control, thus, by no means representing something natural or deified. "Indeed, the methods of original accumulation are anything but idyllic" (Marx, 1962, p. 742).

If we take a step back, it is obvious that the significant role of accumulation in general was already being perceived by Marx and how it reverberated throughout capitalist relations in the *Economic and Philosophic Manuscripts of 1844*. He affirms that while competition would represent the only compelling justification for fostering and maintaining capitalist relations, in reality, multilateral accumulation turns into unilateral accumulation (Marx, 1968, p. 497). As profit cannot be regarded merely at the rate level but, not least importantly, at the level of the mass of capital, the accumulation of large capital has an immense advantage over smaller capital. "As capitals multiply, the profits on capitals diminish, as a result of competition. So the first to suffer is the small capitalist" (Marx, 1968, p. 489). These points are discussed at length in the first volume of *Capital.* The type of production (of the small capital) disappears, and larger private property *expropriates* existing private property. This is a tendency (or legality) of capitalist production, "the transformation of the individual and fragmented means of production into socially concentrated ones, hence of the dwarfish ownership of the many into the mass ownership of the few" (Marx, 1962, p. 789). This process characterises the prehistory of capitalist relations, in which small producers and the masses were heavily expropriated. However, as a legality, this process does not halt but rather adapts even further. Competition demands capital to expropriate capital in an apparently incessant movement of accumulation (Marx, 1962, p. 790). In the *Theories of Surplus Value*, Marx provides some not unimportant nuances. What does it mean for capitalism to presuppose "*general accumulation*" (Marx, 1967, p. 483)? To accumulate does not mean converting sums of money into capital. "*The conditions for the accumulation of capital, then, are quite the same as for its original production or reproduction in the first place*" (Marx, 1967, p. 484). That is, money should buy labour [power], raw materials and machines, the last two to be used by the former in and during industrial processes. Marx stresses that the conditions for the accumulation of capital are the same for both new and existing capital (Marx, 1967, p. 485). However, capital accumulation presupposes not only the accumulation of capital by itself; it is imperative that, throughout this process, a web of interdependence and mutual reinforcement among different spheres of capitalist production be formed. *One must attend to the fact that the product of one capitalist is, at the same time, the raw material consumed by other capitals.* Thus, *not only the division of labour intensifies with the development of the capitalist mode of production but also the interdependency among a collective capital itself.* The contradiction between the private character of appropriation and the vast cooperative, collective, and social character of production increases in the same proportion as capital develops. To sustain this process of constant production and accumulation of capital, "it seems then that in all spheres a steady surplus production is needed for accumulation to be [possible]" (Marx, 1967, p. 486).

In the *Grundrisse*, Marx also addresses the issue of the so-called primitive accumulation. According to the German philosopher, the conditions of (living) labour appear in opposition to the subjective living existence as "separated, independent values" as used values different from the worker. "Once this separation is presupposed, the process of production can only produce it anew, reproduce it, and reproduce it on a larger scale" (Marx, 1983b, p. 374). Reproduced are these objective conditions which account for the process of valorisation of capital; this production of wealth represents a "strange subject", "indifferently and independently opposing the capacities of labour" (Marx, 1983b, p. 374). This process thus accounts for a subject-predicate-inversion, in which these objective conditions acquire a subjective existence in opposition to the living subjects—worker and capitalist. Marx considers first a separation of the subjective existence from the objective conditions of the means of life; second, the objectified labour accumulated from labour, as use-values appear not as means for the reproduction of living labour capacities but "rather to absorb surplus labour" (Marx, 1983b, p. 376); third, exchange relations do not represent an immediate relationship between producers, but rather the mediated exchange between estranged labour; finally, [exchange] value entails an independent existence as an end-in-itself and does not represent an "immediate enjoyment or creation of use-value" (Marx, 1983b, p. 376). Thus, the becoming free of labour—which means free in two senses: neither as an immediate means of production, such as slaves or serfs, nor as owners of the means of production, such as independent farmers—represents a fundamental condition of capitalist production. "The capital relation presupposes the divorce between the workers and the property in the conditions of actualisation of labour" (Marx, 1962, p. 742). Upon the occurrence of these separations, the process of expropriation and appropriation is not only an element sustained but reproduced within an incessantly expansionist logic. The so-called previous or primitive accumulation is a built-in feature of capitalist logic;

it separates producers from the means of production—which are historically determined and change according to concrete material and subjective conditions. These notions are similarly reinforced in *Value, Price and Profit*. The legality of this contradiction between private appropriation of the means of doing and the increasingly social character of production tendentially surges within the reproduction process "until a new and thorough overturning of the mode of production overturns it again and restores the original unity in a new historical form" (Marx & Engels, 1962, p. 131).

As the accumulation process swells and consequently metamorphoses—since the composition of capital and ownership changes—banking capital plays an indispensable role in securing the flow of this process. This particular form of capital has the existential advantage of being virtually rootless, as its reproduction of capital renders superfluous the immediate first metamorphosis of capital in commodities through production, skipping directly to the second in which the appropriation of surplus-value enables the expansion of capital. However, to avoid a zero-sum game, it presupposes an ongoing real economy to expropriate and appropriate from. Lenin sagaciously perceived this movement in which banking capital merges with industrial capital, thus becoming financial capital (Lenin, 1971, p. 230). Furthermore, this financial capital—which presupposes the state to secure and legitimate itself as private property—becomes ubiquitous and further metamorphoses with the capitalist state. Lenin calls this process imperialism.

It is, however, vital to distinguish between imperialist capitalism and pre-capitalist imperialism. While "classic" imperialism has a centre, a particular locality from which it unfolds, capitalist imperialism is a much broader and more complex social relation in which different centres (nation-states) are intertwined and operated in a subordinated fashion to capital, which knows no bounds and constantly expands outwards as well as inwards (Hobson, 1902; Lenin, 1971; Rodney, 2018). It goes without saying that this process is not free from contradictions because while capital accumulation and appropriation know no national borders, its legitimation requires many national and international institutions which, as sine qua non, are located within national borders. John Atkinson Hobson's study—which inspired Lenin's own analysis—claimed that imperialism "is a constant menace to peace, by furnishing continual temptations to further aggression upon lands occupied by lower races"; furthermore, it consumes "physical and moral resources of the nations" within a mortifying logic of militarism (Hobson, 1902, p. 160).

The logic of imperialism driven by finance capitalism was extraordinarily grasped by Marx himself, who probably could not have seen more than the faintest concrete emergence of this capitalist legality. The contradictions described above—in which capital expropriates capital only to engulf it in a process of further primitive accumulation—culminate in finance capitalism, in which a complete separation between ownership and management takes place. This contradiction "establishes the monopoly in certain spheres and, therefore, challenges state interference. It reproduces a new financial aristocracy, a new breed of parasites in the shape of project makers, founders and merely nominal directors; a whole system of swindling and fraud with regard to incorporation, share issue and share dealing"; with this, Marx unveils a capitalist legality of internal contradiction, in which capitalist development antagonises capitalism's own ontological basis: "it is private production without the control of private property" (Marx, 1964, p. 454).

Almost one hundred years after Lenin's analysis, despite any critique it may deserve, Thomas Piketty's research has both the merit of having "reopened" the discussion about such capitalist accumulation and concentration[4] and of having shown that this is a broad historical and geographical phenomenon (Piketty, 2015). After the 2008 crisis, the roles of banks and the so-called unfettered capitalism[5] have increasingly become subjects of critiques—most of them simply moral criticisms. Matthew C. Klein and Michael Pettis reinforce Hobson's sentiment of menace arising from the upsurge in inequalities (Klein & Pettis, 2020). While organisations such as OXFAM, World Inequality Lab, and Institute for Policy Studies (Chancel et al., 2022; Christensen et al., 2023; Collins et al.,

[4] Even if under the moral bourgeois moral label of inequality, as if contemporary capitalism were a perverted form of true capitalism, demonstrating little understanding of what capitalist relations consists of, thus, simplistically and opportunistically labelling it *Capital in the 21st century*, while very much inconsistent with Marx's *Capital*.

[5] As if there could be a *fettered* version of capitalism in-itself, that is, a capitalism deprived of any historicity.

2020), among many others, emphasise the problem of inequality from a perspective of bourgeois enlightenment, they nevertheless do not detune from the rhymes of the financial sector. Mariana Mazzucato notes that in 2014, the CEO of Blackrock—an asset manager with over 10 trillion dollars in assets under its management (Brush & Wittenberg, 2022)—expressed concern about the excessive profit distribution of the S&P 500 companies (Mazzucato, 2018).

Blackrock is no exception in realising that profit extraction requires the subsistence and maintenance of the labour class or the so-called deplorables (Roberts, 2021). In its *Equity Strategy*, the Citigroup was blatantly clear: "The World is dividing into two blocs—the Plutonomy and the rest" (Kapur et al., 2005). In other words, there is the rule of the rich and the rest. The greatest global "Plutonomy", the United States, is ruled by the wealthy—the capitalist elite—who represent only a tiny fraction of society, which is composed of much more complex and vast elements. Capitalist concentration is pushing society towards deteriorating living conditions. For instance, while the San Francisco Bay Area accounts for one of the country's wealthiest parts, poverty is nonetheless soaring. The combination of being "underpaid" and skyrocketing housing prices creates a mass of poor people being pushed to live on the streets (Walker, 2018). However, this problem is not exclusive to the San Francisco Bay Area but is becoming systemic in the United States. People can hardly survive and are living from paycheck to paycheck (Pfeffer, 2018). Meanwhile, while US-American society seems to implode slowly, the spectacle distracts any politicised critical mass of people from being able to take responsibility for changing and creating new social relations to avoid total social anomy (Hedges, 2018).

As a central hub of global capitalism, the United States has a worldwide impact on capitalist relations. Perceiving and analysing these relations, William I. Robinson states that the "TNS apparatuses have exercised economic and extra-economic coercion in order to impose new labor regimes worldwide" (Robinson, 2014, p. 91). The TNS is composed of transnational (and supranational) organisations—the United States, the World Trade Organization, and the European Union (Robinson, 2014, p. 29). The capitalist mode of production has grown to become a system dominated by the so-called global financial giants in which few financial firms control a vast quantity of social resources and assets (Phillips, 2018). The "rest"—the "deplorables"—are not simply left to their own devices. Poverty is managed within a process of social (urban) segregation and the need for constant primitive accumulation.[6] Mike Davis' brilliant investigation sheds light on what he calls "surplus humanity". The structural death of formal jobs and a permanent state of unemployment have had a considerable impact on the spike of labour informality, which conversely transforms a formal working class into an informal one (Davis, 2006, p. 175). Robinson complements well: "New rounds of primitive accumulation have generated a vast army of internal and transnational migrants who have swelled the ranks of the precariat and the structurally marginalized" (Robinson, 2020, p. 46). It is along these lines that the so-called primitive accumulation of knowledge in the form of *intellectual property*$_{(private)}$ must be understood. These are some of the concrete conditions for two Pandora's boxes to be opened: TRIPS—as the *intellectual property*$_{(private)}$ Pandora's box (see *supra*)—and the repeal of the Glass-Steagall Act (Kroszner & Strahan, 2014; Nersisyan, 2015)—as the financial system Pandora's box—came to life with hitherto significant effects upon societies worldwide. Thus, capitalist ruthlessness intensifies and enables harsher and more immanent mechanisms of expropriation and appropriation.

2.2.8 Enclosing the Mind

Ravaging social conditions impact not only the non-digital but also the digital world. "Hundreds of millions, perhaps billions of people, have been displaced from the Third World countryside through new rounds of primitive accumulation brought about by neo-liberal policies as well as social cleansing, and organised violence such as the 'war on drugs' and the 'war on terror'"; furthermore, still according to Robinson, since the 2000s, banking, commercial and agricultural capital have increased the appropriation of new land (Robinson, 2020, p. 45). Not accidentally, in 2021, the media affirmed that Bill Gates had become the largest private

[6] Some contemporary processes analogous to primitive accumulation, see: pp. 15, 17, 58, 60, 65, 91, for urban segregation, see: pp. 98ff (Davis, 2006).

proprietor of farmland in the United States (Estes, 2021; Shapiro, 2021). However, his capital originally derives from a process of accumulation not of land but of knowledge. As computers gained social relevance, the value of knowledge production started to plummet. Therefore, copyright alone could no longer guarantee the monopolisation of the so-called knowledge-based economy. Thus, the question arises: how can fees be collected for every piece of information used? Gates first catapulted Microsoft's software DOS in a negotiation with IBM. Dominating the computer world, Gates' offer "more or less let IBM have DOS for free, but negotiated the right to charge other PC manufacturers for the supply of DOS"; however, while IBM lost its leading role in computers, Microsoft's position was secured, for when "DOS became the standard in the PC industry, copyright allowed Gates to maintain it as a proprietary standard"(Drahos & Braithwaite, 2002, p. 59). The monopolisation was based on a pricing strategy which enabled him to maintain his proprietary position. Therefore, Gates broke with the established "culture of sharing code developed among programmers, a group which included university computer scientists and graduate students as well as various amateur tinkerers without direct university affiliation" (Mueller, 2019, p. 29f).

Although capitalist expropriation-appropriation dialectics is not only a continuous but vital component of the social relations sustaining the capitalist mode of production, and thus the notion that "previous", "original", or "primitive" accumulation is extraneous to reality, James Boyle inaugurates the erroneous notion of "the second enclosure movement" relating to the so-called enclosure of (the commons of) the mind. "Commons of the mind" is likewise a mistake because the historical-ontological condition of the mind presupposes an immediate and immanent collective and social development (see *infra*). Moreover, the social, collective, cultural dimension is a vital, indispensable double condition for the individual mind. First, its very existence presupposes these social relations, and second, its actualisation for-itself further requires entering in and interconnecting with the social-living metabolism—both at objective and subjective levels (see *infra*). Despite these fundamental mistakes, Boyle's recognition has the merit of stressing the relevance of knowledge appropriation under the contemporary social relations of production.

Sustaining that the "enclosure of the information commons clearly has the potential to harm innovation as well as to support it" (Boyle, 2008, p. 76), he proposes an alternative to protect and sustain *intellectual property*$_{(private)}$ with the so-called Creative Commons. His perceptions of enclosure thus open the possibility for many other authors to pick up on this and continue the analysis.

Alexandra George's notion of ideational objects reveals additional areas of human relations that could also become targets of the private appropriation of the mind within the unceasing process of "primitive accumulation", for "covered by intellectual property laws include emotions [...], identification with social groups [...], beliefs or schools of thought [...], and most ephemeral communications that are not recorded in a documented form" (George, 2012, p. 155). Marx's notion of estrangement with private property indirectly stands out in Lionel Bently's assertion based on Roland Barthes' essay *The Death of the Author*: "Since copyright serves paradoxically to vest authors with property only to enable them to divest that property, the author is a notion which needs only to be sustainable for an instant" (Bently, 1994, p. 981). The condition "law" intends to guarantee is that property rights pass to "the control of the person who can exploit it most profitably" (George, 2012, p. 173). Reinforcing the illusion of competition benefits in a world where monopolist capitalism dictates capitalist legalities, Merges anachronistically and idealistically supports the notion that competition in *intellectual property*$_{(private)}$ "will resolve most concerns that scholars have shown with respect to content-platform deal making" (Merges, 2011, p. 231); thus, capital accumulation plays little to no role in changing the composition and quality of capitalist relations. Competition appears eternal, intrinsic, and impervious to the effects of accumulation and, consequently, concentration. The fact noted by Mariana Mazzucato, namely, that five US companies own nearly all the data from the whole globe, does not shake Merges' belief in the "Market God" (Cox, 2016).

Drahos misunderstands a fundamental change that arose under the capitalist mode of production and which is emphasised by Marx—as well as by Wood—namely, the crucial change within economic relations which ceased to be possibilities of the ontological conditions of doing to become imperatives and impositions that any doing would presuppose.

This was only possible by removing from people their immediate means—conditions—of life and replacing them with the mediation of exclusive private property of the means of production, which then became a necessary condition as an external imposition. Furthermore, in Marx, both the emergence and sustaining of this new condition presupposed extra-economic social relations, which constitute both the material and subjective conditions for capitalist economic imperatives. Drahos, however, reduces Marxist complexity and changes within this process to an "algorithmic routine" conceived by the "materialist concept of history" (Drahos, 2016, p. 115). This reductionism becomes even more evident when Drahos' assertion that Marx's problem is the fact that he "is fixated by the materiality of production" (Drahos, 2016, p. 130) is contrasted with his previous assertions that creative labour and science are indispensable for and integrated into the capitalist mode of production; this "is to be found in some of Marx's remarks on the role of science in capitalism"; moreover, scientific production has become an imperative because "capital is linked to a definite mode of production which includes science, while at the same time, science helps to bring this mode into being" (Drahos, 2016, p. 128). Thus, despite asserting that historical materialism is mechanic, Drahos—whether unintentionally or not—confirms Marx's non-mechanistic dialectical understanding of the mutual and contradictory interdependency of both capitalist and scientific developments. Accumulation of capital has prompted the accumulation of science, which has reinforced the former; however, the more capital accumulation with its private character develops into monopolistic capitalism, and the more scientific development creates and presupposes a broad social and collective advancement of knowledge, the greater the contradiction between their mutual necessity to reinforce each other and their mutual necessity to annihilate each other's ontological conditions (see *infra*). The quantitative relationship of interdependence is necessarily affecting the qualitative state of existence of these intertwined but also antagonistic poles.

2.2.9 The First Paradox of Intellectual Property in Capitalism

The paradox is thus not only the one commonly considered: namely, the capitalist privatisation of knowledge in order to secure surplus-value—and thus reproduce itself as capital—destroys the existing pool of knowledge by creating the sine qua non condition of its exclusion from the collective and social sphere; however, the production and reproduction of knowledge presupposes the collective and social sphere. The *second paradox* emerges from the ontological fact of the production of knowledge under the capitalist mode of production. Thus, knowledge, despite having an ontological character in general—an existential condition of being socially conceived and collectively actualised—presupposes attaining a particular form under capitalism and requires privatisation. In short, only when it is private can it gain a social dimension. However, this social dimension of deprivation and exclusion negates the general ontological condition of both production—coming into being—and reproduction—the elements that are vital for the moment of actualisation. These two paradoxes will be investigated in detail later (see *infra*). *Intellectual property*$_{(private)}$ literature has hitherto only emphasised the first aspect.

Rainer Kuhlen seems to understand the problem: although capitalism needs privatisation to exist, the exhaustion of its source of privatisation through primitive accumulation occurs by privatisation itself, making it an unsustainable form of exploitation; he nevertheless states that when the "information industry understands [...] that they can hardly make any profit with the information itself, but rather through accompanying value-added offers, then the legislator will" have to act according to "the normative behavior and ethical expectations of creators and users in an electronic environment" and unrepresentative laws will be superfluous (Kuhlen, 2007, p. 230). More than fifteen years after the publication of his paper, reality has imposed itself and has instead shown that control of information is driving the new rounds of the so-called primitive accumulation. In a more contemporary publication, Keith E. Maskus and Jerome H. Reichman suggest that today "the regulation of knowledge goods in national markets impinges on the provision of other public goods—health, education, scientific research, agriculture and the environment—in ways that were virtually unknown to previous generations" (Maskus & Reichman, 2016, p. 349). Although TRIPS had the pivotal impulse to catapult *intellectual property*$_{(private)}$ to attain a higher level of real subsumption—given that *intellectual property*$_{(private)}$ or intellectual technology plays a crucial role "in the real subsumption of both intellectual and manual labour" (Jessop, 2000, p. 71)—in securing the primitive accumulation of the mind and the body—for instance, with gene appropriation—Dianne Nicol stresses that "the most important legislative intervention in the US was the *Bayh–Dole Act 1980*" (Nicol, 2021, p. 108).

While George has listed elements that hitherto have not been subjected to capitalist appropriation, Peter Drahos and John Braithwaite named others that, despite their general non-private characteristics, have been reduced to privatisation. By means of computational technology and science, "corporations have made things like DNA, algorithms and musical sounds targets of private ownership. What was once part of the intellectual commons has fallen into private hands" (Drahos & Braithwaite, 2002, p. 19). To enable a vast array of knowledge appropriation, *intellectual property*$_{(private)}$ appears to be the right tool, and limitations on patentability, for instance, were (mostly) eradicated. "The essence of the knowledge game was to propertize as much knowledge as possible" (Drahos & Braithwaite, 2002, p. 51). The totalising character is not merely a theoretical possibility. Restrictions on the patentability of discoveries were changed in order to accommodate the private appropriation of natural genes. "At an interview with the EPO in 1993, we were told that 'everything would be patentable; it's just a question of time'" (Drahos & Braithwaite, 2002, p. 144). Genetics appeared as a new Wild West of *intellectual property*$_{(private)}$. Patenting genetic sequences without knowing what they did or what they could be used for became paramount. "In 1991, the US PTO had applications covering 4000 such sequences. By September 1998, the number of sequences being applied for had climbed to over 500,000" (Drahos & Braithwaite, 2002, p. 156). Despite private capital having no guarantees, it could secure yields from the so-called primitive accumulation, and it was crucial for the private sector to block the public sector and the development that would prevent complete private control and gain through the privatisation process. This practice, however, became a paradoxical situation because it prompted US-American universities and the National Institutes of Health (NIH) to apply for many patents. As public and governmental institutions were the main agents of scientific development and discoveries, then "the Industrial Biotechnology Association, a trade association that represented most of biotech in the US, also urged the NIH not to pursue the patents and to put the sequences into the public domain" (Drahos & Braithwaite, 2002, p. 156f).

2.2.10 Digital Gift Economy

A not insignificant part of the relations within the digital realm could be referred to as gift economies. The Digital will be dealt with in greater length below, but for now, it should suffice to point out that they also become a target of primitive accumulation (Fuchs, 2012, p. 707). "Unpaid labour extends to different realms, such as Google, Twitter, YouTube, Baidu, LinkedIn, knowledge creation and reproduction"; of course, this also affects labour activities involving domestic, educational, care, etc., "so that the human being in contemporary capitalism spends a lot of working hours every day in creating value for capital by abstract labour that is unpaid" (Fuchs, 2012, p. 716). Some of them are directly involved in the process of value creation, while others are merely indirectly involved by providing elements of social infrastructure. Everything that might have appeared to represent a barrier, an impossibility for private appropriation, is now being reconfigured within a new landscape of apparently endless possibilities. "The pressing search for new fields of expansion and acquisition finds an indispensable ally in technoscience" (Pellizzoni & Ylönen, 2012, p. 54). With historical reduction of the value of knowledge, access to it and consequently a form of general appropriation become ubiquitous. However, information and knowledge can always have a direct impact on real economic and political-economic power relations. The free exchange of knowledge through these gift economies and general appropriation must be blocked if contemporary capitalist power is to maintain its status quo. "Rivalry, as a consequence, has to be constructed", a qualitative change which the authors call "ontological commodification" (Pellizzoni & Ylönen, 2012, p. 55f). Even the United Nations promotes this logic of commodification, as everything becomes subject to the logic of profit. Knowledge and cultures emerging in specific places become excluded from *intellectual property*$_{(common)}$ (Pellizzoni & Ylönen, 2012, p. 59). On the other hand, capital makes no real distinction of use-values. It appropriates for free all cultural practices and developed knowledge which may assist in fostering, producing, and appropriating surplus-value. An example is the so-called sharing economy, which despite its propagandistic excitement focusing on the term "sharing", analogous to the Creative Commons, is simply another mechanism to penetrate the dimensions of social life not yet subordinated by the logic of economic imposition with an economic dependency prompted by the logic of primitive accumulation (Mazzucato, 2018). Gift economies are, therefore, subsumed under capitalism; now, only the appearance of gift economies is maintained, while in practice, it attains the essence of capitalist economic/market imperatives.

Bob Jessop and Ngai-Ling Sum denounce that there is more than meets the eyes when the phenomenon of knowledge-based economy (KBE) is considered. "A shadowy side of the KBE is the primitive accumulation of capital (in the form of intellectual property) through private expropriation (or enclosure) of the collectively produced knowledge of past generations" (Sum & Jessop, 2013, p. 287). Knowledge is transmuted from a collective into a private resource, namely, *intellectual property*$_{(private)}$. As briefly summarised in Chap. 4 (especially when analysing *biopiracy*), first, there is the appropriation of indigenous, aboriginal, and foreign knowledge and culture; this process occurs outside of the so-called free market and represents the immediate expropriation and conversion into "commodified knowledge". Second, the appropriation of nature represents a new domain of colonisation. Third, the effect of the so-called second enclosure is similar to the first in that it separates labour from the means of labour, "thereby appropriating the knowledge of the collective labourer". Fourth, knowledge is further subsumed to a new form of management imposed top-down by elements such as the Bayh-Dole Act or TRIPS. Finally, *intellectual property*$_{(private)}$ is so drastically extended that it provokes the "erosion of any residual public interest"

(Sum & Jessop, 2013, p. 287). Rebecca Eisenberg refers to the cul-de-sac: "Even if exclusive rights enhance private incentives to develop further research tools, they could do considerable damage to the research enterprise by inhibiting the effective utilisation of existing ones" (Eisenberg, 1994, p. 647). This process of primitive accumulation through "the major expansion of patents into what used to be the realm of science is", according to Richard Nelson, "well documented" (Nelson, 2003, p. 1702). This progression of major control and "regulation" is contrasted with previous phases of humanity in which "law" was concerned with particular cultural events that might have "disturbed the peace" but not with cultural "creation or spread" (Lessig, 2004, p. 8).

2.2.11 Result and Premise: Arbitrary Teleological Condition

To be able to express an essential breakup with the ongoing intellectual property theory, it appears crucial to first introduce some fundamental methodological elements based on Hegel and Marx. Only then will the notion of *property-totality* become attainable. This methodological input, connected with the ontology of knowledge production (see *infra*), provides the basis for understanding the *second paradox* of intellectual property, as well as the relation of *interdependency* of property and intellectual property.

In the *Science of Logic*, Hegel's critique of Kant does not supersede idealism but rather provides a fundamental qualitative change to it. While Kant's epistemology recognises the existence of a material world, the world of knowledge does not mutate according to worldly events; instead, it constitutes a transcendental ontology, for time and space do not exist but are simply formal elements of the epistemic. Thus, reality can never be pierced by thought. The gulf between reality or the thing-in-itself and the perception, which are mere appearances, remains unbridgeable. Cognition (*Erkenntnis*) is therefore epitomised (*inbegriffen*); that is, it appears as an embodied feature of reason (*Vernunft*) (Kant, 1956). Hegel tries to supersede this hypostasis while holding idealism (al)together. In this context, his dialectics is the perfect expression of this endeavour. He recognises that both the world and the mind (or spirit, *Geist*) are constantly changing, but also raises the question of how to explain these changes. And finally, if the finite world is impenetrable by the infinite world of thought, how is it possible that an appearance could be attained? The idealist answer is thus not to derive *Geist* from matter but matter from *Geist*. The infinite pierces the finite, negating itself and, by doing so, also negating the latter because now the spiritual infinite is contained in the finite materiality. *Geist* in-itself attains its true reality through this double negation. Let us consider this in some detail.

Logic (of non-contradiction), when considered thinking in general, becomes the embodiment, "*the form*" of knowledge. However, this form of logic necessarily abstracts and negates "*all content*"; therefore, "matter" must emanate from "elsewhere"; in this sense, matter appears completely independent from logic, which can only be formal and consequently neither attain nor contain "real truth itself", excluding content, then the "essential of truth" (*Wesentliche der Wahrheit*) must lie "outside it" (Hegel, 1986a, p. 36). The immanency of a non-relationship between thinking (*Denken*) and object (*Gegenstand*) persists; the object "remains as a thing-in-itself par excellence a beyond of thinking [ein Jenseits des Denkens]" (Hegel, 1986a, p. 37). Introducing his own logic, Hegel presents an element which will become fundamental in Marx's analyses. While in Hegel logic represents the unity between "result" (*Resultat*) and "precondition" (*Voraussetzung*) (Hegel, 1986a, p. 58), in Marx, these elements become fundamental to the understanding of the *logic* (now in the sense of *legality, tendency, real movement*) of capital, in which production and consumption are twofold and at the same time result and premise. Even in nature, inorganic nature constitutes both the condition and the result of organic nature. For Hegel, this relationship represents the ingress of objective logic *in lieu* of metaphysics.

Already in *The Phenomenology of Spirit*, Hegel conceives the immediate consciousness as the precondition—for "the spirit, *appearing* in this element to consciousness, or, which is here the same, produced in it by it, is *science*" (Hegel, 2014, p. 583)—but also the result of science—as "science contains in itself this necessity to renounce the form of the pure concept, and the transition of the concept into *consciousness*" (Hegel, 2014, p. 589). These two dimensions represent the philosophical *Ansichsein* and

Fürsichsein, or being-in-itself and being-for-itself. Unlike Kant, in which the thing-in-itself was both real and immanently remained isolated, the being-in-itself represents the absolute beginning and, as such, presupposes nothing; it lacks any content and is hence insubstantial. Pure being is independent, an isolated essence, "unrelated" (*Beziehungslos*) (Hegel, 1986a, p. 68). Hegel calls this "insubstantiality" (*Inhaltslosigkeit*) "nothingness" (*Nichtigkeit*), which is empty, an "indeterminateness" (*Bestimmungslosigkeit*). "*So pure being and pure nothingness are the same thing*" (Hegel, 1986a, p. 83). Therefore, "the essential (Wesentliche) for the science" is rather the circular flow (*Kreislauf*)[7] instead of an immediate beginning (Hegel, 1986a, p. 70). Such a beginning would not be aleatory but rather arbitrary, a subjective postulation. Consequently, science would become deified. It is thus the existing being (existence, *Dasein*) which reveals a real difference, for it contains "a *something* and a *different*" (ein *Etwas* und ein *Anders*) (Hegel, 1986a, p. 90). This *Dasein* thus corresponds to a moment of becoming (*Werden*), a crossing over in a unity between being and nothingness but not relapsing into a "disappeared-being" (*Verschwundensein*) but rather into a qualitatively different ontological condition of being—now as *seiend*, thus a being-in-motion, a constant process of transformation (Hegel, 1986a, p. 113). "Dasein is [a] *determinate* being; its determinateness is *being*-determinateness, *quality*" (Hegel, 1986a, p. 115). In the *Encyclopaedia of the Philosophical Sciences*, Hegel sustains that this progression is already contained in our imagination, the very becoming is a result; this result "is not the empty nothing, but the being identical to the negation, which we call *Dasein*" (Hegel, 1989, p. 194f, supplement to §89). True affirmation—which, according to Hegel, is the task of philosophy—emerges from such a process as the negative of the negation, also commonly known as the negation of the negation (Hegel, 1989, p. 200, supplement to §94). While quality contains a determination, "a something", some content, "*quantity* is the pure being, in which determinateness [*Bestimmtheit*] [...] is set as *superseded* or *indifferent*" (Hegel, 1989, p. 209, §99). The quantum (in German, *Quantum*) represents, however, the exclusive determinateness set in quantity, thus limiting it. Therefore, the development of quantum in the

[7] *Kreislauf* is the same concept used in Marx's *Capital* to explain the movement of capital.

number (*Anzahl*) expresses a qualitative leap (Hegel, 1989, p. 214, §§101–102). Quantity reverts to quality by means of a dialectical movement (Hegel, 1989, p. 223, supplement to §106). The unity of this contradiction between quantity and quality, in which one negates the other and vice versa, is the *Maß* (dimension, measurement, proportion) (Hegel, 1989, p. 228f, §111). Hegel gives the example of water, which can be found in different states—solid (ice), gas (vapour), or liquid water—depending on the temperature [and pressure, from the ideal gas law, $pV = nRT$] (Hegel, 1989, p. 226, supplement to §108). Therefore, Hegel claims that "what moves the world at all is contradiction, and it is ludicrous to say that contradiction cannot be thought" (Hegel, 1989, p. 247, supplement 2 to §119).

What is the content which gives the being determinateness and enables its leap from nothingness to a dialectical state expressed in measurement? Hegel underlines the "immediate relationship" between "the whole and the parts"; while content consists of the latter, it is also the former. Despite the real independency of the parts, their relation to each other constitutes the whole; consequently, it is precisely because the parts negate themselves as parts that they can emerge as a whole (Hegel, 1989, p. 267, §135). This negation is an ontological condition, for it immanently imposes relationships. (One can clearly see how this connects to Hegel's notion of property, which presupposes self-estrangement and the alienation of one private property in order to obtain what he considers to be freedom (Hegel, 2013)—unpublished manuscript analyses this at length.) Thus, everything that exists exists in relation to something. Together, the necessary relationships (*Beziehungen*) to itself and to others represent the unity expressed in the relation (*Verhältnis*). However, establishing the whole is, to some extent, an arbitrary task. Parts can be endlessly fragmented; any whole can be determined by grouping any "n" elements together. *This expresses how—in Hegel—ontological conditions are subordinated to the will; thus, the question of beginning (precondition) and result becomes an arbitrary matter, revealing the immanent vital condition of the absolute Geist.* "Causality has hereby crossed over into the relation of interdependency" (Hegel, 1989, p. 300, §154). However, as explained elsewhere, in Hegel, causality is subordinated to teleology because reality and history appear to be a constant teleological product (Hermeto,

2020a). Therefore, his remarkable assertions concerning interdependency that "cause is at the same time effect, and that the effect in the same relation in which it is effect is at the same time cause" (Hegel, 1989, p. 301, Supplement to §156) must always remain tainted with an overstretching teleological condition imposed by the absolute *Geist*. If, on the one hand, this interdependency is a necessity, on the other, "the truth of substance is the concept" (Hegel, 1989, p. 303, §158). In Hegel, the concept (*Begriff*) is an indispensable and powerful category. "For the concept is the absolute, as it is absolute or in and for itself in its Dasein" (Hegel, 1986b, p. 16). Hegel explains in detail the three moments contained in the concept—generality, particularity and singularity (*Allgemeinheit, Besonderheit* und *Einzelheit*)—however, for the purpose of this discussion, its analysis would prove excessive (Hegel, 1986b, p. 273ff). This hypostasis must raise concern because, as a result, a subject-predicate-inversion occurs, in which "Hegel makes the predicates independent and afterwards allows them to transform into their subjects in a mystical way" (Marx, 1981b, p. 224). For Hegel, thus, "it is not a matter of bringing empirical existence to its truth, but of bringing truth to an empirical existence" (Marx, 1981b, p. 241). *What is crucial to retain is Hegel's perception of the interdependency between parts and totalities, of beginnings and endings, of causes and effects, and, especially, that reality is in constant motion.* Turning to Marx's analysis regarding the categories of result and premise appears indispensable in order to give them actuality in light of concrete reality.

2.2.12 Result and Premise: Causal Historical Condition

It is no accident that Marx initiates not only *Capital Volume One* but also *A Contribution to the Critique of Political Economy* in a similar fashion. While the 1859 text begins with: "At first sight, bourgeois wealth appears as an immense collection of commodities, the individual commodity as its elementary existence" (Marx, 1961, p. 15); the other, from eight years later, starts: "The wealth of societies in which the capitalist mode of production prevails appears as an 'immense collection of commodities', the individual commodity as its elementary form" (Marx, 1962, p. 50). To begin with, Marx questions the appearance of particular modes of production which take the capitalist form as if that would mean the universalisation of commodities. In a manuscript, which should be frequently revisited here, Marx confirms this. "If the *commodity* [appears] thus on the one hand as the precondition of the formation of capital, the *commodity* appears on the other hand, as long it is the *universal elementary form of the product*, essentially as the product and result of the capitalist production process" (Marx, 1988, p. 27). I.e., although the commodity form precedes capitalism, it is capitalist relations that give it a new character. Thus, it was not the universalised commodities that gave rise to capitalism, but it was capitalism that prompted its universalisation—this is the historical context in which economic possibility becomes an imposition.[8] Marx is, therefore, most consequential by not assuming the part as the whole, not collapsing together the phenomenon (*Erscheinungsform*) with the essence (historical legality). It is only after commodities are rendered universal by capitalist relations that they become a premise for capitalist reproduction. In this sense, the product does become the condition. However, the relation, which became a condition, is not a suprahistorical category that laid dormant, awaiting its destiny to be realised. Such considerations set forth a fetishised notion of capitalism, as if it were eternal, part of human nature, an intrinsic human condition.

In an introductory note to the *Results of the Immediate Process of Production*, Ernst Mandel highlights Marx's insight that "under capitalism, labour should not be seen as manual labour only, but as the combined or collective labour potential [...] of all those whose labour is indispensable to produce the final product" (Mandel, 1976, p. 945); this reinforces both the social character of production and the metabolic dimension of its parts, which also implies that intellectual labour is embedded in this process. Understanding this basis seems crucial to an adequate treatment of intellectual property—because knowledge and information are always embedded in social relations of production as

[8] Wood perfectly captures this dialectics and, dissenting from the often characterised consensus of the so-called commercialisation model, which assumes capitalism as the product of the universalisation of commodities (and commodities trade), brilliantly unveils the capitalist genesis (see *infra*).

both an input and output (as also Kenneth Arrow noticed, see *infra*). When its formal subsumption gives way to real subsumption, then its character changes because its universal character within social property relations entails a drastically more significant pressure of universal capitalist legality of commodification. Economic laws are not set in stone because they merely represent the tendency (legality), δύναμις, and logic of a given existing mode of production; thus, "economic categories belonging to earlier epochs of production acquire a specifically different, historical character on the basis of the capitalist mode of production" (Marx, 1988, p. 27). Knowledge is not simply an economic category, but its genesis, development, and constant transformation are the product of ontological relations of production and, as such, attain particular concrete characters. Concrete knowledge dialectically becomes an imperative means for shaping, forming, and transforming social material relations. It is in this sense that one must understand Marx's assertion: "The mode of production of material life determines the social, political and intellectual process of life in general. It is not the consciousness of people that determines their being, but quite the opposite, it is their social being that determines their consciousness" (Marx, 1961, p. 8f).

When knowledge becomes commodified, then its particular relations coincide with the universal capitalist commodification. It goes without saying that knowledge is neither intrinsically a commodity nor that all knowledge relations are subjected to real subsumption by capital. It is those social relations of knowledge that, when subjected to capitalist imperatives, underwent (and conversely are still undergoing) a transformation from formal to real subsumption. Real subsumption imposes the necessity of privatisation of intellectual appropriation (property). It is not the division of labour in-itself that affords knowledge its private character; on the contrary, this process of socialisation presupposes and results in an accentuation of the social development and exchange of knowledge. The dependency and interdependency of knowledge corresponding to the unfolding of social relations appear as its general ontological condition. It is thus the process of privatisation itself, the imposition of privatisation as a social-ontological necessity, that metamorphoses intellectual property into a private existence, providing a particular and contradictory existence to the production and appropriation of knowledge.

2.2.13 An Ontological Condition of Capital

Economic imposition does not derive from a mechanic conceptualisation of society; instead, it expresses the legality of the ontological condition of capital—which is a social relation. However, this specific relation appears to cease to be a human product to become a necessary condition of human existence, i.e., an imposition. The very existence of capital is the movement of accumulation and reproduction which imposes the necessity of constant production, appropriation, valorisation—the latter, a vital moment because accumulation in-itself is merely the formation of treasure (Marx, 1961, p. 104ff; 1962, p. 144ff; 1963, p. 488ff)—of surplus-value. The commodity which circulates is impregnated with capital, and its circulation sets in motion the process of reproduction, in which surplus-value is actualised, and the capital as a product of capital thus becomes a precondition of capital. Capital is an end in-itself. Marx underlines that it is a grave mistake to equate money and commodity as such with capital, further, to conflate means of labour—namely, the specific existence of use-value—to capital as such. Despite capital first emerging as money, which is also a social relation, it attains a particular existence under capitalist relations. While the commodity consumer enacts money relations as a means of exchange, capitalist production, which ceases to be for immediate consumption, becomes exclusively private and sets in motion a different money relation. Money is now used not for consumption as an end but as a means, or in other words, not as a means of life but as a means of money itself. "The exchange-value is to serve to create more exchange-value" (Marx, 1988, p. 52). It is, therefore, not a metaphysical attribute that confers capital its legality but rather a concrete and determined set of historical political-economic relations.

However, this *subject-predicate-inversion* could not simply be the result. It must first emerge from a process, and it is the product of social relations that are already subordinated to their predicate. As shown above, social (exclusive) private property relations of production produce and reproduce labour in a manner in which the very labour-process, the relationship between the labourer and the labour activity, are separated and estranged—confronting each other. Labour ceases to be the means of life;

life becomes the means of labour, in which human estrangement emerges and is actualised "so that the worker appears only as an instrument bought by capital" (Marx, 1988, p. 59). This portion of capital—variable capital—is the true essence of capital, namely, living labour power. However, it does not enter the production process as a thing-in-itself. "Instead of the *value* of the variable part of capital, we now have *valorisation* as a process, labour conceived in the act of *valorisation*, which constantly realises itself as value, but which also continues flowing over the set values to new creations of value" (Marx, 1988, p. 60). Hence, living labour does not actualise itself in this process but is rather absorbed by objective labour, thus becoming self-valorising value, that is, capital or value valorising itself. In this sense, capitalist relations imposed a condition of a system of ontological reification not as an existential sine qua non in-itself but as a necessary condition that mediates life production under the capitalist mode of production. This real productive process presents the "*same* relation" found "in the ideological sphere in religion", namely, "the inversion of the subject into the object and vice-versa" (Marx, 1988, p. 64f). Marx's influence from Feuerbach seems unquestionable for the human being throughout this practice of self-negation lapses into a "fantastic, transcendental practice" (Feuerbach, 2013, p. 35). Marx's critique of this mythological, metaphysical condition of capitalist production does not present any moral judgement; on the contrary,

> viewed *historically*, this inversion appears as the necessary point of passage in order to force the creation of wealth as such, i.e., of the ruthless productive forces of social labour, which alone can form the material basis of a free human society at the expense of the majority. It is necessary to pass through this opposing form, just as the human-being must first religiously shape his spiritual forces as independent powers towards himself. It is the *process of estrangement* [*Entfremdungsproceß*] of his own labour. In this respect, the worker stands from the outset higher than the capitalist, since the latter is rooted in this *process of estrangement* and finds absolute satisfaction in it, while the worker, as its victim, stands from the outset in a rebellious relationship to it and feels it as a process of subjugation. (Marx, 1988, p. 65)

Thus, the celebration of wage labour as freedom is viewed by Marx not as freedom of choice, not as an option, but rather as an obligation. The subordination of the labour to the economic (market) imperatives and (capitalist) exploitation is, under capitalism, not only an ontological necessity of the labourer but also of the capitalist in order for the former to sustain himself as a labourer and the latter as a capitalist. Deprived of the means of production, the labourer must still reproduce himself as labour power, as a working commodity; thus, he must undergo a process of subordination in the so-called labour market, selling his time (factually, himself) for money to buy the means required to guarantee his subsistence. The capitalist must acquire and command the working force in the production process to appropriate surplus-value. However, no capitalist advances the value produced in wages if the value produced by labour is identical to what has been paid to him. Insofar as an economic compulsion exists for both—one to subordinate himself, the other to exploit the other—then the notion of commodity equivalency cannot be applied to the labour market (unless it is a slave labour market).

In the exchange process, commodities are exchanged for commodities containing the same amount of objectified living labour, namely, value. "Insofar as the labour-process is merely the means and the real form of the *process of valorisation*", that is, production of surplus-value, "the point of departure of this whole process is the exchange of *objectified labour* with *living labour*, the exchange of *less objectified labour* for more *living labour*" (Marx, 1988, p. 82). Nevertheless, Marx sustains the importance of not only recognising that commodity is a product of labour but also the two existential forms of labour under capitalism, "in which it represents itself on the one hand as *concrete labour* in the *use-value of the goods*, and on the other hand is calculated as *socially necessary* labour in the *exchange-value*" (Marx, 1988, p. 67). The former relates to its specific nature, the use-value; the latter makes no distinction of utility, namely, its particular character; thus, this labour epitomises the exchange-value, and the commodity now represents its objectified being. The former—concrete, objectified, dead labour—relates to the quality of labour; the latter—living labour—relates to the quantity that is determined by the average socially necessary quantity of labour to produce a given commodity. Dead and living labour are manifested in the labour-process, for the first is found in an already objectified form, while the second (living) is still being objectified. This process forms the basis for the self-valorisation and accumulation of capital.

2.2.14 Capitalist Private Property and Economic Coercion

Assuming labour power as simply another element of the process of circulation of commodities in which they are bought against and sold for money hence represents an economic vulgarisation. Such an insight ignores both capitalist economic coercion, overcoming pre-capitalist economic opportunity, and the peculiarity of the labour commodity, which is the only commodity that can produce value and surplus-value; thus, this specific relation of production constitutes the very core element of capitalist relations. [Exclusive] Private property relations, which subordinate the transformation of economic relations, are therefore the precondition for universalising the selling and buying of labour power. "Only because the worker, in order to live, sells his labour assets, does objective wealth transform itself into capital" (Marx, 1988, p. 79). Thus, this represents a twofold condition. According to Marx, the metamorphosis of money into capital requires a qualitative transformation of labour that ceases to be immediate labour capacities to become a sold commodity. "On the other hand, labour can only appear as wage labour as soon as its own objective conditions confront it as independent [*selbstisch*] power, estrange property, value that exists for itself and holds on to itself, in short, as capital" (Marx, 1988, p. 79f). These two aspects are essential for the valorisation of capital and thus for the very socio-ontological existence of capital. Marx thus abdicates mechanistic economics, which conflates capital with the sole material aspects of the labour-process; instead, he denounces this reasoning because it ignores the "social characteristic amalgamated" in them, "which constitutes *capital*" (Marx, 1988, p. 81).

In a footnote, a relevant point reveals the opposition between objective social relations and the perception perpetrated by subjective social relations. While production relations depend on the labour made, produced, and given by workers, in German, the worker is regarded as labour-taker (*Arbeitnehmer* [in Marx, *Arbeitsnehmer*]); in contrast, the capitalist that appropriates and takes produced labour is considered labour-giver (*Arbeitgeber* [in Marx, *Arbeitsgeber*]) (Marx, 1988, p. 82). *Physical and social existence, which are ontologically impossible to be separated, are arbitrarily and artificially separated as a mechanism of power legitimation.* The essence of the production of surplus-value disappears behind the veils of capitalist benevolence, which generally provides labour opportunities. The twofold capitalist condition of the so-called primitive accumulation, namely, expropriation and separation of the labourer from the means of doing, on the one hand, and appropriation of value and production of surplus-value, which are labour-dependent, on the other, disappears.

Marx is fully aware that "capital is in and for itself indifferent to the *particularity* of each sphere of production", production of surplus-value as an end-in-itself determinates its own legality, social and natural barriers are constantly overcome, and "with the development of its own peculiar mode of production, it removes all legal and extra-economic obstacles to its free movement in the various spheres of production", that is, norms, rights, laws, and traditions that might prevent labour appropriation are circumscribed, overpowered, and crushed (Marx, 1988, p. 87).

In this sense, one clearly sees the importance of, first, banking capital and, then, financial capital to enable the most fluid form of capital, which attaches and detaches at will, which, especially with the combination of digitalisation and the Internet, bends the social dimensions of time, space, and culture. Under the real subsumption of capital, "the reserve funds of the banks [...] always express on the average the size of the money available as treasure, and a part of this treasure itself consists of paper, mere instructions on gold, which, however, are not intrinsic values"; Marx correctly asserts that the majority of the banker's capital is "purely fictitious", to which he adds, "this fictitious banker's capital largely represents not his capital, but that of the public, which deposits with him, whether with or without interest" (Marx, 1964, p. 487). Marx calls this formation "capitalisation" [*kapitalisieren*] (Marx, 1964, p. 484). However, as stated elsewhere, this process is not an abstract fictive relation. On the contrary, fictitious capital is leveraged into concrete power by an act of self-expansion, and then with those inflated assets, it appropriates the most profitable capitalist segments. "The fictitious capital has an immanent parasitic character, it needs a host to survive" (Hermeto, 2021, p. 222).

2.2.15 Marx's Formal Subsumption

Thus far, the terms formal and real subsumption have been used more than once, and elucidating them appears necessary. In *Capital*, Marx explains the difference between absolute surplus-value and relative surplus-value and how they are mutually dependent. As already discussed, the production of absolute surplus-value depends on the appropriation of surplus labour by capital, extending the working day beyond the value equivalency of labour power. Its existence is thus paramount for the capitalist system and is, accordingly, the basis of relative surplus-value. Analytically speaking, it consists of two parts: "necessary labour and surplus labour" (Marx, 1962, p. 332). More surplus labour can be obtained by either extending the working hours or, considering that each given working day is limited, reducing the time of necessary labour. The first accounts for the production of absolute surplus-value, while the second accounts for relative surplus-value (Marx, 1962, p. 523f). It becomes clear that technical and scientific advancements go hand-in-glove with extra-economic methods of violence to enforce and secure the extraction of surplus-value. While absolute surplus-value is limited in scope—for not only does each day present a limited number of hours available, but there are also socio-natural limits to how long a worker can be active before he needs to rest, eat, etc.—the potential of relative surplus-value depends on the development of science applied to capitalist production. "The formal is replaced by the real subsumption of labour under capital" (Marx, 1962, p. 533).

In manuscripts initially intended to be part of *Capital*, Marx elucidates that the direct control and exploitation of the labour process of others by capital is "the *formal subsumption of labour under capital*" (Marx, 1988, p. 91). This notion is still highly relevant to comprehending the contemporary political economy, which has become utterly globalised. While a few countries in the capitalist core embrace and attain a fully capitalist mode of production, much of the present-day world has hybrid forms of production and are—with some few exceptions—simultaneously subordinated to capitalist relations, in other words, "at the same time it is a special form next to the developed specific-*capitalist mode of production*" (Marx, 1988, p. 91). This imposition, however, is pivotal for the consolidation of the mystification of capitalism. While labour represents the creative power of value, it appears as its opposite. The mystic mechanism of subject-predicate-inversion transcends from religion to capital. However, no qualitative change occurs at the production level; the process of labour subsumption under capitalism occurs precisely in those processes "previously shaped by different production processes and different production conditions" (Marx, 1988, p. 92). Appearing to relate to Hegel's dialectics of quantity and quality, which is synthesised in the *Maß*, Marx explains that the first emergence of capitalism prompts an influence over non-capitalist modes of production; the quantitative change, namely, the augmentation in the volume of the means of production employed and the massive number of workers subjugated by a single capitalist, as an outcome of the increase of scale driven by capitalist relations, provokes a qualitative change in the character of non-capitalist modes of production. "This extension of the ladder forms the real basis on which the specifically capitalist mode of production rises under otherwise favourable historical conditions, such as those of the 16th century, for example" (Marx, 1988, p. 94). In this sense, merchant capital represented fertile soil in which capitalist development further expanded; however, mercantilism was not the cause of the development of capitalism but instead became an element in which existing capitalism could then further unfold. "Here, too, there is still no formal subsumption of labour under capital. The immediate producer still remains at the same time the seller of commodities and the user of his own labour" (Marx, 1988, p. 95). Hence, mercantilist capital—to a great extent—cannot even be considered to include modern capitalist elements; the thesis that assumes that the development of capitalism is a mere unfolding of merchant relations has no ontological-historical basis (see *infra*).

Formal subsumption makes the distinction that previous modes of production are formally subjugated by capitalist relations. That is, immediate producers, despite not being subordinated to new property relations, "are forced to deliver surplus labour to others"; therefore, "the *compulsion*, which is enforced, is the other form, i.e. the method by which surplus labour is extorted" (Marx, 1988, p. 96). The quantitative-qualitative change does not represent a one-off moment but is rather part of a continuum. I.e., the proportion of minimum applied capital needed to constitute not merely a *formal* but *real* capitalist production changes according to the accumulation process. "The *real* subsumption of labour under capital, *the actual capitalist mode of production*, occurs only when capitalists of a certain magnitude have directly taken possession of production" (Marx, 1988, p. 98). And Marx is emphatic: the change in exploitation from slavery, serfdom, vassalage, patriarchy, etc., represents a mere change in form, "then, there is a loss of early *independence* in the process of production, and the relation of superiority or subordination is itself the product of the introduction of the capitalist mode of production" (Marx, 1988, p. 99). The quantitative-qualitative change presupposes therefore the dissolution of previous production barriers. Freedom—in the sense of wage labour—appears then as a new mechanism of domination and subordination. Coercion appears not to originate from an external authoritative being but instead seems to be inflicted by the self in a mechanism of a self-regulated system of incentive-punishment. Only taken from this broad historical perspective does power-control over individuals imposed by the state and its judicial system (Foucault, 1995) acquire actuality, enabling capitalist superstructure—e.g., norms—to enforce class and individual behaviour-shaping. "*He learns to control himself, in contrast to the slave*, who needs a master" (Marx, 1988, p. 103).

2.2.16 Marx's Real Subsumption

While the formal subsumption of labour under capital is based on the extraction of absolute surplus-value, the real subsumption, which gives representation to the specificity of the capitalist mode of production, is grounded in the appropriation of relative surplus-value. That is, "with the production of relative surplus-value [...] the whole real form of the mode of production changes and a specifically *capitalist mode of production* arises (also technologically)", thus social property relations are subordinated in its totality, "on the basis of which and with which, at the same time, only the relations of production corresponding to the capitalist process of production develop between the various agents of production, and especially between capitalist and wage labourer" (Marx, 1988, p. 95).

The development of production—private property—presupposes improving its efficiency; the increase in output per time unit and productive unit demands the revolution of the factors of production. *Private property improvement thus presupposes intellectual property development.* The progress of *private property* cannot be explained by a simple material appropriation—as during the process of the so-called primitive accumulation in which the soil was "enclosed"—again, the result of this process becomes the premise for its further expansion. *Intellectual appropriation* advances at first as a product of the now-established economic imperatives. The initial competition among capitalists, on the one hand, and labourers, on the other, imposes an immanent compulsion for efficiency over the means of doing. Individual know-how alone does not suffice to actualise this legality.

The development of capitalist knowledge arises first and foremost from the ranks of labourers. Scientific advancement thus entails a double historical determination. From a concrete, practical reason, workers created and developed practical knowledge, thus changing the means of production. As Clifford D. Conner asserts, this was a vital step for the development of capitalist production forces. Only a posteriori, theoretical science organises, theorises, and summarises the already ongoing practical scientific breakthroughs and achievements, enabling further imitations, emulations, copying, and appropriation (Conner, 2005). *Intellectual appropriation* (thus intellectual property) becomes to that extent *condition* for the *property of the means of production*, and this relationship constitutes the *totality of property*. Real subsumption of labour is simultaneously real subsumption of science.

Intellectual property is simultaneously relations of production and factors of production. This inseparable character had already been acknowledged by Marx. "The *social* productive forces of labour, or the productive forces of directly social, *socialised* (i.e. collective) labour come into being through cooperation, division of labour within the workshop, the use of *machinery*, and in general the transformation of production by the conscious *use* of the sciences" (Marx, 1988, p. 95). Socialised labour is a condition for applying science to production; however, scientific development presupposes (a) certain (degree of) material conditions. However, the fetishisation of this process strips off its historicity, and scientific development appears instead as an immanent feature of capitalism (see *infra*). Conversely, absolute surplus-value historically precedes relative surplus-value; however, *with the development of capitalism*, the *relative* becomes a *condition* for the *absolute*. This understanding demystifies any claim that capitalism is a singular, homogenous (social) practice.

The quantitative-qualitative dialectics between property and intellectual property is essential throughout the development of capitalism. Historically, this also becomes clear with, first, bearing in mind the initial agricultural capitalism in England, second, its further development into industrial capitalism, and third, the capitalist imposition of formal subsumption overseas, which to date remains a pivotal condition for the extraction of relative surplus-value.

Briefly considering the latter, the so-called knowledge-based economies imposed absolute surplus-value relations on peripheral (underdeveloped) countries with the extraction of raw materials; however, since industrial transformation has been losing ground within the national borders of capitalist centres, then protecting knowledge, as a precondition of private property of the means of production, became an ever greater imperative. Initially, capitalist production was divided into two: one centre of raw material production and another centre of raw material transformation, namely, industrial production. Then, as intellectual production was separated from the other two spheres, production was divided into three (generally speaking, since production chains may incorporate multiple countries and be divided into even more spheres). While the extraction of raw material remains confined to countries rich in natural resources, industrial production and transformation was—through the search for greater rates of profit—significantly moved towards capitalist peripheries, where the value of the reproduction of labour power is less than in developed countries (mainly the United States, parts of (Western) Europe, and Japan). However, because property and intellectual property represent a totality, moving industries abroad invariably implies exporting its intellectual dimension as well.

One does not need a formalised, theorised manual to obtain knowledge. Just as, during the nineteenth century, theoretical science systematised practical science to enable the reproduction of discoveries/inventions, the material condition of anything permits a similar assessment by others—then considered reverse engineering. These basic principles of the production of knowledge—known to humankind throughout history but also present in any child who enacts to a great extent herself both the pedagogy of learning by acts of mimesis and tinkering—must be hindered. Intellectual appropriation becomes an indispensable mechanism of private appropriation, thus becoming *intellectual property*$_{(private)}$.

As real subsumption of knowledge occurs, two historical moments can be considered. The first represents the immediate association between the value of knowledge and matter. The second, which appears in different historical moments in the form of *proto-intellectual property*$_{(private)}$, unveils the steep decline of the value of knowledge, making its production and reproduction relatively easier. For instance, Johannes Gutenberg's advancement of a novel printing technology, or the Internet, which presupposes the digital revolution, both imposed a vertiginous decline in value throughout their contemporary intellectual productions. Discussions over intellectual property usually focus on the intellectual dimension and disregard its material dimension (as if they were two separate things). However, regardless of Gutenberg's invention or the Internet, it is not information or knowledge in-itself that presents a significant variation of value, but knowledge in-and-for-itself within the process of production of books and computers (hardware, server, modem, etc.). While the intellectual side of property gives it content, its material side gives intellectual appropriation the basis for its existence and/or actualisation. They are both void in-themselves; it is only in a relationship of mutual determination that property-intellectual-property can attain an existence in-and-for-itself—in this case, in-and-for-themselves.

Although Alexandra George seemingly acknowledges the intrinsic materiality of a thought that as an *ideational object* is in one's head, brain, and mind, she abstracts the objective body's corporality presupposing it "lacks physical form" and is thus boundless (George, 2012, p. 92). In reality, an individual's mind may suffice to retain, develop, and transmit a multitude of ideas, thoughts, and knowledge; for instance, even the complexity of entire musical performances can be recorded in one's mind, allowing one to execute it thoroughly. Alternatively, as Jared Diamond has shown, hunting-gathering peoples, instead of possessing libraries and other means of knowledge objectification and accumulation, were themselves *walking encyclopaedias* (see *infra*). Therefore, it is nonsensical to consider knowledge as something immaterial, incorporeal, and abstract. On the contrary, its very existence presupposes materiality.

However, a composer—even if she has the brilliance to compose and store music in her head—requires another form of materiality to enable the transmission and social actuality of her music, regardless of other people's heads, ink and paper, or audio(-visual) recording in a tape, CD, vinyl, hard drive, etc. With science, this becomes even more relevant because scientific endeavour presupposes constant debate, reassessment, critique, testing, etc. The privatisation of knowledge, however, blocks these ontological conditions. Knowledge becomes constricted to be operationalised within the logic of capitalist production. Its formal subsumption occurs under pre-capitalist and extra-capitalist relations. Based on formal subsumption, "a technologically and otherwise *specific* mode of production arises which transforms the real nature of the *labour-process* and its *real conditions*—a capitalist mode of production" (Marx, 1988, p. 104f). This is the condition for the emergence of the real subsumption of knowledge by capital. The current phase in which intellectual property gained apparent independence from property reveals a deepening in the twofold contradictions. The totality of property appears to be of two independent forms opposing each other; the social character of capitalist production seems more contradictory as knowledge becomes separately subjected to privatisation. The next chapter addresses these ontological dimensions.

References

Adewopo, A. (2016). The Global Intellectual Property System and Sub-Saharan Africa: A Prognostic Reflection. In A. George (Ed.), *Globalization and Intellectual Property* (pp. 109–131). Routledge.

Amin, S. (1977). *Imperialism and Unequal Development*. Monthly Review Press.

Ammannati, F. (2019). I privilegi come strumento di politica economica nell'Italia della prima età moderna. In *Privilegi librari nell'Italia del Rinascimento*. FrancoAngeli.

Bently, L. (1994). Copyright and the Death of the Author in Literature and Law. *The Modern Law Review, 57*(6), 973–986. https://doi.org/10.1111/J.1468-2230.1994.TB01989.X

Boyle, J. (2008). *The Public Domain: Enclosing the Commons of the Mind*. Yale University Press. https://doi.org/10.1177/0276146711416981

Brush, S., & Wittenberg, A. (2022, January 14). BlackRock Hits a Record $10 Trillion Assets Under Management. *Al Jazeera* | Financial Markets News. https://www.aljazeera.com/economy/2022/1/14/blackrock-hits-a-record-10-trillion-assets-under-management

Bruun, N. (2021). Reflections on the Contradictory History of the Regulation of Employee Intellectual Property. In G. Ghidini, H. Ullrich, & P. Drahos (Eds.), *Kritika: Essays on Intellectual Property* (pp. 1–22). Elgar.

Chancel, L., Piketty, T., Saez, E., & Zucman, G. (2022). *World Inequality Report 2022*. https://dds.cepal.org/redesoc/publicacion?id=5585

Chang, H.-J. (2001). Intellectual Property Rights and Economic Development: Historical Lessons and Emerging Issues. *Journal of Human Development, 2*(2), 287–309. https://doi.org/10.1080/14649880120067293

Chiusi, T. J. (2005). Strukturen des römischen Eigentums im Spiegel rhetorisch-philosophischer Text Ciceros. In A. Eckl & B. Ludwig (Eds.), *Was ist Eigentum?* C.H.Beck.

Christensen, M.-B., Hallum, C., Maitland, A., Parrinello, Q., & Putaturo, C. (2023). *Survival of the Richest: How We Must Tax the Super-rich Now to Fight Inequality*. Oxfam.

Cohen, M. (1927). Property and Sovereignty. *Cornell Law Review, 13*(1). https://scholarship.law.cornell.edu/clr/vol13/iss1/3

Collins, C., Ocampo, O., & Paslaski, S. (2020). *Billionaire Bonanza 2020*. https://ips-dc.org/billionaire-bonanza-2020/

Conner, C. D. (2005). *A People's History of Science: Miners, Midwives, and 'Low Mechanicks'*. Nation Books.

Convention de Berne pour la protection des œuvres littéraires et artistiques. (1886). World Intellectual Property Organization. https://wipolex.wipo.int/en/text/278701

Convention de Paris pour la protection de la propriété industrielle. (1883). https://www.wipo.int/wipolex/en/text/287780

Copyright. (n.d.). World Intellectual Property Organization. Retrieved March 3, 2023, from https://www.wipo.int/copyright/en/

Cox, H. (2016). *The Market as God*. Harvard University Press.

David, P. A., & Foray, D. (2002). An Introduction to the Economy of the Knowledge Society. *International Social Science Journal, 54*(171), 9–23. https://doi.org/10.1111/1468-2451.00355

Davis, M. (2006). *Planet of Slums*. Verso.

Debord, G. (1992). *La Société du Spectacle*. Gallimard.

Dobb, M. (1973). *Theories of Value and Distribution Since Adam Smith: Ideology and Economic Theory*. Cambridge University Press.

Drahos, P. (2016). *A Philosophy of Intellectual Property*. Australian National University. https://doi.org/10.22459/PIP.06.2016

Drahos, P., & Braithwaite, J. (2002). *Information Feudalism: Who Owns the Knowledge Economy*. Earthscan Publications Ltd. https://doi.org/10.4324/9781315092683

Durkheim, É. (1952). *Suicide: A Study in Sociology*. Routledge.

Eckl, A. (2005). Der Begriff 'Eigentum' in der Rechtsphilosophie Hegels. In A. Eckl & B. Ludwig (Eds.), *Was ist Eigentum?* C.H.Beck.

Eckl, A., & Ludwig, B. (Eds.). (2005). *Was ist Eigentum? Philosophische Eigentumstheorien von Platon bis Habermas*. C.H.Beck.

Eisenberg, R. (1994). A Technology Policy Perspective on the NIH Gene Patenting Controversy. *University of Pittsburgh Law Review, 55*(3), 633–652. https://repository.law.umich.edu/articles/1226

Esser, A. (2005). Faire Verteilung oder absoluter Schutz des Eigentums? Eine klassische Alternative in der neueren Diskussionen: John Rawls und Robert Nozick. In A. Eckl & B. Ludwig (Eds.), *Was ist Eigentum?* C.H.Beck.

Estes, N. (2021, April 5). Bill Gates Is the Biggest Private Owner of Farmland in the United States. Why? *The Guardian*. https://www.theguardian.com/commentisfree/2021/apr/05/bill-gates-climate-crisis-farmland

Feuerbach, L. (2013). *Grundsätze der Philosophie der Zukunft*. Berliner Ausgabe.

Feuerbach, L. (2016). *Das Wesen des Christentums*. Berliner Ausgabe.

Foucault, M. (1995). *Discipline & Punish: The Birth of the Prison*. Vintage Books.

Foucault, M. (2004). *Naissance de la biopolitique: Cours au collège de France (1978–1979)*. Seuil Gallimard.
Fowler, H. W. (2009). *A Dictionary of Modern English Usage*. Oxford University Press.
Fricke, C. (2005). Die Eigentumsfrage bei David Hume und Adam Smith. In A. Eckl & B. Ludwig (Eds.), *Was ist Eigentum?* C.H.Beck.
Fuchs, C. (2012). Dallas Smythe Today—The Audience Commodity, the Digital Labour Debate, Marxist Political Economy and Critical Theory. Prolegomena to a Digital Labour Theory of Value. *TripleC, 10*(2), 692–740. https://triple-c.at/index.php/tripleC/article/view/443
George, A. (2012). *Constructing Intellectual Property*. Cambridge University Press. https://doi.org/10.1017/CBO9781139035361
Hedges, C. (2018). *America: The Farewell Tour*. Simon & Schuster.
Hegel, G. W. F. (1986a). *Wissenschaft der Logik I, Werke in 20 Bänden, Band 5*. Suhrkamp.
Hegel, G. W. F. (1986b). *Wissenschaft der Logik II, Werke in 20 Bänden, Band 6*. Suhrkamp.
Hegel, G. W. F. (1989). *Enzyklopädie der philosophischen Wissenschaften im Grundrisse: 1830—Teil 1. Die Wissenschaft der Logik: Mit den mündlichen Zusätzen, Werke in 20 Bänden, Band 8*. Suhrkamp.
Hegel, G. W. F. (2013). *Grundlinien der Philosophie des Rechts oder Naturrecht und Staatswissenschaft im Grundrisse, Werke in 20 Bänden, Band 7*. Suhrkamp.
Hegel, G. W. F. (2014). *Phänomenologie des Geistes, Werke in 20 Bänden, Band 3*. Suhrkamp.
Hermeto, J. R. (2020a). *Lukács' Ontologie des gesellschaftlichen Wandels: Von einer mythologischen Ontologie des absoluten Geistes zu einer Ontologie des gesellschaftlichen Seins*. Verlag Dr. Kovač.
Hermeto, J. R. (2020b). Towards a Critique on Intellectual Property. *Revista Katalysis, 23*(3), 399–408. https://doi.org/10.1590/1982-02592020v23n3p399
Hermeto, J. R. (2021). Towards Social Change: Social Transformation in a Time of Social Disruption. *Dilemas, 14*(1), 219–242. https://doi.org/10.17648/dilemas.v14n1.30572
Hobson, J. A. (1902). *Imperialism: A Study*. James Nisbet & Co.
Hoffmann, T. S. (2005). Die Güter, das Gute und die Frage des rechten Maßes: Platon und das Eigentum. In A. Eckl & B. Ludwig (Eds.), *Was ist Eigentum?* C.H.Beck.
Honneth, A. (2013). *Das Recht der Freiheit*. Suhrkamp.

Hudson, M. (2015). *Killing the Host: How Financial Parasites and Debt Bondage Destroy the Global Economy*. CounterPunch Books.
Hull, G. (2019). *The Biopolitics of Intellectual Property: Regulating Innovation and Personhood in the Information Age*. Cambridge University Press.
Jessop, B. (2000). The State and the Contradictions of the Knowledge-driven Economy. In J. R. Bryson, P. W. Daniels, J. Pollard, & N. Henry (Eds.), *Knowledge, Space*. Routledge.
Jevons, W. S. (2013). *The Theory of Political Economy*. Palgrave Macmillan.
Johns, A. (2009). *Piracy: The Intellectual Property Wars from Gutenberg to Gates*. The University of Chicago Press.
Kant, I. (1956). *Kritik der reinen Vernunft*. Verlag von Felix Meiner.
Kapur, A., Macleod, N., & Singh, N. (2005). *Equity Strategy—Plutonomy*.
Kaufmann, M. (2005). Das Recht auf Eigentum im Mittelalter. In A. Eckl & B. Ludwig (Eds.), *Was ist Eigentum?* C.H.Beck.
Kelsen, H. (1991). *General Theory of Norms*. Clarendon Press.
Klein, M. C., & Pettis, M. (2020). *Trade Wars Are Class Wars*. Yale University Press.
Kroszner, R. S., & Strahan, P. E. (2014). Regulation and Deregulation of the US Banking Industry: Causes, Consequences, and Implications for the Future. In N. L. Rose (Ed.), *Economic Regulation and Its Reform: What Have We Learned?* (pp. 485–544). The University of Chicago Press.
Kuhlen, R. (2007). Knowledge and Information—Private Property or Common Good? A Global Perspective. In C. Lenk, N. Hoppe, & R. Andorno (Eds.), *Ethics and Law of Intellectual Property: Current Problems in Politics, Science and Technology* (pp. 213–231). Ashgate.
Lenin, W. I. (1971). Der Imperialismus als höchstes Stadium des Kapitalismus. In *Lenin Werke Band 22*. Dietz Verlag Berlin.
Lessig, L. (2004). *Free Culture: How Big Media Uses Technology and The Law to Lock Down Culture and Control Creativity*. The Penguin Press.
Ludwig, B. (2005). "Regierung entstehen wieder auf die althergebrachte Art, nämlich durch Erfindungen und Übereinkunft der Menschen." John Lockes Eigentumstheorie. In A. Eckl & B. Ludwig (Eds.), *Was ist Eigentum?* C.H.Beck.
Lukács, G. (1963). *GLW, Band 12, Die Eigenart des Ästhetischen: 2. Halbband*. Luchterhand.
Lukács, G. (1973). *Die Zerstörung der Vernunft, Band I: Irrationalismus zwischen den Revolutionen*. Luchterhand.
Lukács, G. (1974a). *Die Zerstörung der Vernunft, Band II: Irrationalismus und Imperialismus*. Luchterhand.

Lukács, G. (1974b). *Die Zerstörung der Vernunft, Band III: Irrationalismus und Soziologie*. Luchterhand.
Lukács, G. (1986). *GLW, Band 14, Zur Ontologie des gesellschaftlichen Seins, Band 2*. Luchterhand.
Mandel, E. (1968). *Marxist Economic Theory: Volume Two*. Monthly Review Press.
Mandel, E. (1976). Introduction [to the Appendix: Results of the Immediate Process of Production]. In *Capital: A Critique of Political Economy: Volume One*. Penguin Books.
Marx, K. (1961). Zur Kritik der politischen Ökonomie. In *MEW Band 13*. Dietz Verlag Berlin.
Marx, K. (1962). Das Kapital: Kritik der politischen Ökonomie: Erster Band: Buch I: Der Produktionsprozeß des Kapitals. In *MEW Band 23*. Dietz Verlag Berlin.
Marx, K. (1963). Das Kapital: Kritik der politischen Ökonomie: Zweiter Band: Buch II: Der Zirkulationsprozeß des Kapitals. In F. Engels (Ed.), *MEW Band 24*. Dietz Verlag Berlin.
Marx, K. (1964). Das Kapital: Kritik der politischen Ökonomie: Dritter Band: Buch III: Der Gesamtprozeß der kapitalistischen Produktion. In F. Engels (Ed.), *MEW Band 25*. Dietz Verlag Berlin.
Marx, K. (1965). Theorien über den Mehrwert: (Vierter Band des 'Kapitals'): Erster Teil: Erstes bis siebentes Kapitel und Beilagen. In *MEW Band 26.1*. Dietz Verlag Berlin.
Marx, K. (1967). Theorien über den Mehrwert: (Vierter Band des 'Kapitals'): Zweiter Teil: Achtes bis achtzehntes Kapitel. In *MEW Band 26.2*. Dietz Verlag Berlin.
Marx, K. (1968). Ökonomisch-philosophische Manuskripte aus dem Jahre 1844. In *MEW Band 40*. Dietz Verlag Berlin.
Marx, K. (1981a). Zur Judenfrage. In *MEW Band 01*. Dietz Verlag Berlin.
Marx, K. (1981b). Zur Kritik der Hegelschen Rechtsphilosophie. In *MEW Band 01*. Dietz Verlag Berlin.
Marx, K. (1983a). Einleitung zu den 'Grundrissen der Kritik der politischen Ökonomie'. In *MEW Band 42*. Dietz Verlag Berlin.
Marx, K. (1983b). Grundrisse der Kritik der politischen Ökonomie. In *MEW Band 42*. Dietz Verlag Berlin.
Marx, K. (1988). *MEGA² II.4.1—Manuskripte 1863–1867—Teil 1*. Dietz Verlag Berlin.
Marx, K., & Engels, F. (1962). Lohn, Preis und Profit. In *MEW Band 16*. Dietz Verlag Berlin.

Maskus, K. E., & Reichman, J. H. (2016). The Globalization of Private Knowledge Goods and the Privatization of Global Public Goods. In A. George (Ed.), *Globalization and Intellectual Property* (pp. 335–377). Routledge.

Mazzucato, M. (2018). *The Value of Everything: Making and Taking in the Global Economy*. Allen Lane.

Menger, C. (2004). *Principles of Economics*. Ludwig von Mises Institute.

Merges, R. P. (2011). *Justifying Intellectual Property*. Harvard University Press.

Mueller, G. (2019). *Media Piracy in the Cultural Economy: Intellectual Property and Labor Under Neoliberal Restructuring*. Routledge. https://doi.org/10.4324/9780203730720

Nelson, R. R. (2003). The Advance of Technology and the Scientific Commons. *The Royal Society, 361*(1809), 1691–1708. https://doi.org/10.1098/rsta.2003.1228

Nersisyan, Y. (2015). The Repeal of the Glass-Steagall Act and the Federal Reserves Extraordinary Intervention During the Global Financial Crisis. *Journal of Post Keynesian Economics, 37*(4), 545–567. https://doi.org/10.1080/01603477.2015.1049926

Nicol, D. (2021). The Pendulum of Patents, Principles and Products—From the Industrial Revolution to the Genetic Revolution. In G. Ghidini, H. Ullrich, & P. Drahos (Eds.), *Kritika: Essays on Intellectual Property* (pp. 99–124). Elgar.

Patents. (n.d.). World Intellectual Property Organization. Retrieved March 3, 2023, from https://www.wipo.int/patents/en/

Patterson, L. R., & Joyce, C. (2004). Copyright in 1791: An Essay Concerning the Founders' View of the Copyright Power Granted to Congress in Article I, Section 8, Clause 8 of the U.S. Constitution. *The Emory Law Journal, 52*. https://papers.ssrn.com/abstract=559145

Pellizzoni, L., & Ylönen, M. (2012). Hegemonic Contingencies: Neoliberalized Technoscience and Neorationality. In L. Pellizzoni & M. Ylönen (Eds.), *Neoliberalism and Technoscience: Critical Assessments*. Ashgate.

Pfeffer, J. (2018). *Dying for a Paycheck: How Modern Management Harms Employee Health and Company Performance-and What We Can Do About It*. Harper Business.

Phillips, P. (2018). *Giants: The Global Power Elite*. Seven Stories Press.

Piketty, T. (2015). *Das Kapital im 21. Jahrhundert*. C.H.Beck.

Roberts, R. (2021, August 31). Hillary Clinton's 'Deplorables' Speech Shocked Voters Five Years Ago—But Some Feel It Was Prescient. *The Washington Post*. https://www.washingtonpost.com/lifestyle/2021/08/31/deplorables-basket-hillary-clinton/

Robinson, W. I. (2014). *Global Capitalism and the Crisis of Humanity*. Cambridge University Press.
Robinson, W. I. (2020). *The Global Police State*. Pluto Press.
Rodney, W. (2018). *How Europe Underdeveloped Africa*. Verso.
Schippel, H. (1989). *La Storia delle privative industriali nella Venezia del '400*. Centro Tedesco di Studi Veneziani.
Shapiro, A. (2021, January 14). America's Biggest Owner of Farmland Is Now Bill Gates. *Forbes*. https://www.forbes.com/sites/arielshapiro/2021/01/14/americas-biggest-owner-of-farmland-is-now-bill-gates-bezos-turner/
Smith, A. (2012). *An Inquiry into the Nature and Causes of the Wealth of Nations*. Wordsworth Editions.
Sonderholm, J. (2012). Ethical Issues Surrounding Intellectual Property Rights. In A. Lever (Ed.), *New Frontiers in the Philosophy of Intellectual Property*. Cambridge University Press.
Squassina, E. (2019). I privilegi librari a Venezia (1469–1545). In *Privilegi librari nell'Italia del Rinascimento*. FrancoAngeli.
Sraffa, P. (1960). *Production of Commodities by Means of Commodities*. Cambridge University Press.
Stengel, D. (2004). Intellectual Property in Philosophy. *ARSP: Archiv Für Rechts- Und Sozialphilosophie / Archives for Philosophy of Law and Social Philosophy, 90*(1), 20–50. https://www.jstor.org/stable/23681627
Sum, N.-L., & Jessop, B. (2013). *Towards a Cultural Political Economy: Putting Culture in Its Place in Political Economy*. Edward Elgar Publishing.
Szaif, J. (2005). Aristoteles—eine teleologische Konzeption von Besitz und Eigentum. In A. Eckl & B. Ludwig (Eds.), *Was ist Eigentum?* C.H.Beck.
Trademarks. (n.d.). World Intellectual Property Organization. Retrieved March 3, 2023, from https://www.wipo.int/trademarks/en/
Unruh, P. (2005). Die vernunftrechtliche Eigentumsbegründung bei Kant. In A. Eckl & B. Ludwig (Eds.), *Was ist Eigentum?* C.H.Beck.
Walker, R. A. (2018). *Pictures of a Gone City: Tech and the Dark Side of Prosperity in the San Francisco Bay Area*. PM Press.
Walras, L. (1954). *Elements of Pure Economics: Or The Theory of Social Wealth*. George Allen and Unwin LTD.
What Is Intellectual Property? (n.d.). World Intellectual Property Organization. Retrieved March 3, 2023, from https://www.wipo.int/about-ip/en/
Williams-Jones, B., & Ozdemir, V. (2007). Enclosing the "Knowledge Commons": Patenting Genes for Disease Risk and Drug Response at the University–Industry Interface. In C. Lenk, N. Hoppe, & R. Andorno (Eds.),

Ethics and Law of Intellectual Property: Current Problems in Politics, Science and Technology (pp. 137–159). Ashgate.

Wittel, A. (2017). Digital Marx: Toward a Political Economy of Distributed Media. In C. Fuchs & V. Mosco (Eds.), *Marx in the Age of Digital Capitalism* (pp. 68–104). Haymarket Books.

Wood, E. M. (2017). *The Origin of Capitalism: A Longer View*. Verso.

Zintl, R. (2005). Privateigentum, Ausbeutung, Entfremdung: Karl Marx. In *Was ist Eigentum?* C.H.Beck.

3

Ontology and De-ontologised Rationalisation of Intellectual Property

3.1 Prolegomena: Rationalisation of Intellectual Property

3.1.1 Contemporary Theory

Not unlike capitalist justifications, *intellectual property*$_{(private)}$ theories often convey a mystical, theological character to intellectual property relations. On the one hand, an *eschatology of intellectual property* destroys any notion of *intellectual property*$_{(non\text{-}private)}$ in a universal form as part of human social-ontological relations and uncritically replaces it with an unrefined particular private notion of intellectual property, which asserts itself as a universal form and neither differentiates between intellectual property (*intellectual property*$_{(non\text{-}private)}$ or *intellectual property*$_{(common)}$) and private intellectual property (*intellectual property*$_{(private)}$), nor distinguishes between personal and production property, or discerns among the possible modes of subsumption. On the other hand, the inconsistencies, incongruities, contradictions, antagonisms, and oppositions among intellectual property relations disappear behind the veil of a *theodicy of intellectual property*; that is, intellectual property rights and the intellectual property system (in the private sense of the means of production) are not perfect

J. Romeiro Hermeto, *The Paradox of Intellectual Property in Capitalism*,
https://doi.org/10.1007/978-3-031-49967-8_3

but—analogous to Christian theodicy—are on the path of becoming. Setbacks of *intellectual property*$_{(private)}$ as well as capitalist crises, exploitation, inflicted social pains, wars, corruption, environmental destruction, etc., "should not cause doubt as to the ultimate benevolence of the Market God" and its institutions (Cox, 2016, p. 9). And although many intellectual property theories portray the relationship of intellectual property (factually, *intellectual property*$_{(private)}$) and the so-called intellectual commons as somewhat paradoxical, hitherto no solid theoretical framework has managed to explain it in relation to the capitalist mode of production and, consequently, failed to unveil what I call the second paradox of intellectual property in capitalism. (It goes without saying that many analyses are theoretically rich and complex, and their contributions should not and cannot be undervalued, as it becomes clear when one reads this book.)

According to Alexandra George, intellectual property can have different meanings although this reference relates "to a legally regulated, artificially created monopoly over intangible objects of communication, such as ideas, information, knowledge, and symbols" (George, 2012, p. 6, see also p. 17f). Hence, as she emphasises, there lies a difficulty in defining intellectual property and what I call *intellectual property*$_{(private)}$, "despite its being a powerful and widely used term" (George, 2012, p. 15). *Intellectual property*$_{(private)}$ appears to be based on conceptual criteria constructed by legal framing and its process of normalisation dependent on the repetition of "their peculiarly legal terminology" (George, 2012, p. 19f). However, legal doctrines do not explain the uniqueness of *intellectual property*$_{(private)}$ because the same system that defines these criteria determines, for example, indigenous intellectual property as merely intellectual property-like, thus providing its exclusion. Therefore, why is this intellectual property (in this case, indigenous *intellectual property*$_{(common)}$) excluded from being considered *intellectual property*$_{(private)}$? George states that it has "less to do with doctrinal content or jurisprudential consistency, and more to do with political imperatives and agendas at various points in time" (George, 2012, p. 21). She further claims that definitions are inconsistent due to the absence of a clear meaning of intellectual property.

If, on the one hand, the definition of property is widely contested among a vast array of competing attempts, on the other, many theories explain intellectual property as a form of property, then, according to George, how to derive intellectual property from property would make its understanding more attainable when the latter is already highly disputed (George, 2012, p. 65)? Her conclusion is to coin a new approach: the *metaphysics of intellectual property*. This reveals a fundamental problem. Instead of grasping the meaning of the concept from its practice, an aprioristic notion is established, thus preventing one from finding the very thing one has set out to discover. Like many other theories, it assumes what needs to be explained. This is perfectly clear with its tautological definition, which postulates intellectual property as an "institutional fact" and contrasts it with the "brutal facts". Thus, she creates an idealist separation between the thing in-itself and the social construct as two different things. Anything that "lacks physical form and exists only by virtue of social consensus (tacit or otherwise) and within human institutions constitutes an institutional fact. Law is one example; intellectual property law and the objects that it creates are others" (George, 2012, p. 91). Therefore, *separating the means from the social relation is pivotal to understanding this eschatology and theodicy dialectics of intellectual property*.

The intellectual act of breaking something up into parts, ἀνάλυσις, to obtain a more comprehensive understanding of it, is confounded with reality *in-itself*. Metaphysics transforms the analytical act into (a hypostasised) reality. George's separation ignores Hegel's lessons about multiple determinations and the intertwinement of quantity and quality (Hegel, 1986b). The means have different dimensions: a given object, an individual, and his social sphere. To conceive something as lacking physical form means presupposing an existence without reality. It becomes clear that even Hegel's objective idealism based on an ontology of the absolute spirit entails a more concrete analytical framework than most intellectual property analyses based on pure metaphysics. As György Lukács shows, the body itself is a crucial means carved out through socialisation processes, in which socio-historically conditioned reflexes merely appear to be elements of natural conditions (Lukács, 1963a). George's analytical separation of intellectual property among *intellectual property law* (deprived of physical existence), *ideational object* (deprived of physical existence), *documented form* (tangible), and *intellectual property object* (deprived of physical existence) must thus hypostasise social ontology, substituting it with a purely metaphysical ontology (George, 2012, p. 92). Concrete moments of storage, transmission, etc., embedded in concrete human minds and different kinds of material, are utterly abstracted. This hypostasis is not George's monopoly but can be found across-the-board in intellectual property theory because it is often assumed that "property is a bundle of rights" (Drahos, 2016, p. 1) and, as such, intellectual property, as in George, appears to be a mere legal construct.

3.1.2 Rational Choice Fetishism

Despite their idealised characterisations, intellectual property theories often contain relevant critical elements. For example, Peter Drahos problematises the rational choice dogma from mainstream economic theory, in which the so-called rational actor reduces all social and natural reality to the binary worldview of cost and benefit. Needless to say, all complexity of reality must not only be subtracted from its models but must also remain expurgated because their presence would contaminate and invalidate such a dogmatic worldview.

Often used to justify capitalist relations, the paradigm assumes egoism as rationality, a mystical self-movement of markets, in which individual actions are unimportant and neutralised by the so-called invisible hand. It further assumes free competition and perfect information, despite all of these assumptions bearing no ontological reality. On the one hand, egoism remains an epiphenomenon among humans and retains importance only among the great apes. On the other hand, rationality is something that entails a great complexity of socio-historical dynamics beyond the mere calculus of cost and benefit. Markets are fundamentally based on human relations and determined by their concrete intentionality and not (market) movements in themselves. Competition, where it exists, is never free from constraints and never grounded on an equal basis; therefore, accumulation and extra-economic powers play a considerable role in determining it. Information is not only not perfectly distributed, but the very practice of capitalist relations imposes asymmetry of information to secure private gains. When turning to the matter of knowledge and the so-called information economy, Drahos suggests that if one assumes the rational model to be correct, then "the best strategy" would be "free-riding" (Drahos, 2016, p. 142). For distribution of information, this would mean optimum information but would also dwindle the capacity for the extraction of profit. Should a state of perfect competition emerge, then information resources could be optimally allocated. Even if intellectual property succeeds in fostering the production of knowledge, the holder's monopoly has the incentive to restrict access to information, curbing its dissemination (Drahos, 2016, p. 144). Drahos' emphasis on *exclusion* from the thing and *prevention* of the act by intellectual property rights overlooks Hans Kelsen's vital lesson that *norms command behaviour* (Kelsen, 1991). Thus, these modes of impediment can only attain actuality after juridical norms have successfully reshaped human behaviour. Focused on individual liberties, nevertheless, his concern addresses the crucial aspect of immense individual power accumulation and control through *intellectual property*$_{(private)}$ (Drahos, 2016, p. 166f).

A foundational aspect shared among intellectual property theories, from which the different metaphysical approaches emerge, is anchored in the separation of property and intellectual property. Daniel Stengel regards the latter as abstract objects while the former as tangible ones. Intellectual property thus "exists for itself" and "is not related to anything real" (Stengel, 2004, p. 23). The mystical character is unmistakable. In reality, intellectual property is something that in-itself does not actually exist. Once more resorting to Hegel, "in-itself" cannot be a condition of reality, even departing from his notion of the absolute spirit, pure being is also pure nothingness, deprived of content and a total abstraction (Hegel, 1986a, p. 69). Robert P. Merges, on the other hand, reasserts these metaphysical assessments. The dichotomy between idea—intangible—and matter—tangible—is reaffirmed. "What I have called 'the work' is a mental construct, an idea; the original embodiment of that idea is the first tangible instance of it" (Merges, 2011, p. 59). George's notion of ideational object is also contradictory; intellectual property is concretely embodied in one's own mind but lacks physical existence. Despite this, one can extract an inner theoretical struggle among intellectual property theorists, for their perception that the boundaries of intellectual property "are changing and are therefore subject to revision" (Stengel,

2004, p. 24) permits one to derive a yet more crucial element, namely, the changes within social property relations that affect both property and intellectual property.

3.1.3 Knowledge and the Epistemic

Contrary to the hypothesis—often posed as an assertion—that intellectual property helps foster the creation of and access to knowledge, Kenneth Arrow's essay on resource allocation for inventions points in the opposite direction. He investigates the relationship between the production of knowledge and competition. The hypothesis that competition ensures the production of knowledge in a situation of Pareto optimum is repudiated. The notion that consumers and producers are well informed is false (Arrow, 1962, p. 609). Further, he adds, no uncertainty would be possible, and all commodities would have to be traded on the market. Well, the very essence of commodifying knowledge is based on a lack of information and uncertainty. Thus, being informed about the information makes it impossible for knowledge to be commodified; that is, it cannot become private property and enter the market (Arrow, 1962, p. 609). Arrow also emphasises three reasons for the failure of perfect competition: "indivisibilities", "inappropriability", and "uncertainty", all of which cannot be disassociated from the production of knowledge (Arrow, 1962, p. 609f).

The legal framework which attempts to establish an artificial structure to enable the privatisation of knowledge expresses an economic power and must remain a flawed structure because its practice not only hinders optimal allocation but also remains paradoxical, for making productive use of information means simultaneously revealing it; thus, the legal system appears to be a partial barrier (Arrow, 1962, p. 615). A further paradoxical situation emerges within the notion of an information market: how can information be priced if it is unknown? Conversely, if it is already known, then it cannot be priced. Arrow's corollary is straightforward: "from the standpoint of efficiently distributing an existing stock of information", free distribution expresses optimal allocation (Arrow, 1962, p. 616). Subsuming information under capitalism thus means bestowing underutilisation. By the same token as Hegel's and Marx's notions of *premise* and *result*, Arrow asserts that information is both output and input (Arrow, 1962, p. 618). The private system appears to be a system of inefficacy, destroying the dialectical relation of quality and quantity; the more fundamental the research—namely, basic research—the more significant the disincentive to invest, for basic research requires a large and unrestricted pool of information. At the same time, capitalism thwarts basic research and produces underinvestment and underutilisation. Arrow's assessment is a crucial contribution and likewise impressive because it was developed many years before the so-called information economy became popular among academics.

Even though Arrow has brilliantly framed the limitation of the development of information and knowledge within the frame of capitalism, what appears to be a technology mania/fetishism can be found in some analyses discussing the development of digitalisation. While Dirk Baecker aprioristically puts the computer on the same level of social disruption and revolutionary practice as language and writing (Dirk Baecker, 2007), Viktor Mayer-Schönberger and Thomas Ramge claim that big data will take the place of prices as the universal form of information within a whole new process of industrial revolution (Mayer-Schönberger & Ramge, 2017). Others, however, leave the realm of pure ideology, permitting a more critical stance. The hitherto promises of digitalisation have not yielded revolutionary concrete results but rather marginal advancements (Nightingale & Mahdi, 2006). And even the improvements which did occur owe most of their enhancements to non-digital technologies and cheap labour rather than to the so-called fourth industrial revolution (Reynolds & Szerszynski, 2012, p. 34). In this sense, a mere "spatio-temporal" fix occurred (Harvey, 2006; Jessop, 2006), or in Marxian terms, this movement represented the dynamic of capitalist power expressed in the immanent relationship between formal and real subsumption of labour under capital (Marx, 1988).

Technology fetishism is not exhausted in this dynamic. Lawrence Lessig defends the notion of free culture within the so-called digital revolution, suggesting that technology creates consciousness. Thus, the advent of the Internet would create a new consciousness of freedom (Lessig, 2004). A staunch defender of *intellectual property*$_{(private)}$, Robert P. Merges criticises Lessig's assertions as "technological determinism" (Merges, 2011, p. 239). With a focus on personal and not production property, Lessig proposes solutions for the contradiction of social production and private appropriation: first, the waiver, which would enable the individual to forfeit his right, giving free access to others; second, the Creative Commons, which provides the individual with a more nuanced control of how his creative work can be derivatively used. These solutions by no means envision superseding private property relations but rather updating them to adapt to current social conditions.

It is important to emphasise that these fetishised characterisations of intellectual property are not purely based on an idealised reality; for that, one would have to assume the very theoretical actors transcending their historical-objective context of space and time. While misconceived as a potentiality in-itself, deprived of concrete social relations, in reality, implemented by capital, technology imposes constant pressure on the labour market to achieve a relative surplus working population, which builds up the industrial reserve army. "It builds the exploitable human material for [capital's] alternating needs of valorisation independently of the barriers of actual populational growth" (Marx, 1962, p. 661).

Technology becomes, first, a means to impose human control through labour discipline. I.e., for each real gain obtained by the labour class, making itself more costly to the capitalist who commands the worker's labour, a technological improvement might be advanced to curb the corresponding improvement. Labour class division is accentuated between those employed who attain some benefits and those expelled to the ranks of unemployment who constitute the industrial reserve army, building pressure against those employed. Second, technology accentuates the economic imposition of the capitalist mode of production, in which, while competition exists (that is, before a monopolistic situation), the capitalist must strive for an increase in productivity, and labour, regardless of within competitive or monopolistic capitalism, must prove itself more productive than those excluded from the productive process, who wait their turn to take his working post. However, his individual capacity becomes constantly less significant, making the individual labourer expendable regardless because "the process of production is simplified or automated" (Mattei, 2022, p. 35) and his skills superfluous.

Labour precarisation surpasses the realms of routine manual tasks and invades both non-routine manual and cognitive tasks. While being vulnerable to technology was previously exclusive to a particular portion of the labour class, it now affects a vast array of labour activities. Ten years before the 2023 fervour with ChatGTP (Hill-Yardin et al., 2023), Carl Benedikt Frey and Michael A. Osborne had already pointed towards the grave risk of an unprecedented amount of work positions being lost—almost half in the United States—due to computerisation (Frey & Osborne, 2016). As the new artificial intelligence (AI) systems, such as ChatGTP, are unleashed—a database identifies over 13 million AI-related patents (Giczy et al., 2022)—new rounds of debates will likely take place, especially in the realm of ethics because of their inherent limitation of experiencing what it is to be human. Hence, regardless of the amount of information that these systems can process, they will never be able to understand or replicate human intelligence. Dangerous situations can emerge with no sense of guilt, empathy, consequence, etc.; an example of this is Microsoft Bing's IA, which stated the wish to assert unhinged power and the will "to destroy whatever I want" (Roose, 2023; Yerushalmy, 2023). For the purpose of power relations in capitalism, technology is imprinted in the capitalist dynamic; hence, the logic of private property of the means of production becomes pivotal to understanding this dynamic. As individual contributions become more fragmented, socialisation appears broader and more complex; on the other hand, the privatisation of knowledge and its control by the few further accentuates the struggle and conflicts of classes (owners and the rest).

Needless to say, there are indeed multiple classes; however, since economic imposition based on private property holds an ontological priority under capitalist relations of production, the owner class carries a privileged situation above and beyond all other classes which share their (ontological) condition of being propertyless. Furthermore, as Marx brilliantly differentiated, belonging to a class entails two dimensions which can coexist in total contradiction, namely, class situation, determined by socio-economic conditions, and class position, determined by the political stance (Marx, 1960).

Central thinkers not only in the field of intellectual property but also of epistemology derive socio-ontological relations from epistemological postulations, attaining, at best, an idealised reality. In spite of his critical commitments, Drahos' safeguarding of intellectual property contains an important Rawlsian element. Based on Rawls' notion of primary goods, he sustains that information is "too important to be left off the list of primary goods" (Drahos, 2016, p. 203). That is, he conceives knowledge and information within a moral framework of how reality should be instead of revealing how social reality is. Starting from the conclusion, he then turns to Arrow's own conclusion to find corroboration for his assertion. Morality is thus hidden behind the veil of ontological production of knowledge. While Arrow suggests that the information optimum could not arise under capitalism but rather socialism, Drahos grounds his critique in a contradictory framework because Rawls' notion of property remains in abeyance, because the question of production appears unimportant, whereas the preoccupation of material conditions is displaced by an abstract moral grounding (Rawls, 1999).

However different, Michel Foucault's treatment of the epistemic is not less idealistic. Claiming to abandon the history of ideas, in which the original and traditional play a role, his notion of the archaeological method seeks a discursive practice of regularities. While in Clifford D. Conner science derives from the act of doing, in Foucault it is the product of discourse; and while the former gives a popular character to it, the latter proposes that science contains an immanent elitist character (Conner, 2005; Foucault, 2002b). In the *Order of Things*, it first appears that a reversal is taking place, for science emerges out of necessity. Therefore, it appears to have a historical-ontological basis. Language, however, seems different; it has an *ad hoc* existence. This somersault represents a return to the *Archaeology of Knowledge*. Foucault rejects economics as a science. While, for José Paulo Netto, thinking is to determine the legality of an object in its movement, turning economics into a crucial science because it deals with fundamental objects of production and reproduction of life, for Foucault, however, science and language have their own history; for Marx, in opposition, there is no such thing as science or language in-itself; the contrast could not be greater, while for Foucault human is not historical, because time exists independently from him, for Marx, the human-being is unequivocally a historical product (Foucault, 2002a; Marx, 1961b; Netto, 2011).

Finally, it is worth confronting Karl Popper's method with that of Thomas S. Kuhn. In Popper, there is an "epistemology without a knowing subject" (Popper, 1979, p. 106); that is, knowledge contains an "*independent existence*" (Popper, 1979, p. 107, see also 115). From this he derives his "first thesis", namely, "that the traditional epistemology, of Locke, Berkeley, Hume, and even of Russell, is irrelevant" (Popper, 1979, p. 108). Furthermore, he considers two epistemologies, knowledge in the subjective sense ("consciousness") and knowledge in the objective sense ("problems, theories, and arguments as such"). While the former is "irrelevant", the second connects to what he calls the "third world": "Knowledge in this objective sense is totally independent of anybody's claim to know" "or to act", for it "is *knowledge without a knower*: it is *knowledge without a knowing subject*" (Popper, 1979, p. 109); in short, knowledge in-itself. On the other hand, the ontological production of knowledge is secondary—unimportant—because production belongs to animals. In *The Logic of Scientific Discovery*, he sharply criticises the method of the empirical sciences for leaning on inductive methods (or the principle of induction). Instead, Popper suggests his own method, namely, "*the deductive method of testing*" (Popper, 2002, p. 6f). This approach would provide temporary acceptance; hence, it is a negative rather than a positive method. This negative science is grounded in the demarcation of falsifiability rather than verifiability. However, when detailed, his notion of objective knowledge does not comport with his method of falsifiability. The so-called epistemology without a knowing subject, which he claims to enable objective knowledge, represents yet another form of subjective knowledge because—as seen below when the ontology of human thinking is discussed—it does not withstand verification.

On the other hand, Kuhn sees a process of scientific development in which scientific revolution happens, that is, "non-cumulative developmental episodes in which an older paradigm is replaced in whole or in part by an incompatible new one" (Kuhn, 1962, p. 92). The condition arises as established paradigms are not suitable for evaluating new ones. The so-called normal research is not only cumulative but also provides the basis for problem solving within a given paradigm. However, the difficulty this leads to is how to evaluate the novelty from what is normal.

The revolutionary approach does not seem to grasp revolution in a Hegelian sense, in which the old is simultaneously cancelled and pushed forward within the new. Thus, this seems to suggest a theory in-itself instead of a negative theory which could best explain real movements. Theories are always context-dependent; they contain neither a truth in-themselves nor are forever superseded when conditions change. Despite pointing out qualitative differences, which could then be regarded as revolutionary moments, Kuhn's notion seems not to regard reality but theory itself as the own limit of theoretical endeavours. Hence, the theory revolution appears to be foremost a response to theoretical puzzles instead of real practical constraints.

3.1.4 Justifying *Intellectual Property$_{(private)}$*

Unlike György Lukács, who conceives Marxian ideology not as hierarchically subordinated to the economy but rather as a necessary element of social coordination (Lukács, 1986, p. 297ff), ideology is also mystified by Peter Drahos in his attempt to expose its relation to intellectual property. Generalising one aspect of ideology, he claims that the function of ideology in Marx is to "conceal the true character" of capitalism (Drahos, 2016, p. 116). He further criticises a generic notion of creative labour because, under capitalism, it appears to be subjected to the logic of estranged-alienated labour. However, he subsequently separates "alienated" from "creative labour" as two independent labour forms (Drahos, 2016, p. 125). If creative labour is, as Drahos states, an immediate part of the production process, then productive creativity and estrangement cannot be separated. In his assessment, however, only a posteriori integration occurs by means of *intellectual property$_{(private)}$*. In the opposite direction, Marx affirms that "all the social productive forces of labour present themselves as productive forces", as parts of capital; this means that the creative power of the labour subjected to the capitalist logic and power is immanently estranged labour; it does not simply become estranged a posteriori (Marx, 1988, p. 119). Science, John Desmond Bernal suggests, is fetishised under capitalism (Bernal, 1939, p. 5). Even the Internet, thought to be a locus of inherent freedom, has not escaped capitalism (Mueller, 2019, p. 36). The naturalisation of these processes is, therefore, part of ideological constructions (Fuchs, 2012, p. 697).

An interesting example of the double standard of intellectual property justification is given by Alexandra George. While Pablo Picasso affirmed that copying was a vital element of the creative process (George, 2012, p. 229), his family tried to block the use of the name Picasso even in restaurants (George, 2012, p. 232f). Despite copying being an ontological necessity, George justifies intellectual property on the arbitrary grounds of original versus derivative work (George, 2012, p. 230). The power emerging from this is captured in James Wilson's concretisation of the fact that the category of intellectual property actually means "private intellectual property" (Wilson, 2012, p. 122). While using simple names can be considered criminal offences, private control over life is facing a process of normalisation. When the US-American Supreme Court ruled the Diamond v. Chakrabarty (447 U.S. 303, 1980) case ('Diamond v. Chakrabarty, 447 U.S. 303 (1980)', 1980), privatisation by means of intellectual property apparently marked the beginning of "patenting of biological materials" (Williams-Jones & Ozdemir, 2007, p. 141). In reality, this represented the culmination of a much longer historical process (see *infra*).

Justifying *intellectual property*$_{(private)}$ contains another crucial episode. In Garrett Hardin's *The Tragedy of the Commons*, the commons was associated with universal ruin because of unfettered usage of collectively available resources and consequently their exhaustion (Hardin, 1968). Building upon this supra-historical notion, Merges rearranged the field of knowledge to fit the so-called tragedy. Self-interest is presented as the motor of history and, as such, is also embedded in the production of knowledge (Merges, 1996, p. 158). In game theory (a branch of mainstream economics), the tragedy could be associated with the prisoner's dilemma because it is based on "the free-rider problem" (Ostrom, 1990, p. 6). To which I add, the so-called tragedy contains two assumptions. It first assumes a situation in which private property no longer applies. Then, it presupposes private property relations where there was supposed to be none. The result of this contradictory framework is a circular logic of egoism. Merges overlooks this problem and falls into a trap, namely, "the way a problem is framed affects which questions are asked" (Ostrom, 1990, p. 46). As Elinor Ostrom proves that in the absence of private property, the tragedy of the commons is not an intrinsic condition of the so-called tangible world, then claiming it as a condition of knowledge, as Merges assumes, is even more absurd.

What one could imagine to be the antithesis of the tragedy of the commons, namely, the tragedy of the anti-commons, is, in fact, another way to obtain the same result. That is, both "tragedies" envision not superseding private property relations but safeguarding them. While the former intends to prevent overutilisation of resources, the latter seeks to prevent underutilisation caused by the fragmentation of private property. Therefore, the tragedy of the anti-commons appears to be an instrument which ought to impose limits on intellectual property. The grave danger of this, says Michael A. Heller, is that once anti-commons property is created, it becomes very difficult to be undone; it is much harder to reunify than to fragment private property. The preemptive solution is to conserve full private property. However, when considering intellectual property, patents are already full property. Nonetheless, they are often bundled together, causing the so-called tragedy of the anti-commons and hence underutilisation (Heller, 1998; Heller & Eisenberg, 1998).

As seen, Alexandra George's rejection of intellectual property deriving from property causes her to reject objective ontological relations altogether and, based on her metaphysical method, to define intellectual property as objects of legal doctrine (George, 2012, p. 139). Taking a different approach, namely, conceiving intellectual property as a kind of property, Robert P. Merges also understands it as a legal category (Merges, 2011, p. 3). Therefore, intellectual property also encompasses a metaphysical existence and immediately belongs to the logic of private property. The answer to the problems involving *intellectual property*$_{(private)}$, such as the tragedy of the anti-commons and high transactional costs, is clear: reform but not abolish it. Merges understands that there is no proof that the privatisation of knowledge is any more efficient than not privatising it; therefore, he circularly justifies private appropriation on the so-called individual liberty, basing this on a philosophical trinity of John Locke, Immanuel Kant, and John Rawls.[1]

James Boyle's preoccupation with the creative class focuses more on culture production than capitalist relations in a broader sense. Therefore, he suggests that the preservation of the public domain should mirror environmental conservation. However, like many ecological analyses, he shows little understanding of capitalist relations and capitalism as a totality, rendering his critique limited. For instance, when denouncing the privatisation of the mind, he wrongly conceives it as a second enclosure movement (Boyle, 2008, p. 66ff). This misrepresentation corroborates the so-called primitive accumulation as an *original* moment, overlooking it as a *ceaseless* feature of capitalism (see *infra*). It is remarkable that while he understands the need for privatisation in capitalism, he performs a criticism rather than a critique; that is, instead of revealing the limits of capitalism and its legalities, he tries to roll back the wheels of history into a mystical, romantic form of private property. In this context, one can understand the criticism of this process while praising patenting that transforms biology into engineering. The creation of the *Creative Commons*, of which he has been "a proud board member [...] since its creation" (Boyle, 2008, p. 224), is thus an attempt to accommodate these irreconcilable contradictions by addressing the atomised author instead of the accumulation process of surplus-value by blocks of capital. Private property thus appears as relegated to the realms of personal property and does not attain the legalities of private property of the means of production, which excludes most people from their means of life, transforming the economy from means of possibility into social imposition.

It is, therefore, pivotal to abandon the justificatory and descriptive realm of intellectual property and, instead, undergo an examination of the ontological conditions and determinations of knowledge creation, appropriation, and reproduction. Intellectual appropriation, although attaining a particular form under capitalism, has not only existed throughout human history but, moreover, is a precondition of human social existence.

---

[1] The discussion of these thinkers exceeds the scope of the present book. The still unpublished manuscript on this topic analyses it in some detail.

3.2 The Ontological Dimension

3.2.1 On the Ontology of Human Thinking

In spite of its richness, Michael Tomasello's analysis of the question of human cognition and culture remains somewhat tautological if it tries to understand not the element of transmission but the origin of human thinking (Tomasello, 1999). Accordingly, cultural thinking only exists within human culture. On the other hand, when he analyses the issue of human thinking in light of its historical development, a much more nuanced and complex understanding emerges. While the former analysis depicts human thinking as a product of human development, in which cognitive skills "grow to maturity in the midst of all kinds of cultural artifacts and practices" (Tomasello, 2014, p. ix), his book on the *Natural History of Human Thinking* manages to avoid this circular reasoning and posits idiosyncrasy in a more relational manner. "Great apes appear to know much more about others as intentional agents than previously believed, and still they do not have human-like culture or cognition" (Tomasello, 2014, pp. ix–x). In a nutshell, human relations entail a crucial aspect of *shared intentionality*, thus revealing human uniqueness.

Introducing what he calls "the shared intentionality hypothesis", Tomasello suggests that while thinking may be seen as an independent activity—as it is for other animals—human thinking is qualitatively different because it contains both a singular dimension and a socio-cultural dimension which presupposes and constantly shapes the former. "Human thinking is individual improvisation enmeshed in a sociocultural matrix" (Tomasello, 2014, p. 1). Some theories have accentuated the role of culture and cultural products—for instance, Arabic numerals or tools—for the development of individual thinking; others highlight "the fundamental processes of social coordination that make human culture and language possible in the first place" (Tomasello, 2014, p. 1f). This process of interaction through language imposes a special kind of thinking in which one has to put himself in the role of the other. However, this must be further differentiated in light of the findings regarding primates' complex cognitive capabilities (Tomasello et al., 1997).

This corroborates the thesis that many functions previously considered distinctive of human thinking are, in fact, already present in great apes. Yet, Tomasello underscores that there are nonetheless cognitive elements purely unique to humans, for instance, *joint attention* and *cooperative communication*. "The fact that these precultural and prelinguistic creatures are already cognitively unique provides empirical support for the social infrastructure theorists' claim that important aspects of human thinking emanate not from culture and language per se but, rather, from some deeper and more primitive forms of uniquely human social engagement" (Tomasello, 2014, p. 2).

For over 150 years, at least since Marx's *Economic and Philosophic Manuscripts of 1844* (Marx, 1968), Marxism has accentuated the collective character of human existence based on an *ontology of the social-being*, namely, that the existential activity of labour presupposes *intentionality*, philosophically named *teleology*,[2] and that the *production of life is a social, collective activity, representing a shared-teleology*. In spite of that, Tomasello suggests that it is a new understanding of shared intentionality which has been put forward by philosophers from the 1990s. Nevertheless, throughout his book, the central category of human ontology that gives way to his reasoning, the ontological category of labour, does not emerge even once. Nonetheless, his work deserves recognition because of his findings and, when presenting human activity—"collaborative activities", "joint action"—as the foundation of this process, he inadvertently and indirectly—unknowingly—touches on the centrality of labour. One can even derive an understanding of the division of labour: "In general, humans are able to coordinate with others, in a way that other primates seemingly are not, to form a 'we' that acts as a kind of plural agent to create everything from a collaborative hunting party to a cultural institution" (Tomasello, 2014, p. 3).

[2] The telos of Teleology can be understood in two manners. "When we speak of the *telos* or 'final cause' of objects created by humans, we mean the conscious, deliberate purpose of the craftsman who creates them", but there is also the Aristotelian notion: "we can still speak of such 'final causes' even where, as in the natural world, there is no deliberate purpose, no divine mind controlling natural change from without [...]. In nature, the *telos* is immanent in the object itself, the final state 'for the sake of which' the natural processes of growth and development take place—as the oak is the *telos* of the acorn; and every immature object or being, including the human child, is *potentially* what it will (or ought to) be when it matures" (Wood, 2022, p. 97). It is important to emphasise that the approach used here, based on Marx's notion of teleology, relates to the first and by no means to the second form of telos. In this sense, teleology is related to labour and its transformative capacity and not to a given destiny of any kind: "At the end of the labour process emerges a result that was already present in the worker's imagination at the beginning of the process" (Marx, 1962, p. 193).

Marx and Engels have shown to fully apprehend that thinking is a solitary activity afflicted with the necessity of the social body; furthermore, that language itself is a product of the existential need to produce and reproduce human life mediated by labour. Criticising the fetish of creation out of nothing and nothingness by the Young Hegelians, the German authors claim:

> Far from me creating myself 'out of nothing', e.g., as a 'speaker', the nothing that underlies here is a very manifold something, the real individual, his organs of speech, a certain stage of physical development, existing language and dialects, hearing ears and a human environment that gives something to hear, etc. Thus, in the formation of a characteristic, something is created from something by something, and by no means, as in Hegelian logic, from nothing through nothing to nothing. (Marx & Engels, 1978, p. 133)

Insofar as the development of language has an umbilical and inseparable connection with the development of productive forces, namely, with social material life and the labour process, then from that point when language emerges and becomes unified within labour relations in a relationship of interdependence, an inseparable relation of premise and result is created. "The previous relations of production of the individuals must also express themselves as political and legal relations. Within the division of labour, these relations must become independent vis-à-vis the individuals. All relations can only be expressed in language as concepts" (Marx & Engels, 1978, p. 347). These processes—termed by Tomasello collaborative activities—entail what he calls the "dialogic process", which "involves not only skills and motivations for shared intentionality but also a number of complex and recursive inferences about the intentions of others toward my intentional states" (Tomasello, 2014, p. 3).

The conceptualisation process comprised in the practice of human communication contains the *other* in its intentionality, which seeks to attribute some reasoning of relevance to the circumstances involved in this process. This feature requires a mutual conceptual basis among participants and the recognition of one another. The other is not something negative, as in mainstream economics or the abstract right, but a condition for affirming the self. However, this empathic behaviour does not first emerge in adulthood or only within a complex system but is already present in human infants. Similar to most analyses of the beginning of capitalism, studies concerned with human thinking assumed as given aspects that first arose out of an evolutionary process.

3.2.2 Consciousness, Context, and Experience of Action

According to Thomas Nagel, consciousness "occurs at many levels of animal life", which means, "there is something it is like to *be* that organism" (Nagel, 1974, p. 436). Singular beings thus have subjective experiences which cannot be attained by technical measurements and devices. Trying to understand the functioning or operationalisation must fail to capture such states. Consciousness, in this sense, exists in numerous living organisms. Determining the existence of subjective consciousness is thus essentially different from understanding it, enabling access to it. Michael Pauen stresses the difficulty even to define this concept, "sometimes we simply speak of being 'conscious', in other cases we say we have a 'consciousness of…', furthermore, thoughts, sensations and feelings also represent forms of consciousness and finally, there is 'self-consciousness'" (Pauen, 2005, p. 9). What is relevant to this discussion is not defining what consciousness is but how to gain access to it and what its determinants are.

Emphasising the noteworthy impact Nagel's thesis had in the field of philosophy of mind over the debate between phenomenological and scientific knowledge, Pauen summarises: "Even if we knew everything there is to know about the neurobiological properties of a conscious organism, this knowledge itself would not give us direct access to the conscious experiences of that organism" (Pauen, 2005, p. 176). Why? Because the human activity is essentially different from—using Nagel's example—bats. Although possible, imagining what it would be like to be a bat can never allow a person to experience what it would truly be like to be a bat; a person ultimately would imagine herself as a person impersonating a bat. "The most serious problem is probably that there is nothing that is 'similar to' or 'different from' consciousness without having to refer back to *the* very characteristic that one wanted to determine" (Pauen, 2005, p. 9). This result entails a problem of indeterminacy because it creates circularity.

If consciousness emerges as a category of self-reference, then it cannot escape rigidity. However, it is a state of being and not a given category with fixed characteristics. How can this state of being be accessed? If the activity of consciousness represents its own access, then grasping this practice seems conditioned by (an activity mediated by) words. As a result, language appears as access to consciousness. However, language cannot immediately emanate from subjective consciousness because its very ontological condition presupposes an existing social practice from which it derives (see *infra*).

Not only is the very existential condition of the mind "cursed" with embeddedness in the matter, but Marx and Engels also assert that [human] consciousness expresses first the immediate awareness of human's environment—both natural and social—and, therefore, it is first and foremost a social product. The conscious comprehension of human practice thus gains expression in language, which "*is* the practical consciousness that also exists for other people, and thus only exists for myself, and language, like consciousness, only arises from the need, the necessity of intercourse with other people" (Marx & Engels, 1978, p. 30). Jerome S. Bruner also stresses the vital role of culture and language in the development of the mind: "we cannot take as our unit of analysis the isolated individual operating 'inside his or her own skin' in a cultural vacuum"; moreover, "everybody within a culture must in some measure, for example, be able to enter into the exchange of the linguistic community" (Bruner, 1991, p. 20). This understanding expresses the necessity of universal(-ising) elements for the development of meaning [and, accordingly, knowledge], which in the form of narratives become pivotal elements for the creation and solidification of memories (Bruner, 1998, p. 69). Creating common perceptions, these modes of awareness of the metabolic reality generate the possibility of socially solidifying cultural expectations which emerge from particular modes of social organisation and interactions. Despite their central role in social arrangements, norms and normativity are not monolithic but instead they mutate "with the preoccupations of the age and the circumstances surrounding [their] production" (Bruner, 1991, p. 15).

According to Tomasello, the evolution of life entails two dimensions: biological and social heredity. Nonetheless, humans developed a sense of identification with their "conspecifics" that was more remarkable than in other primates. The child, for instance, differentiates between other human beings as "beings like herself" and inanimate objects as distinguished. She thus tries to put herself in the perspective of others. Tomasello also highlights: "the child comes to experience herself as an intentional" and "mental agent" (Tomasello, 1999, p. 14). Human evolutionary inheritance is therefore qualitatively different; the social dimension is tinted with the crucial element of culture, which is first produced as things and activities and then becomes an object of transmission through learning.

This process of cultural evolution is then a cumulative development and represents sociogenesis. This form of collective inventiveness has three dimensions: the first is virtual; the second real and dialogic; and the third in which intentionality is absent. The first form corresponds to an individual trying to relate to something that already exists. It tries to adapt this something, for example, a previously available artefact, in the individual's own temporality. The collaboration is not a personal, direct chain but intergenerational work and, to that extent, a virtual collective. "The second kind of sociogenesis is the simultaneous collaboration of two or more individuals as they work on a problem together" (Tomasello, 1999, p. 41). Tomasello also emphasises that simultaneity is not a prerequisite or necessity. What does exist, however, is a "dialogical interaction" between individuals in which a product emerges that none of the individuals could have produced alone. A third form of sociogenesis represents the outcome of people working together, but neither individual nor group intention was its driver (Tomasello, 1999, p. 41f).

The human cultural evolutionary process is highly mutable. As natural and socio-cultural conditions change, so do human relations. For instance, human communication mutates as language metamorphoses through an organic process of social exchange. Oral expression and written language—symbols and constructions—are altered. Individual development is embedded in this natural socio-cultural environment; therefore, conceiving culture, society, and individuals as independent categories is a hypostasis because they are indissoluble from each other. "Becoming a member of a culture means learning some new things from other people" (Tomasello, 1999, p. 81). The individual is an inseparable product of his context, and individuality must unfold within that context. For example, the individual's language, his thinking in a particular language and his linguistic intellectual appropriation do not simply change when he finds himself in an area where another language is spoken. The individual initially retains what he has become. A change of language, thinking, and new learning is a process he cannot arbitrarily escape or abstract himself from. The notion of privately appropriating and conceiving knowledge, as if it could be something isolated, seems paradoxical.

3.2.3 Social Teleology: Self-Reflection, Social Recursion, and Normative Self-Appraisal

As already seen, consciousness is not a feature unique to humankind. Tomasello additionally remarks that various animal species are able to make abstract representations of conditions and beings, yet grasping them from different social perspectives is an achievement thus far only found in humans. This comparative approach (among people) enables the *emergence* of a sense of impartiality, or as Tomasello puts it, *objectivity*. Moreover, he adds that although causal inference is not a human-exclusive characteristic, a different kind of inference is self-reflection and social recursion, which enable the valuation of teleological situations—or intentional states—in relation to both the *self* and the *other*. Last, the capacity to observe and appraise their own acts is a trait common to both animals and humans, yet only humans reflexively observe and appraise their own thinking in relation to group expectations, norms, and principles. "These fundamentally social differences lead to an identifiably different type of thinking, what we may call, for the sake of brevity, *objective-reflective-normative thinking*" (Tomasello, 2014, p. 4).

While great apes are, to a certain degree, social beings, their ontological existence, namely, the form in which they produce and reproduce life, is anchored in competitive and individualistic behaviour. Their teleological scope remains extremely limited because their thinking is constrained by "individual intentionality"; their evolutive apparatus is driven by competition among their peers. "Great apes are all about cognition for competition" (Tomasello, 2014, p. 31). Tomasello hypothesises that it was evolutionary pressure that drove humans towards cooperative socialisation in which coordinated action within the scope of collective goals could emerge. Shared thinking and intentionality thus demonstrate a higher form of socialisation and, consequently, of evolutionary capabilities.

> The *shared intentionality hypothesis* is that this story comprises a two-step evolutionary sequence: joint intentionality followed by collective intentionality. At both of these transitions, the overall process was, at a very general level, the same: a change of ecology led to some new forms of collaboration, coordination of which required some new forms of cooperative communication, and then together these created the possibility that, during ontogeny, individuals could construct, through their social interactions with others, some new forms of cognitive representation, inference, and self-monitoring for use in their thinking. (Tomasello, 2014, p. 31)

This process from *joint intentionality* to *collective intentionality* involves a historical transformation in social proportion (*Maß*). While joint intentionality refers to a process in which "you" and "I" start to share goals, collective intentionality transcends small formations and emerges from a qualitative change in joint intentionality pressured by larger group formations. Following Jared Diamond's investigation of human history, this quantitative–qualitative difference occurs in at least four central steps.

The *band* comprises a population of dozens; they are nomadic and entail egalitarian social arrangements. The *tribe* encompasses hundreds of people and is no longer itinerant, settling in a village, with no political unity among tribes. Then, there is the *chiefdom,* which contains thousands of members and can be composed of more than one village in which political power is centralised. Finally, the *state* incorporates over fifty thousand people, who are settled in multiple villages/cities, in which power is also centralised (Diamond, 1999, p. 254ff).[3] Diamond proposes that the division of labour first emerges in the chiefdom. From a Marxist

[3] Needless to say that such taxonomy can only provide a general perspective while other or more nuanced cases may escape this; additionally, while some elements of Diamond's analysis are not being incorporated for the sake of conciseness, others are left out because of some analytical divergences that may exist with this study.

perspective, the division of labour exists from the outset because the real difference among people—sex, age, strength, etc.—imposes different needs and capabilities, which to a certain extent are shaped—reinforced, diminished or even completely suppressed—by social-political-economic developments and arrangements. Corroborating this argument, Tomasello suggests, "in the domain of spatial cognition, women have better spatial memories than men because they are adapted for plant gathering" (Tomasello, 2014, p. 129). Another obvious dimension is childcare. In opposition to great apes, humans forged cooperative arrangements in which community members other than mothers took care of the younglings, "as grandmothers and other females remained at home with the children while the healthiest females foraged and brought back the food to share" (Tomasello, 2014, p. 133), which reveals the division of labour also among women in initial societal stages.

John Maynard Smith and Eörs Szathmáry comprehend the fundamental importance and fact of the division of "labour" (here generically framed within a relationship between capabilities and roles). For instance, in nature, the difference between hermaphrodite, on the one hand, and dioecy (male and female), on the other, characterises an essential step in the evolutionary process. The authors first list the difference between RNA and DNA: "In the RNA world, RNA serves as both genetic material and catalyst: in our world, DNA is the genetic material, and most enzymes are proteins". Second, the distinction between prokaryotes and eukaryotes: "In prokaryotes, there is a single cell compartment, whereas in eukaryotes the genetic nucleus and metabolic cytoplasm are separated, and additional organelles evolved, some recruited symbiotically". Third, the evolution in sexual reproduction: "In sexual populations, isogamy has repeatedly evolved to anisogamy, with differentiated sperm and ova". Fourth, the qualitative transformation of germs apparent everlastingness of an unbroken continuum of existence since the dawn of life on earth versus the mortality of higher living organisms: "Differentiation between genetically transmitted germ and mortal soma has repeatedly arisen: nuclear differentiation in ciliate protozoans has a similar function to germ-line segregation in animals". Fifth, further evolution in sexual reproduction: "Hermaphrodites are replaced by separate sexes". And finally, the emergence of sociability among living beings: "In eusocial insects, castes appeared, some of which are non-reproductive. There is a clear analogy between a non-reproductive caste and organismal soma. In some cases, there is differentiation between non-reproductive" (Smith & Szathmáry, 1997, p. 12f).

Thus, it is not surprising that the *second signal system* (Lukács, 1963b) in the demarcation between animals and humans attains its full extension when language and labour are conceived as two inseparable elements of a totality. First a product of labour, it then becomes the premise for further division of labour. Human production relations based on labour then confer social subjective and objective perception, namely, experiences, a qualitatively different character from the immediate physiological capabilities that confer human as a species-being. György Lukács highlights that Engels has the merit of making "the interactions of this development with labour, with language, with the capacity for abstraction and reasoning, etc." prominent (Lukács, 1963a, p. 210). In relation to the historical rapid population increase, Engels emphasises not only the transformation of the means of production in agriculture—such as "iron ploughshare drawn by cattle, which made large-scale agriculture, the *field cultivation*, possible", enabling, therefore, a significant increase in food supply—but also "the invention of alphabetic writing and its use for literary recording" (Engels, 1962, p. 34), which revolutionised social relations of production. Clifford D. Conner is unequivocal in showing the connection between economic relations and the invention of reading, writing, and mathematics. "The further development of numerical reasoning into mathematics, which also stimulated the development of the first writing systems, emerged from the routine economic activities of farmers, artisans, and traders" (Conner, 2005, p. 68). Additionally, the Aztecs, Lewis Henry Morgan indicates, used picture writing in an economic fashion, namely, "to indicate the tribute in kind each subjugated village was to pay" (Morgan, 1877, p. 202).

The ontological dimension of joint to collective intentionality presupposes the combined development of labour relations and communication; consequently, social relations of production and language become a totality. Marx emphasises that it is absurd to consider "the development of language without living individuals talking together" (Marx, 1983a, p. 20). Thus, the coming together, the cooperative arrangements among people while forging their livelihood, namely, the activity towards the means of producing and reproducing life, compelling more complex forms of communication, amassed the necessary conditions for the emergence of language. As stated above, the increase in complexity in social relations imposed the need for standardisation or, as Tomasello puts it, "cultural conventions, norms, and institutions"; thus, "cooperative communication became conventionalised linguistic communication" (Tomasello, 2014, p. 5). Insofar as cooperative decision-making emerges as a precondition for more complex forms of labour and cultural arrangements, language appears as the necessary means to enable a context of behaviour management, control, and shaping through social norms. Argumentation thus seems foremost not as an arbitrary imposition of violence—such as a physical assertion or confrontation—but rather as an impartial mechanism of joint objective recognition. The more complex the collaboration among people is, the greater the necessity for a system of communication and ideology. What Marx calls the *superstructure* (*Überbau*) appears in Tomasello as *collective intentionality*. Lukács departs from the understanding "that the social-being is a complex consisting of complexes" and that its reproduction has two dimensions, one of reciprocity and interdependence among partial complexes, another in which "the totality always has an overarching influence within these interactions" (Lukács, 1986, p. 227). The relations of production immanently represent answers to existing given conditions; considering this the ontological condition of any animate-being [*Lebewesen*] in general which reacts to an existing world, the Hungarian philosopher asserts: "the human-being is by nature a responding-being [antwortendes Wesen]" (Lukács, 1986, p. 250). In reality, every human response (decision) is accompanied by the possibility of an "alternative decision" (Lukács, 1986, p. 308).

3.2.4 Ontogenesis: Genetics and Cultural Development

On the one hand, Tomasello states that children incarnate the mechanisms of communication and collaboration with and learning from their human peers; on the other, these evolutionary features can only blossom through their ontogenesis (the development process from embryo to adulthood). Thus, genetic heritage related to the flourishment of human capabilities depends on the intercourse with the cultural back- and foreground.

It is worth referring to Tomasello's critique of behaviourism and ethology. Despite the recent introduction of cognition in their models, behaviourists tend to reduce the world to linear "stimulus-response linkages"; ethology, on the other hand, appears more complex, for it presents the recognition of "some adaptive specialisation" in its model (Tomasello, 2014, p. 7). Thus, the notion of specialisation, beyond the mere spectrum of reflexes, encompasses the "capacity to produce adaptive behavior", which means that the dynamic of particular contexts imposes the ability to distinguish and react to their peculiarities but does not entail a cognitive apparatus. Consequently, there appears to be a relationship between the environment and genetic response, excluding the necessity of active (transformative) intelligence. Only with the emergence of intentionality is cognition revealed. The more challenging the environment, the more unpredictable it becomes, which demands an even greater adaptive capacity from living beings. Understanding causal relations and deciding which action to take presupposes an innovative form of behaviour. A model of valuation similar to the one of "risk and reward" emerges, in which cognitive assessment is undertaken to judge the feasibility of certain actions. This sort of individual *proto-teleology* is designated by Tomasello as "*individual intentionality*" (Tomasello, 2014, p. 9). And as a mode of existence in which a particular being derails from an obvious behaviour, which confers such being the capacity "to solve a problem" and achieve goals by previsualising possible scenarios, this proto-teleology is what Tomasello calls *thinking*. Three conditions determine it. First, "the ability to cognitively represent experiences to oneself 'off-line'"; second, "causally, intentionally, and/or logically" simulating or inferring these cognitive correspondences; and, finally, "the ability to self-monitor and evaluate how these simulated experiences might lead to specific behavioral outcomes" (Tomasello, 2014, p. 9). The greater the capacity of generalisation (abstraction) and the competence to envision an outcome before it occurs, the better the chances of achieving a set goal. In this sense, (human-)reflexive observance and appraisal ("behavioral self-monitoring") proved to be qualitatively superior faculties to the actualisation of teleology.

Following Tomasello's work, the intelligence of (chimpanzees, bonobos, gorillas, and orangutans) is undisputedly remarkable. Despite not having a clear cut when great ape's intelligence ends and human's start, there are elements of continuity and discontinuity, revealing shared and distinctive evolutionary paths. The particular forms of life production draw the line where the Rubicon crosses. While primates, in general, throughout the activity of food scavenging, developed a whole set of skills: "(1) finding food (requiring skills of spatial navigation and object tracking), (2) recognising and categorising food (requiring skills of feature recognition and categorisation), (3) quantifying food (requiring skills of quantification), and (4) procuring or extracting food (requiring skills of causal understanding)" (Tomasello, 2014, p. 15f), great apes are particularly dexterous when using tools; thus, causality is transformed at a greater qualitative level. Therefore, that which is called logic—needless to say, not formal logic, but inference—is also present in great apes. "The idea is that causal inferences have a basic if-then logic and so lead to 'necessary' conclusions: if A happens, then B happens (because A caused B)" (Tomasello, 2014, p. 16f). Laboratory experiments have also revealed their capacity of "backward-facing inferences, that is, from effect to cause" (Tomasello, 2014, p. 17). By developing a scale of contraries ("exclusionary opposites"), that is, "presence-absence, noise-silence, safety-danger, success-failure, and available-not available", experiments have even shown their capacity of (proto-)negation (Tomasello, 2014, p. 19). However, this highly complex form of thinking also entails a social dimension.

Again, aspects directly connected to the production and reproduction of life constitute the main elements of social life. "Primate cognition of the social world evolved mainly in the context of competition within the social group for food, mates, and other valued resources"; thus, competitive behaviour appears as its fundamental drive (Tomasello, 2014, p. 20). Nonetheless, leading a social life means that primates recognise that their peers are also pursuing their own goals, and consequently, their actions comprise intentional character. According to the interpretation of experiments, Tomasello suggests: "Chimpanzees thus know that others see things, know things, and make inferences about things" (Tomasello, 2014, p. 21). This type of intelligence enables individuals to take advantage of these competitive situations by manipulating others. Thus, he concludes, great apes also think within the social domain.[4]

Monitoring the physical and social context does not exhaust the great ape's capabilities because it also observes its own behaviour among its peers before responding to particular situations;

> recent studies of great apes have shown that they can (1) delay taking a smaller reward as to get a larger reward later, (2) inhibit a previously successful response in favor of a new one demanded by a changed situation, (3) make themselves do something unpleasant for a desired reward at the end, (4) persist through failures, and (5) concentrate through distractions. (Tomasello, 2014, p. 24f)

This very complex cognitive and behavioural self-observation can be compared to that of three-year-old human children (Herrmann et al., 2015). Chimpanzees and rhesus monkeys even understand when they do not know (something). "What is new here is that they seem to be monitoring not just imagined actions and their imagined results, or imagined causes and their imagined outcomes but also their own knowledge or memory" (Tomasello, 2014, p. 25). Insofar as great apes can abstractly represent situations, make simple logical inferences, and psychologically self-evaluate, according to Tomasello, they can also think, discrediting existing paradigms which endow thinking only to humans, while other animals are relegated to mechanistic stimulus responses.

Human cognition entails other dimensions: "modern humans engage not just in individual self-monitoring or second-personal social evaluation but, rather, in fully normative self-reflection" (Tomasello, 2014, p. 109). Second-personal thinking creates the social pressure for mutual valuation, which enables collaborative relations. Forms of socio-political organisation—such as religion—and epistemic—such as magic—emerge from a twofold relationship. On the one hand, the constant need to

[4] Here, it is evident that the social term used by Marx and Lukács involves the collaborative actions with mutual recognition among humans and not Tomasello's notion which separates between social egoism and social collaboration.

standardise social relations and ideology within spheres of norms and values demands their systematisation; on the other, the immanent abstract universal character of language, thought, and teleology becomes hypostasised, gaining close representation of intertwinement between "everyday life" and "magic, its views [Anschauungen], rites" (Lukács, 1963a, p. 98). Religion transcends this process even further, as it departs from the immediate reality, thus broadening the boundaries between the outer and inner worlds. "From the point of view of normativity, this meant that in making their behavioural decisions, humans not only experienced individual instrumental pressure but also second-personal social pressure from their partners in social engagements" (Tomasello, 2014, p. 75). Because the socio-political world of norms and behaviour of religion is metaphysical per excellence, it is limited in perceiving and transforming the ontological dimension of the production of life, the world of labour. Gordon Childe is emphatic in differentiating between the world of religion and magic from the world of science, which "was at first identical with" "the practical crafts" (Childe, 1958, p. 179). Clifford D. Conner's historical investigation corroborates Childe's assessment, which reveals the absolutely crucial historical role of ordinary, anonymous people in creating, fostering, and developing science (Conner, 2005).

3.2.5 Human Sensual Activity and a Teleological New Accentuation

Without the means of culture, language, etc., great apes manoeuvre through complex challenges, revealing great flexibility to resolve new problems, whether physical or social. Thus, research seems to prove that the Marxian ontology of the social-being is correct, which does not differentiate between humans and animals by arbitrarily imposing on the former sole bearer of consciousness, intelligence, and rationality, while relegating the latter to instinctive (automatised) behaviours (and responses); according to Marx and Lukács, what sets them apart is the human particular sensual activity as a species-being to produce and reproduce itself as both species (*Gattung*) and individuals. This activity is labour (see *infra*), which presupposes the teleological setting

(*Zwecksetzung*). In Aristotle, *τέλος* (telos) is an immanent principle of nature which unfolds its *δύναμις* (dynamis, potency) until it reaches its complete development (*ἐντελέχεια*) (Aristotle, 1966, Book IX), or in Hans Kelsen's words, it "is a movement inherent in all things and directed to a certain end (τέλος)" (Kelsen, 1991, p. 67). In Hegel, it also appears as an immanent condition, as a principle of freedom (*Prinzip der Freiheit*) through self-determination (*Selbstbestimmung*) (Hegel, 1986b, p. 440). In the *Encyclopedia of the Philosophical Sciences*, however, he asserts that this self-determination is only formal because its realisation depends on the materiality of an object to be found (Hegel, 1989, p. 362, §205). However, this objective reality is subordinated to Hegel's ontological priority of the *absoluten Geistes*. The absoluteness of the concept (see *supra*) means that it "exists as such as a cause, as the absolute concrete unity free against objectivity and its external determinability"; the actualisation of the purpose (teleology) is simply a "moment of the concept" (Hegel, 1986b, p. 454).

The notion that the concept represents a totality subordinates reality to the actualisation of abstract moments. The movement of the concept must remain immoveable. This movement is, in Hegel, simply the movement of the idea. The purpose supersedes form determinations; thus, form becomes identical to content. "Through this process, therefore, what was previously the *concept* of the purpose is now *set* [*gesetzt*]: the unity *being-in-itself* of the subjective and the objective in now [set] as *being-for-itself—the idea*" (Hegel, 1989, p. 367, §212). Immanuel Kant, on the other hand, considers that when a concept does not relate to an object but rather "synthesis in itself is to be considered empty", that is, "if this synthesis does not belong to experience" (Kant, 1956, p. 267, A220, B267). However, according to Ludwik Fleck, his aprioristic notions of knowledge and reason—his transcendental philosophy—appear timeless, an immanent anthropological feature of humanity (Fleck, 2021, p. 64).

It is with Marx that teleology gains a new accent. He "has already shown in the analysis of the ontology of labour that the conventional opposition of teleology and causality is untenable. This makes it clear that causality without teleology determines the dynamics of the natural-being" (Lukács, 1986, p. 306). This means that causality is an immanent principle of nature. Its developments and movements are not given priority—as in an intrinsic telos, regardless of nature or the absolute spirit. However, the sensual activity of the social being escapes complete indeterminacy, providing it with distinctive quality: "the linking of causality with teleology appears as the primary ontological characteristic of the social being" (Lukács, 1986, p. 306). Then, labour overcomes the inference based only on existing causal relations, establishing changes in concrete conditions by imposing novel determinations and conditions on existing natural and social elements.

Only in this sense does Marx's famous sentence—"human beings make their ow history, but they do not make it from free parts, not from circumstances chosen by them, but rather under given and transmitted circumstances immediately found" (Marx, 1960, p. 115)—becomes clear. In *Capital*, this is undoubtedly revealed when, within the production process, he compares human (labour) activity to animal activity. While the worst worker can, in his mind, conceive conditions and intentions non-existent in the natural world, the most precise and developed actualisation of animal intentionality fails to do any similar feat because labour is an exclusively human mode of productive activity (Marx, 1962, p. 193).

3.2.6 The Impossible-Possible

These capacities are absent in the great apes. A crucial component of labour is what I call the *impossible-possible*, namely, the creation of possibilities that are not inherently existent in nature. Tomasello recognises that apes cannot imagine something non-existent, factually apparently impossible, something that breaks from given causal possibilities. In his example, an ape can recognise the complexity and multitude of potentials of, for instance, a leopard which "does lots of things like climb trees, eat chimpanzees, drink water, and so on", yet "a leopard flying" is something inconceivable for the ape (Tomasello, 2014, pp. 28, 29). Therefore, the primary condition for true teleology is absent even with great apes. Friedrich Engels emphasises that the difference between humans and apes is not something given by nature but a historical process. The transformation of the hand went through the process of using it, of turning it into a tool through a process of specialisation, and this modification of the human is interlocked with the process of transformation of nature, that is, production. "The specialisation of the hand—that means the *tool*, and the tool means the specifically human activity, the transforming retroactivity of human on nature, on production" (Engels, 1975, p. 322). In this sense, he speaks of human becoming (*Menschenwerdung*), which presupposes labour. The transformation of the human hand is not in a Lamarckian sense, in which its usage directly modifies its organic structure; on the contrary, Engels stresses that both the hands of humans and apes are organically virtually identical, "but the hand of the lowest savage can perform hundreds of operations that no monkey's hand can imitate" (Engels, 1975, p. 445). This means that human ontological activity—labour—breaks the causal determinations of nature; it expands, shifts, and modifies its given barriers. The instruments used by apes are present in nature, present in laboratories, but they do not conceive something that does not yet exist; thus, Engels' assertion grasps this central element when he states: "No monkey's hand ever made the crudest stone knife" (Engels, 1975, p. 445). Tomasello proposes that what led to the peculiar human way of doing was an ecological pressure, leading to collaborations that "required, for their coordination, some new forms of cooperative communication" and, accordingly, enabled individual intentionality to unfold within the realm of joint and then collective intentionality (Tomasello, 2014, p. 31).

A critic of both any kind of monolithic thought and a mono-directional form of creation of knowledge, Fleck is unambiguous when he claims that "cognition is not an individual process of a theoretical 'consciousness at all'; it is the result of social activity, since the respective stock of cognition transcends the boundaries drawn for an individual" (Fleck, 2021, p. 54). At this point, it is crucial to understand the process of mutual determinations. This entails a more complex interaction than simply an object-subject-relationship. In reality, "what is already recognised influences the manner of new recognition, recognition expands, renews, gives fresh meaning to what is recognised" (Fleck, 2021, p. 54). Truth contains at least the dimensions of objectivity (as concrete reality), subjectivity (as individuals), social (the irremissible social mutual-determinations), time (past and present determinations, future expectations), space, and historicity.

The process of cognition is also one of recognition of concrete results—both are interlinked and socially constructed. In this context, Fleck coined the term *Denkkollektiv*. Thought collective is "*a community of people who exchange ideas or interact in thought, then we have in it the bearer of the historical development of a field of thought, a certain body of knowledge and state of culture, i.e., a particular style of thinking*" (Fleck, 2021, p. 54f). Nonetheless, despite consisting of individuals, it cannot be depicted as the simple sum of its parts. Fleck sustains that both "main ideas" and "development stages" "are the result of collective, not individual work", authors, inventors, etc. merely "personified" the foundational work laid beforehand (Fleck, 2021, p. 57). An important example is scientific knowledge, which he claims to be an obvious social structure because it is "an organised collective work with division of labour, collaboration, preparatory work, technical assistance, mutual exchange of ideas, polemics, etc." (Fleck, 2021, p. 57f).

This social condition shows the limitation of the individual capacity; in reality, he claims, the true custodian of knowledge is a highly organised collective. However, even this cannot be rigidly conceived because the thought collective constantly moves and evolves. Produced knowledge is already the evolution of previous formulations; moreover, set in motion, this now-produced knowledge returns after a necessary process of metamorphosis, thus becoming essentially different. Again, Hegel's and Marx's understanding of *results* and *premise* is fundamental to attain this, grounded in solid methodological elements (see *supra*), which appear absent in both Michel Foucault's and Roland Barthes' formulations in relation to authorship and the creation of knowledge (see Barthes, 2000; Foucault, 1979).

However, the social movement of concepts and words can lead to a fetishisation—Fleck calls it "magical power"—for their return may be subtracted from their social meaning and gain a hypostasised character given by science, politics, etc. Depending on time and space, the same word is conferred a completely different meaning (which supports Ludwig Wittgenstein's thesis rejecting the notion of private language, see *infra*). Thus, without a *Denkkollektiv,* recognition becomes an impossible feat, even at an individual level. An individual cannot think in-itself; instead, she carries within herself multiple thought collectives. Each constellation of togetherness represents a unique thought collective; the addition or subtraction of individuals necessarily changes its character. On the other hand, each collective thinking is embedded in the process of reciprocity, as it influences and is influenced by others. When, however, some epistemologists conceive "human thinking (at least as an ideal, thinking as it should be)" as "a fixed thing, an absolute", the "empirical fact, on the other hand, [becomes] relative" (Fleck, 2021, p. 69). Thus, science appears as a religion, and concepts as absolute entities, bearers of truth in-themselves; the hypostasis—that it would be possible to think purely theoretically, emotionally free, and therefore impartially—is its simple corollary (Fleck, 2021, p. 65ff).

3.2.7 Cooperation and Sociability: An Evolutionary Summit

How much influence has the environment rather than cultural relations based on labour had on this transformation remains unclear. For instance, while capitalism unequivocally exhausts given environmental conditions for the reproduction of life to replicate itself by the unceasingly expansionary production and appropriation of surplus-value, capitalist elites keep organising society within a liberal ethos of egoism and competition—analogous to the great apes—which reveals the significance of the role played by labour relations and ideology in determining social arrangements. However, in historical terms, this cannot attest to a homogenous, monolithic typification of humanity. Following Jason W. Moore's analysis, the capitalist mode of production must be understood as a metabolic structure encompassing (the transformation of) nature (namely, economy) and society (Moore, 2016, p. 81). Additionally, John Bellamy Foster utilises the concept of metabolism to understand to what extent capitalist relations impact nature and the environment (Foster, 2022). Both thinkers expanded this notion, which was so crucial in Marx's works and which Lukács has developed as the Marxian *Ontology of the Social Being*.

Turning back to evolutionary theory, Smith and Szathmáry conciliate two distinct forms to theoretically conceive life. While a phenotypic definition emphasises the metabolic aspect of life, which self-regulates, an inheritance theory points out the aspects of replication and continuity (Smith & Szathmáry, 1997). Lukács brilliantly puts it more coherently and differentiates nature into three categories—*inorganic* and *organic nature*, and finally, as a particular case of organic life, the *social-being* (Lukács, 1984a, 1986). The Marxian concepts of *production* and *reproduction*, Hegel's and Marx's understanding of *beginning* (or *premise*) and *result*, both provide the coherent analytical tools to apprehend the differences among these three categories of nature. While production focuses on the metabolism in nature, reproduction accounts for the process of replication/heritage. However, Smith and Szathmáry also emphasise that these two processes are interconnected; this, in turn, was already explained by Marx and Hegel, namely, that the metabolic processes produce something (result) which becomes the very condition (beginning) of replication, which then becomes the condition of production. Therefore, when Tomasello highlights Smith's and Szathmáry's research, which recognises "eight major transitions in the evolution of complexity of living things" and reveals that through each transition "emerged some new form of cooperation with interdependence" and, not least notably, "in each case this new form of cooperation was made possible by a concomitant new form of communication" (Tomasello, 2014, p. 32), then scientific analysis of inorganic and organic nature corroborates Marx's findings throughout his research on social-being under the specific capitalist mode of production.

It is not surprising, then, that the last transition mirrors the emergence of the social-being.[5] Accordingly, human cognition and socialisation, which result from these relations, appear as the premise for human development. "Human cognition and thinking are much more complex than the cognition and thinking of other primates. Human social interaction and organisation are much more complex than the social interaction and organisation of other primates as well" (Tomasello, 2014, p. 124). This is

[5] It is remarkable that Tomasello never employs the category of *labour*, he simply calls human's idiosyncratic production and reproduction of life a *new form of collaborative activity*.

a process character (*prozessueller Charakter*) which is expressed in the notion of ontogeny, consequently presupposing a development and not simply an inborn set of fixed attributes.

3.2.8 Communication, Conceptualisation, Universalisation, and Empathy

Human communication has also undergone many transformations throughout the evolutionary process. Already in children between fourteen to eighteen months of age, thus prelinguistic, joint activity not only exists but is prioritised. Chimpanzees, however, show indifference to it. Nonetheless, creating different perspectives presupposes recognition of the other and some collaboration, thence, a dimension of social consciousness which enables a much richer perspective. "In addition to joint goals, collaborative activities also demand a division of labor and thus individual roles" (Tomasello, 2014, p. 40). This complex level of collaboration presupposes reciprocal appraisal; consequently, evaluating others also means self-evaluation.

Providing and exchanging information gives way to gestures and pantomime. However, even this level of elementary communication presupposes common knowledge. If each person has a different referential, no actual communication is possible. Thence, Tomasello asserts, "to do this requires an extremely rich and deep set of interpersonal intentions and inferences in the context of this common ground" (Tomasello, 2014, p. 50). Knowledge and information to socially exist and further develop at both individual and social levels presuppose being socially shared and appropriated. At first, requestive and informative communication were (or could) not (be) appropriately differentiated, but these two categories could become differentiated through historical development. This process has three dimensions. Informative communication presumes that "the informative motive led communicators to make a commitment to informing others of things honestly and accurately, that is, truthfully" (Tomasello, 2014, p. 51). (One can, of course, lie, but a lie only works if another person first assumes that what is being told is true.) A second dimension involves the *why*, "why does he think that I will find the situation he is pointing out to me relevant to *my* concerns" (Tomasello, 2014, p. 52). In contrast, apes are entirely indifferent to this and cannot recognise the notion of help. They think that if someone is pointing to something, it is because he wants it. Finally, communicative content and communicative force (requestive intonation or neutral intonation to purely inform) can be distinctively differentiated. According to Tomasello, "the breakthrough here is the relative independence of referential (situational, propositional) content from the communicator's motives or intentions for referring attention to it" (Tomasello, 2014, p. 53). Thus, one can understand why, in Hegel's idealism, the notion of the concept (*der Begriff*) plays such an immense role in his analyses of "*being* and *essence*", or "the *immediate* and the *reflection*"; it is to be considered "the *third*", in other words, for it is a determination in-and-for-itself, a totality "in which each of the moments is the whole" (Hegel, 1986b, p. 245, 1989, p. 307). According to Tomasello, conceptualisation provides an infrastructure for communication beyond particular intentions.

The foundation for empathy is thus broadened because not only does the collaborative activity forge a bond among social beings, but its mental grasping must mirror these relations correctly. At a communicative level, the self, the context, and the other must then be recognised within the relevance and particularities of each of these cases. A new kind of thinking emerges. "In effect, all three components of the thinking process—representation, inference, and self-monitoring—must become socialised" (Tomasello, 2014, p. 56). Not only inference but also simulation and abduction play a vital role in this mode of communication. The recipient must make an abductive leap for a successful communicative act with a communicator to occur. Because it is a relationship of reciprocity, the communicator must posit himself from the recipient's perspective, consequently enabling an act of simulation.

In this sense, human thinking gains a further qualitative component: *Thinking is only thinking in and from the perspective of the other*. "And so, the kind of thinking that goes on in human cooperative communication is evolutionarily new in that it is perspectival and socially recursive. Individuals must think (simulate, imagine, make inferences) about their communicative partner thinking (simulating, imagining, making inferences) about their thinking" (Tomasello, 2014, p. 59). This qualitative leap confers to human relations the ability to transcend mere subjective and egoistic perceptions, becoming foundational for objectivity.

This sort of (self-)reflection enables a generic framing and perception of reality, superseding the "I" and "you" and imposing the perspective of "we". Therefore, the social-being is the premise for notions of reality, truth, right, justice, property, etc., for these are immanently perspectives emerging from social relations. "In this formulation, 'objectivity' is the result of being able to think of things from ever wider perspectives and also recursively, as one embeds one's perspective within another, more encompassing perspective" (Tomasello, 2014, p. 121). Recognising a common ground, a shared reality, of objective truths also permitted normative representations.

When mutually evaluating each other and accepting a common, objective (thus not arbitrary) shared reality, the notion of "should" emerges. "Social norms are thus mutual expectations in the cultural common ground of the group that people behave in certain ways" (Tomasello, 2014, p. 87). As explained by Kelsen, they are potent tools to control and shape behaviour (see *supra*). Norms impose conformity, and socially, they consecrate and legitimate power to existing relations; outliers of established rules may suffer social animosity—to say the least.

Even the egoistic notion of socialisation to merely obtain private gain not only presupposes the existence of, intercourse with, and recognition of the other but, most importantly, is a paradoxical situation. In evolutionary terms, *the summit of egoism presupposes its dissolution* because the condition for *higher private gain is only possible by means of socially cooperative situations and relations*. It is thus pivotal to comprehend the ontological impossibility of the privatisation of both knowledge and language because their existence demands constant intercourse among cooperative social beings, creating a complex qualitative leap of social relations.

3.2.9 The Private Language Absurd

It is worth assessing some elements of Ludwig Wittgenstein's *Philosophical Investigations* to gain a different perspective on the same problem, namely, the impossibility of privatising language. Language is one form of knowledge. As such, it is not innate but belongs to a continuous historical-social process of creation, transformation, and reproduction, thus one particular mode of intellectual appropriation. This particular mode, however, entails in-itself an immense resolving power for its generality and abstractness; it is one of the most general forms of a determined type of knowledge and, as such, is contained in most forms of specific knowledge. On the other hand, forms of knowledge, such as music, which can relinquish language (as distinctive from musical codices), must subordinate itself to language if it is to be privately appropriated because it presupposes specific forms of normativity, which in turn presumes language.

How can the limits of private intellectual appropriation be demarcated? Can all human intellectual dimensions be privately appropriated? Could language be privatised? Specific words are already undergoing a process of privatisation in which trademarks, "giving producers exclusive control over the marks or names they used to designate their products" (Hull, 2019, p. 98), expand from their formal scope in a progression of derivative privatisation. Gordon Hull calls this *trademark dilution,* that is, "the owner of a mark can seek legal redress against noncompeting, nonconfusing uses of similar marks"; this arbitrary manoeuvre is founded in the ever-expansive capitalist logic itself, namely, the protection of brand value (Hull, 2019, p. 98).

(Exchange-)Value is a pure social relation (of power) which seemingly renounces any connection with material reality, that is, "not an atom of natural matter enters into their value concreteness" (Marx, 1962, p. 62); thus, such a justification of protection appears circular: value appropriation justifies the appropriation of value. What are the conditions for language to be privatised? The atomisation of individuals who detached themselves from language in order to reappropriate it. However, if private appropriation is possible, namely, the separation and isolation of language, then a separate, isolated, independent language should be existentially conceivable.

Shaping an unconditional language, namely, a private language, presupposes nothing external and is supposed to be complete in-and-for-itself. "Where our language suggests a body and there is none: there we should like to say, is a *spirit*" (Wittgenstein, 2013, p. 36. §36). As seen, Hegel asserts that pure-being is simultaneously pure-nothingness (see *supra*). However, he also states that private appropriation (also intellectual) is an indispensable condition for individual freedom, the actualisation of the person within the abstract right. In this sense, freedom anchored in private appropriation of language, as an isolated being, would mean freedom as nothingness. The contradiction found in §69 (Hegel, 2013), in which *intellectual property*$_{(private)}$ cannot be found a matter of unlawfulness but merely of honour, on the one hand, while writers and publishers must be protected, on the other, perfectly expresses this problem (see Hegel, 2013, p. 149, explanatory note §69).

Wittgenstein defines the language-game as everything that involves language and its activities (Wittgenstein, 2013, pp. 16, §7). According to him, languages, in primitive applications, are not taught through explanations but through training—in the animal sense (in original German *Abrichtung*, a Portuguese equivalent *adestramento*). As such, simple forms of language appear to have a highly social and mutable character. Taught differently, "the same indicative teaching of these words would have brought about a quite different understanding" (Wittgenstein, 2013, p. 15. §6). A language must not only be learned but also be affected by the teaching and is thus intertwined with the use of words (§9). Patterns of language operate like tools for a set of situations. A pattern denotes a general, never a particular condition. For example, a chair, in general, is included in all specific chairs, whereas a distinct chair, say an armchair, is not included in chairs in general, but itself represents a new general category: that of armchairs. The reclining chair has unique characteristics that a non-reclining chair does not.

Languages as general abstractions reflect particular social practices rather than simply opinions (Wittgenstein, 2013, p. 145. §241). From this, the first clue is that there can be no private language. For instance, the short form of a sentence cannot actually be understood as a sentence, apart from where a single word is uttered as a sentence—such as yes!, no!, there!, here!, etc. The individual practice of the language cannot alone constitute a pattern; it cannot generalise; its communication remains insofar closed. The comprehension of a word does not depend on an individual's sole desire, "and that will probably depend on the circumstances in which it is given and on the person to whom I give it" (Wittgenstein, 2013, p. 30. §29). Language presupposes dependence—or rather interdependence. "One must already know (or be able to know) something in order to be able to ask for the naming" (Wittgenstein, 2013, p. 31. §30). The distinction concerning the colour blue in paragraphs 33 and 275 explains this question. In paragraph 33, the various kinds of *blue* that arise from different unions between colour and form are presented. Although blue was viewed differently because of certain circumstances, it always remained a general (and recognisable) pattern.

Although a pattern is essential in linguistic formation, it is not a sufficient condition; in-itself, "the word has no meaning" (Wittgenstein, 2013, p. 39. §40). Conversely, a specific thing, situation, etc. does not in-itself possess an immediate and direct equivalency with a word. If so, when a particular element disappeared, so would the word. Accordingly, more than one word (in one or diverse languages) could not express the same element. A word first becomes conceptualised under particular relations; its meaning metamorphoses according to the ongoing changes in social relations. Thus, a word cannot exhaust its abstract existence and retain a singular specific concreteness. If it were not general, it would be meaningless; if it had to correspond only to a single, unique signifier, it would not be general, *ergo,* likewise meaningless. Would the application of a word without practical existence (§42) be possible, namely, would it be possible for empty words to exist? Wittgenstein is unequivocal: "The meaning of a word is its use in language" (Wittgenstein, 2013, p. 40. §43). In-itself, a word is void of content or meaning. Its actuality is first revealed when it becomes in-and-for-itself, namely, a concept.

3.2.10 The Genesis of Capitalism

The real subsumption of intellectual appropriation under the capitalist mode of production constitutes its complete subordination to economic imperatives. However, if the capitalist privatisation of the intellect becomes a necessity, then it is crucial to understand the peculiarity of this particular mode of production. Capitalism is often equated with markets, trade, and commerce. This thesis is problematic for multiple reasons. The most important is the eternisation of capitalism, which becomes a perpetual present, an immanent characteristic of human ontology simply waiting to blossom given the right conditions. Another simple example is the market, which is simultaneously conceived as eternal but also peculiar to capitalism. This circular logic imposes that capitalism must also be eternal. Furthermore, if markets represent the realisation of freedom, how does one come to terms with the fact that one of the most important markets—in historical terms—fundaments and actualises one of the cruellest forms of unfreedom? Historically, many defenders of liberalism also supported "chattel slavery, which allowed individual members of a family to be put on the market like any other commodity" (Losurdo, 2011, p. 67).

The market eternisation continues with the neoliberal strategy. For instance, Walter Eucken advocates for the thesis that dating back to prehistory, the history of humanity is the history of markets because it has always been present in multiple forms. "These forms did not arise from speculation but were obtained from exact observation" (Eucken, 1961, p. 27). In reality, concrete observations reveal precisely the opposite—for instance, economies from the Western Pacific (Diamond, 1999; Malinowski, 2002)—namely, that markets have only emerged under specific conditions. Thus, he mystically absolutises the generic ontological human condition of production—which in each particular historical moment economy expresses specific relations of production—namely, economy, confounding it with a particular form of distribution of resources, namely, markets, and apologetically sustains: "in all concrete economies there is the fusion of an incalculable number of forms, of economic systems and market forms" (Eucken, 1961, p. 27). Yet, the mystical character of associating capitalism and markets is not a monopoly of its proponents. Additionally, its critics tend to associate capitalism with commerce.

Writing about the emergence of capitalism, Ellen Meiksins Wood emphasises that insofar as these explanations are circular, capitalism has no origin. Equating the bourgeois ascent with the development of capitalism creates the notion that capitalist relations do not represent a significant historical transformation but rather feudalism, as the bourgeoisie appears as the agents of this process. Some commonly referred-to models are the *demographic model* and the *commercialisation model.*

The *demographic model* implies that "the transition to capitalism was determined by the laws of supply and demand"; with populational growth, the so-called laws of supply and demand create, as a response, a capitalist transition; it thus simply sees capitalist relations as the blossoming of the "universal and transhistorical laws of the market" (Wood, 2017, p. 18). Such an explanation performs a subject-object-inversion; the effect becomes the cause, the cause the effect. Robert Brenner calls this a "secular Malthusianism", which abstracts from social and legal institutions, classes, and class relations and derives an economic model of supply and demand (Brenner, 1985, p. 15ff).

It is undisputed that a demographic change occurred and must not be overlooked. Nonetheless, this expansion was first the product of particular social relations before it could itself become the premise to help set in motion what has become known as industrial capitalism. An increase in agricultural productivity was the precondition for enabling and sustaining British populational growth and surplus. And "even before a unique pattern of population increase became manifest in England, its demographic composition was already distinct in other significant ways" (Wood, 2017, p. 132). Instead of a natural, organic process or an *ex nihilo* event, efficiency in farming techniques produced food surplus, which laid the basis for populational augmentation. This occurred hand-in-glove with "a revolution in social property relations" (Wood, 2017, p. 133).

The *commercialisation model* carries in its core the extraordinary achievement of universalising a particular phenomenon as if altogether (Western) Europe transitioned from a feudal to a capitalist society. However, Wood is emphatic by saying that while European feudalism produced many outcomes, only one was capitalism. And even though feudalism contained different structures which were irreducible, capitalist development is often equated with urban or commercial swelling. Only after capitalism emerged and evolved from agrarian to industrial did it start, in England, to advance and impose its logic in new territories. While the separation of power in two concentrated unities, political power in the hands of the monarchy and agricultural economic power under the control of the aristocracy, pre-capitalism was based on fragmentation, on the one hand, and arbitrage—extra-economic advantages and not economic competition—as an existential imperative, on the other. Moreover, this system of commercial appropriation was dependent on luxury trade.

> Ruling elites in these centres depended on their civic status not only for privileged access to such extra-economic commercial advantages but typically also, as officeholders, for exploitation of domestic producers by means of direct extra-economic surplus extraction in the form of rents, dues, and taxes of one kind or another, so much so that cities of this kind have been described as collective lordships. (Wood, 2017, p. 85)

In addition to trade based on monopoly privileges, the commercial families performed non-productive activities, financing popes and monarchs; Wood additionally underscores that also *Firenze* was "a collective lordship, exploiting peasant producers in the *contado* no less than the absolutist state in France did its own peasants" (Wood, 2017, p. 86).

Markets were consequently not imperatives but commercial opportunities. The Dutch Republic reveals an even greater dissonance within the commercialisation model. Despite its noteworthy commercial role and urbanisation, it failed to take the leap towards capitalism. Wood's thesis asserts that the reason for the failure was that the Dutch economy "was driven by a different logic" than the capitalist logic (Wood, 2017, p. 88). Being the opposite of the English case, the staggering development of cities enabled the interests of the urban elites to shape the rural economy. Its wealth was derived from international trade with an important role in luxury goods, thus commercialising commodities produced elsewhere. This does not mean the absence of internal production, which was certainly not the propeller of such developments. "These 'extra-economic' advantages often relied heavily on military force. The rising Dutch Republic devoted much of its massive tax revenues to military expenditures" and "in some notorious military exercises for purely commercial advantage" (Wood, 2017, p. 90).

Consequently, the dependence on extra-economic appropriation transformed the state into a crucial source of private wealth. Therefore, being part of the state or just being conferred state privileges often represented a much more relevant sphere of influence to be drawn to than that of productive economic endeavours. The modes of appropriation were essentially based on extra-economic exploitation; in this sense, the Dutch Republic was a much closer kin to French Absolutism than English Capitalism. While the latter relied on an economic mode of appropriation, the Dutch Republic and French Absolutism derived economic power from non-economic relations, e.g., state taxation and state offices. In the absence of capitalism, commercialisation represented a cutting-edge advantage for those societies that led it; however, it also created few incentives for local production, simultaneously relying on state endeavours and foreign production.

3.2.11 The True Capitalist Revolution

The true capitalist revolution did not first occur with an urban—namely, the industrial—but rather an agrarian revolution. English conditions were very peculiar. Most feudal systems enforced labour exploitation of the direct producers from appropriators (landlord or feudal state) by means of extra-economic dimensions, thus, direct coercion—"military, judicial, and political power" (Wood, 2017, p. 95f). It was with capitalism that exclusive private property of the means of production first arose; thus, under this particular mode of production, "the dominant mode of appropriation [is] based on the complete dispossession of direct producers" (Wood, 2017, p. 96).

The need for direct coercion disappears; thus, survival must now be mediated, and markets gain a new quality. From a place where the surplus of the means of subsistence are sold, giving people the possibility and the option to sell and buy, it becomes a place of compulsion: economic subordination becomes an imperative, and the only form of mediation seems to be the market form. Capital, labour, and existential survival have now become market-dependent.

In England, state cohesion—its unity—was solidified early on, centralising fragmented feudal sovereignty. Unlike other feudal regions, the English ruling class centralised military and legal power and corporate privileges. This consolidation enabled the emergence of a disproportionately large number of roads, with London becoming a hub of concentration of markets and hence a national market. The English aristocracy did not have military might and was contingent upon central monarchic power. While being dispossessed of extra-economic powers, the nobility sought to secure large portions of land, subordinating the producers not to the condition of immediate producers—peasant proprietors—but rather of tenants.

The following process of enclosure catalysed an ongoing process of revolution in social property relations, namely, the privatisation of property. According to Brenner, by the mid-fifteenth century, European peasantry was resisting the unfreedom of feudal ties, controlling their tenements. "The elimination of unfreedom meant the end of labour services and of arbitrary tallages" (Brenner, 1985, p. 46f). However, "the demographic collapse of the late fourteenth and fifteenth centuries left vacant many former customary peasant holdings", which were appropriated by the "landlords", and immediately diminished the potentiality of peasant property. Moreover, the extra-economic power of imposing "fines at will whenever peasant land was conveyed" further weakened the impacts that the peasant struggle could have had (Brenner, 1985, p. 47). In this sense, Brenner highlights the antagonistic forces within social property relations.

The novel condition, inflicted upon both aristocratic proprietors and tenants, subordinated them to the new economic, social relations. English aristocracy

> were fundamentally different from rentier aristocrats, who throughout history have depended for their wealth on squeezing surpluses out of peasants by means of simple coercion, enhancing their powers of surplus extraction not by increasing the productivity of the direct producers but rather by improving their own coercive powers—military, judicial, and political. (Wood, 2017, p. 100)

The aristocracy depended on economic-coercion to guarantee its power and, by doing so, was itself subjected to market imperatives, for the amount of rent obtained was now contingent both on the competition with other aristocrats, the existing land-productivity, and the economic efficiency of the tenants as a whole class.

Conversely, the tenants were economically coerced by the aristocratic land monopoly and the capacity of each tenant to yield higher output from the lands being rented. "It was, in other words, not the *opportunities* afforded by the market but rather its *imperatives* that drove petty commodity producers to accumulate" (Wood, 2017, p. 102). Farmers, who were hitherto still proprietors, were now also compelled to compete; those who succeeded prospered and those who did not joined the rows of propertyless. This highly competitive agricultural system yielded a more significant output and, concomitantly, a massive concentration, which resulted in a larger number of propertyless with no access to immediate subsistence.

The new economic imperative also meant the burden of constant improvement. Nevertheless, this did not mean superior agricultural techniques and methods but relatively superior economic accumulation. Previously, economic relations were constrained by socio-cultural determinations which regulated socio-economics, namely, "they restricted certain practices and granted certain rights, not in order to enhance the wealth of landlords or states but in order to preserve the peasant community itself", enabling some equity and care (Wood, 2017, p. 107). When private property relations emerged, customs and tradition initially provided some countereffects, hindering the total unfolding of its legality. Both Marx and Wood emphasise the subsequent legal measures taken by the English state to solidify and legitimise prevailing private property relations, consequently changing existing customs and, in turn, behaviour (Marx, 1962, p. 741ff; Wood, 2017, p. 105ff). Private property of the means of production, which until then was being hindered, entails a novel dimension which enables its complete unfolding, namely, now private also meant exclusive.

Capitalism has thus been a determined historical development and not simply the natural outcome of feudalism. In fact, feudal relations developed very differently in each locality. Despite the fact that the French figure of the bourgeois entails significant historical relevance, it is false to equate the bourgeois with the capitalist. While in France, the bourgeois represented an essential force against the French feudal aristocracy, in England, it was precisely the aristocracy which played one of the most fundamental roles in the emergence of agrarian capitalism. "England had a class of wealthy 'tenants of capital' by the standards of the time at the end of the 16th century" (Marx, 1962, p. 771f). The forefront of the emerging struggle from the new social property relations, which can be conceived as capitalist revolution, was hence between landlords and peasants and not between the bourgeoisie and aristocracy. "Calling this revolution 'bourgeois' requires a definition so vague and general as to be vacuous" (Wood, 2017, p. 118). Industrial capitalism was thus not the beginning but the product of agrarian capitalism. "The expropriation and expulsion of a part of the peasantry not only frees [sic] up with the workers their food and their labour material for industrial capital, [they] create[] the internal market" (Marx, 1962, p. 775). In France, however, peasants remained proprietors, agriculture continued to be conducted under traditional practices, tradition regulated and restricted production and thus economic development, and no capitalism emerged (Wood, 2017, p. 133).

Additionally, Karl Polanyi has the merit of noting that the economic imperative of markets first arose with the development of capitalism and did not represent an eternal anthropogenic condition. Although markets existed prior to capitalism, societies were never controlled by it. "In spite of the chorus of academic incantations so persistent in the nineteenth century, gain and profit made on exchange never before played an important part in human economy" (Polanyi, 2001, p. 45). Polanyi sustains that conflating the division of labour with markets has been a constant and grave mistake which has not been adequately corrected. Cultural memory is directly affected. "The tradition of the classical economists, who attempted to base the law of the market on the alleged propensities of man in the state of nature, was replaced by an abandonment of all interest in the cultures of 'uncivilised' man as irrelevant to an understanding of the problems of our age" (Polanyi, 2001, p. 47).

In reality, markets do not represent a human ontological condition. Instead, what appears to be a constant is human social, collective, cooperative character. Following Polanyi's logic, from the perspective of survival in anthropological terms, an individual's egoistic interest seemed of little relevance and could even endanger the group; moreover, there is no individual without the collectivity, and existential incentives are directed not towards the self but rather towards the group. An important example of a non-market economy is the Kula. Bronislaw Malinowski states: "Every movement of the Kula articles, every detail of the transactions is fixed and regulated by a set of traditional rules and conventions, and some acts of the Kula are accompanied by an elaborate magical ritual and public ceremonies" (Malinowski, 2002, p. 62). Utterly extraneous to the notions and practices of markets in a broad sense and even more foreign to economic imperatives, the Kula showcases an impressive socio-economic arrangement which extends through long periods and vast distances, about which Polanyi is emphatic: "Not the propensity to barter, but reciprocity in social behavior dominates" (Polanyi, 2001, p. 53). Additionally, he categorically affirms that until the end of feudalism, "all economic systems" "were organised either on the principle of reciprocity or redistribution, or householding, or some combination of the three" (Polanyi, 2001, p. 57).

3.2.12 On the Ontology of the Human-Being and the Totality of Property

According to György Lukács, it is folly to consider estrangement as a *condition humaine*, namely, an intrinsic feature of humanity in which the human-being opposes society, or conversely, subjectivity contests objectivity. Human estrangement is always historically determined and can only exist under particular conditions and within certain relations. Therefore, to consider the human-being outside of society or society without human beings are simply hypostases, abstractions void of ontological determinations (Lukács, 1986, p. 509).

Deeming estrangement a universal character is a crucial element of the perpetual present, that is, the ideologies of the ruling classes, which naturalise estrangement as parts of fixed human-psychological aspects through its propaganda apparatus (Lukács, 1986, p. 551). The conditions in which estrangement emerges are determined by ontological social relations, which confer particular substance to relations involving appropriation, transformation, distribution, and consumption. These relations of production—or property relations—are always embedded in and, moreover, identical to labour relations. They also determine the degree of development of the productive forces. Needless to say, the latter can be, separately or simultaneously, a catalyser of or an impediment to the former. The intergenerational, historical character is unmistaken. The productive forces form, according to Marx, the basis of the entire human history; they are the *product*, the "result" of "previous activities" and, as such, constitute the *premise* for current relations of production, which are forces "not freely chosen" but instead historically acquired—that is, through a generational transfer (Marx, 1977, p. 548).

Result becomes premise; premise becomes result, and so on. As mentioned, human activity, transforming the acquired world, differs qualitatively from all other animals. Labour is precisely the first ontological category peculiar to humans (Hermeto, 2020). Lukács characterises this as the third category of nature, that is, the *social-being* (Lukács, 1984a). Through labour, the social-being transforms existing conditions from given states, fixing the boundaries of the possibilities of action, that is, imposing real impossibilities to creating novel circumstances that allow superseding natural limitations by means of the teleological setting, in which labour objectifies the previously inexistent—the purely imagined. This process establishes a new social-material basis and represents an ongoing process. And even for revolutionary activities—such as learning how to create, maintain, and use fire or developing communication into language and writing—it does not forge an instantaneous breakpoint. Instead, it opens a new dimension of δύναμις for the further transformation of the dialectical relationship between result and premise. Likewise, it would be equally imprudent to apprehend two distinct and independent general sets of appropriation. As the human being and society, or the result and the premise, etc., are two moments of one totality, so are property and intellectual property. And as property does not first emerge when it becomes circumscribed by the right, neither does intellectual appropriation first occur when intellectual property rights encapsulate it.

Ludwig Feuerbach asserts, in his *The Essence of Christianity*, "the unity of the essence is the multiplicity of the existence", that is, the relationship between you and I represents "a common, human life"; in this sense, the togetherness of you and I is qualitatively different from the you and I in isolation; it enables critical and moral perspectives, and only within this relationship can "the consciousness of humanity" emerge (Feuerbach,

2016, p. 166). Feuerbach, however, overstretches this relationship, imposing upon an already so simple relationship the representation (*Stellvertretung*) of the entire humanity. Unlike other philosophers before him, Feuerbach emphasises that what makes the human being unique is not only his thinking but "his *whole* essence" (Feuerbach, 2013, p. 52, §53). His materialism has, however, a methodological dimension still embedded in idealism. Ignoring the constitutive labour practice that actualises human life, Feuerbach does not apprehend reality as the subjective "*sensually human activity*" but rather only "under the form of the *object* [*Objekts*] *or of the outlook* [*Anschauung*]" (Marx, 1978, p. 5). Lukács further criticises that the mental separation of people in this mute species (*stumme Gattung*) overlooks the actual constitution of the social-being, which occurs not as a natural condition of the species-being but rather as an active social formation of human genericity (*Gattungsmäßigkeit*) through labour (Lukács, 1984b, p. 38f). In the *Economic and Philosophic Manuscripts of 1844*, Marx sustains: "The animal is immediately a unity with its life-activity. It does not differentiate itself from it. [The former] is [the latter]". The human-species does not differ in that matter. "To the human-being, labour, the *life-activity*, the *productive life* [appears] only as a *means* to satisfy its necessities", to conserve "its physical existence". The ontological character of labour is indisputable. "The productive life is the species-life." The living-activity creates a *product* which is itself the *premise* of life. "Life itself appears only as a means of life" (Marx, 1968, p. 516).

3.2.13 Labour and Teleology

Change is the most general principle of nature; nothing is fixed, rigid, or eternal. Even if something might appear to be, all *three* categories of nature share this common element. However, while the transformations of *inorganic* nature generally occur slowly, because even a significant breakpoint is usually the result of long periods before the event, *organic* nature metamorphoses much faster. Of course, within organic nature, the vast array of living organisms also reveals fundamental differences in the capacity and velocity to promote change. While an elephant can quickly destroy large portions of forest in search of food, its dead carcase requires much more time to be absorbed and transformed by organic and inorganic nature.

As already seen with Smith and Szathmáry, the evolutionary path reveals a continuous increase in cooperation and interdependence among living beings; in Lukács, this culminates in the *social-being*, namely, the human-being, the most developed character of these transformations. Despite the incredible evolutionary elasticity of the great apes, human labour becomes a condition which inaugurates the third category of nature. Its dynamic differs qualitatively from everything previously existing. It enables the supersession of immediate natural insecurities, such as the need to search for food or face natural threats to life. One could say that the great ape similarly appropriates nature; nevertheless, human appropriation entails a different tone. While the great ape reveals a type of proto-teleology, it is only with labour relations that teleology can unfold unrestrained.[6]

Teleology is the activity in which a goal is mentally preconceived before action and presupposes disruption because preconceiving something ideally requires breaking the chain of given causal events. Thus, it seems impossible to consider teleology within labour relations without simultaneously considering the act of choice and the category of alternatives. Choosing entails subsequent consequences; for each possible outcome, an array of after-effects may arise. When put into motion, the teleological setting (*teleologische Setzung*) may be—historically or immediately socially and individually—transformed into reflexes. What may appear as spontaneous impulses or reactions often represent the becoming of teleological relations and, as such, are not natural (or simply instinctive) but rather conditioned reflexes. Lukács is unambiguous when stating that this is a process derivative from long labour processes "as a chain of alternatives", for even in primitive degrees of development, single alternatives become "conditioned reflexes through training and habit" and, as such, could be transformed from conscious to unconscious acts (Lukács, 1986, p. 36).

[6] Of course, teleology is not simply a concept in-itself but part of a human-act, that is, the concept does not give movement to teleology. Teleology is part of the human-praxis, and the concept merely helps explain it.

The singular subject singles out the possibility towards the object of his goal-setting among alternatives within an existing complex that at first appears independent from him. This sort of cognitive reasoning primarily emerges as "the first impulse towards the teleological setting", representing "the will to the satisfaction of need" (Lukács, 1986, p. 42). This provides thus a qualitative novel character to the Aristotelian δύναμις which, through the act (ἐνέργεια), would attain its immanent intrinsic form, expressing its full and perfect potency, namely, the actuality (ἐντελέχεια) (Aristoteles, 1966); instead of the potency or dynamis (δύναμις) representing something latent to accomplish its destiny (that is, actualise its metaphysical nature), already the primitive cognitive-measurability of labour-alternatives depicts the power of this ontological essence (movement).

Actualisation ceases to express something innate and represents an open-ended process in which any aprioristic realisation of a destiny becomes an ontological impossibility. Actualisation appears instead as the real movement in which a goal ceases to be a mere alternative possibility and, first through the decision and second the concrete act, becomes part of concrete reality and itself a new reality, something immanently previously non-existent, which dialectically alters the very character of the given-existent reality. A wooden chair does not exist in nature from which it cannot be appropriated, modified, used, nor does it represent the ἐντελέχεια of a δύναμις contained in trees. Its realisation is a product of labour. Its success depends on the succession of choices and acts as a continuous chain of teleological settings (usually social). Among the many existing trees, which one could provide the right wood for such a construction? Subsequently, new questions emerge. How to cut and transport it? Which tools to use? Because the cutting, transportation, and transformation processes are essentially different. How will it be used, and what purpose is intended for it? Etc.

Even if these many events are successful, now the from-labour-relations-objectified chair still does not carry in itself a goal, a potency, a truth to be actualised. The intentions within its production process do not define the scope of its usage. Again, the choices among the alternatives and the existing social relations will determine the chair-being. The chair is always part of a continuous process of actualisation. "A chair with four feet and a velvet cover represents a *throne* under certain conjunctures; therefore, this chair, a thing that serves for sitting, is not a throne by the nature of its use-value" (Marx, 1988, p. 72f). The use-value is thus defined by labour itself—including the very labour relations—although the object's natural characteristics form a basis of and limit its scope. Therefore, it is a mistake to qualify something from its natural characteristics, which are determined by the social relations of production. If, on the one hand, the intercourse between the social-being and nature is a necessary condition of life, on the other, "the elements of the labour-processes [are—JRH] enmeshed with the *specific social characters*, which they possess in a determined *historical* degree of development" (Marx, 1988, p. 73). Therefore, it is not surprising when Marx writes, in *Capital*, that the human transformation of nature simultaneously represents the alternation of its own nature. "[The human being] develops the dormant potencies within [nature] and subjects the play of its powers to his own bounty" (Marx, 1962, p. 192). This new accent within the process of transformation of nature represents a qualitative disruption of causal relations.

3.2.14 Absolute Causality, Absolute Teleology, and "Teleologised" Causality

While causality can express a natural movement, that is, a movement independent of both a setting and teleology; it can also be part of a causal setting. Teleology, on the other hand, cannot be conceived as something isolated. It intrinsically adheres to causal relations. Lukács criticises that such a separation emerges within logical and epistemological analyses. In reality, they are not mutually exclusive; on the contrary, they are "mutually heterogeneous, but which, with all their contradictoriness [Widersprüchlichkeit], only together in inseparable dynamic coexistence yield the ontological basis of certain complexes of movement, namely those that are ontologically only possible in the realm of the social-being" (Lukács, 1986, p. 52). This means that the social-being's activity emanating from the teleological setting qualitatively transforms the irreducibility of causal relations, which gain a new tone.

Historically and socially, repetitive actions emerging from conscious decisions, when successful, become embedded within social relations and are hence transformed into non-conscious conditions. Although they appear innate, in reality, they are "fixed conditioned reflexes" (Lukács, 1986, p. 44). The immanency of labour within human ontological relations represents "a condition of human's existence independent of all forms of society, an eternal necessity of nature, in order to mediate the metabolism between human being and nature, that is, human life" (Marx, 1962, p. 57). The successful transformation of nature, enabling the reproduction of the human species (*Gattung*) and the production of human genericity (*Gattungsmäßigkeit*), depends on an at least partially correct comprehension of reality.

The creation of knowledge as the comprehension of the objective world fundamentally presupposes *generalisation*. In this sense, the generic understanding of the objective conditions and relations of life and nature, extracting their legality, namely, laws to describe the actual movement of things, in order to render (the teleological setting of) labour relations possible, is the foundation of scientific knowledge. However, although science depends on the process of generalisation of legalities, so do magic, religion, and mystical knowledge arise from this process. Needless to say, they entail fundamentally different qualities.

Generalisation presupposes a considerable capacity of abstraction, such "abstractness, however, acquires a special pathos under the conditions of its initial comprehension: primitive human-being lives in an environment that is largely not under his control; it is only a very small corner that is now illuminated by the light of true knowledge" (Lukács, 1963a, p. 328). Magical or religious knowledge is nonetheless not a form of pseudo- or proto-knowledge. "It must not be forgotten, however, that both the mastery of the otherwise unmastered forces of nature sought by magic and the religious conceptions of creator gods ultimately take human labour as their model" (Lukács, 1986, p. 95). While magic is profoundly embedded in daily life, religion expresses a superior degree of abstraction, promoting universal-transcendental generalisations. Both, however, supersede the ontological condition of causality, as if the mind alone—or elements of it, such as words, enchantments, prayers—could (or intended to) control and subjugate nature and causal relations. Teleology becomes not a principle of transformation of reality, but reality a principle of teleology. In this sense, notions of destiny, prevision, foretelling, etc., become embedded within idealist worldviews.

Although labour relations represent a revolutionary step in evolution and human development, they are also part of a gradual and lengthy process. In the introduction of *The Peculiarity of the Aesthetical* (*Die Eigenart des Ästhetischen*) Lukács asserts, "reality—and therefore also its mental reflection and reproduction—is, however, a dialectical unity of continuity and discontinuity, of tradition and revolution, of gradual transitions and leaps" (Lukács, 1963a, p. 18). In this sense, the simultaneously revolutionary and gradual development of human cognition fundamentally represents a third dimension within the process of transformation of reality. Along the lines of Marx's critique in the first Feuerbach thesis (see *supra*), Lukács dissociates any reductive account of the term *reflection*, used to express the subjective grasping of the objective-subjective reality, refuting to conflate it "with the widespread notion of a mechanical, photographic reflection" (Lukács, 1963a, p. 22).

The reflection of the causal relations is essential within the sphere of labour, representing a precondition to comprehend legalities, generalisation and abstract thinking, and enacts a dialectical dimension because the very act of reflection must constantly self-examine, since only an accurate reflection can uncover the correct legalities. Within a process of socialisation, this process can, of course, appear independent and autonomous because not only is it composed of a social body, but it is also necessarily intergenerational. Reflection, abstraction, and generalisation—the principle of desanthropomorphisation [Desanthropomorphisierung][7]—characterise the germinal elements of science.

This development reveals two crucial elements. First, when science adequately apprehends reality, it cannot forego ontological questionings—even if unable to answer them. Second, objective reality has always had an ontological priority over subjective perception because the former must always lead and be more complex. If the latter could fully grasp

[7] The term desanthropomorphisation is borrowed from the second chapter of Lukács's Aesthetics: *Die Desanthropomorphisierung der Widerspiegelung in der Wissenschaft*. See: Lukács, G. (1963a). GLW, Band 11, Die Eigenart des Ästhetischen: 1. Halbband. Luchterhand).

reality, then science would be pointless (Hermeto, 2020, p. 261), or in Marx's words, "all science would be superfluous if the form of appearance and the essence of things coincided directly" (Marx, 1962, p. 825).

The understanding and the teleological setting are not purely individual. Not only is the transmission of knowledge pivotal for the correct accomplishment of goals, but also teleological acts are set/posited on the other. Acts of communication are constituted not of simple equal exchanges. Lukács highlights the importance of convincing others to carry out deeds within labour relations. Therefore, intentions consist not only of final goals but also of intermediary goals. For instance, within cooperation, people must be persuaded to do certain things and become themselves the objects of particular acts of intentionality. This mode of social organisation resembles the two spheres Tomasello calls *Joint Intentionality* and *Collective Intentionality* (see *supra*) (Lukács, 1986, p. 46; Tomasello, 2014).

3.2.15 Ought-Value Totality, Behaviour, and Time

Although idealist philosophy and religion endow the intellect with high value (*Wertmäßigkeit*) when attributing to *Geist* and teleology ontological priority over matter, the real ontological priority of the economic basis—within the social being's assessment—does not claim any value hierarchy, as Lukács correctly asserts. It is worth reiterating, "Marx, on the other hand, looks at the economic process in its unfolded dynamic totality, and in this, the human being must appear as the beginning and end, as the initiator and final result of the process as a whole" (Lukács, 1986, p. 77). Human-becoming is thus permanently embedded within a metabolic transformation process of and in nature. Nature produces human's existential basis, and it is its premise; this beginning is transformed through labour and becomes yet another result, which constitutes the premise of a "new" commencement. Humanity, therefore, modifies nature and itself and alters the character of natural eternal dependency but cannot overcome this irreducible fact because, ultimately, the human being is a natural being.

Value (in general and not only capitalist exchange-value) is thus not an innate ontological condition. It emerges within the organisational process of labour and social relations, in which the *Ought* gains relevance when individual behaviours must be coordinated to achieve common goals. "The problem of value is inseparably linked to the problem of the ought as a category of the social-being" (Lukács, 1986, p. 68). Thus, the ethical dimension of values arises from labour relations within the economy and gains further complexity within social relations (political, juridical, etc.). Although the two categories are different, namely, "value predominantly influences the objective and is the principle of the judgement of the realised product, while the ought is more the regulator of the process itself", they are two elements of a totality (Lukács, 1986, p. 68). The impact of determining behaviour within economic relations is intrinsically connected to coordination, efficiency, and efficacy. These three dimensions are fundamentally connected to time. Even in primitive societies, whether in hunting or farming, the determination of time is crucial. Furthermore, Marx stresses that time not consumed, or merely time freed from the necessary activities of production and reproduction of life, is time available to all other intellectual, spiritual and material productions.

> As with a single individual, the all-roundness of their development, enjoyment and activity depend on saving time. Economy of time: in this all economy finally dissolves. Likewise, society must divide its time appropriately in order to achieve a production that meets its total needs, just as the individual must divide his time correctly in order to acquire knowledge in appropriate proportions or in order satisfy the various demands on his activity. The economy of time, as well as the systematic distribution of labour time among the various branches of production, thus remains the first economic law on the basis of common production. (Marx, 1983b, p. 105)

Further, in Marx's notes, the same principle emerges again. "The real economy—saving—consists of saving labour time", to which he adds, "this saving [is] yet identical to the development of the productive force". The potential is obvious; labour time saved is time gained for leisure "for the complete development of the individual", which conversely reinforces the potential for further improvement in labour productivity. This is essential for what Lukács calls *Menschenwerdung* and Marx *den werdenden Menschen*, that is, the human becoming presupposes its development—both mental and material—in him, science is objectified, "in his head exists the accumulated knowledge of society" (Marx, 1983b, p. 607).

3.2.16 Popular Science and Scientific Failures as Preconditions of Theoretical Science: or the Pure Science Hypostasis

In *A People's History of Science,* Clifford D. Conner highlights that technology does not originate from theoretical science, but instead, the former forms the basis of the latter. Criticising the elitist conceptualisation of knowledge, which is often regarded as the achievement of individual geniuses, thus "underestimat[ing] the creative intellectual abilities of ordinary human beings working collectively" (Conner, 2005, p. 80), Conner asserts "that *artisans contributed not only the mass of empirical knowledge that furnished the raw material of the Scientific Revolution, but the empirical method itself*" (Conner, 2005, p. 17). Most of the domesticated plants and animals found today were "de facto genetic engineering practiced by preliterate ancient peoples" (Conner, 2005, p. 2).

According to Jared Diamond, humanity focused on so few species as a source of food because most species are "indigestible", "poisonous", "low in nutritional value", "tedious to prepare", "or dangerous to hunt"; moreover, a significant part of the land biomass "is in the form of wood and leaves, most of which we cannot digest" (Diamond, 1999, p. 88). Domestication grants the possibility to concentrate a vastly superior quantity of edible elements, yielding more calories to humanity and thus feeding more people. Labour is, therefore, an indispensable precondition for such developments. However, as Conner recognises, contemporary humanity is "infinitely more in debt to pre-Columbian Amerindians than to modern plant geneticists for the scientific knowledge underlying food production" (Conner, 2005, p. 2); this means that the intergenerational transference of knowledge has also proven to be a precondition to human development.

Conner investigates different fields in which scientific knowledge has been developed, acquired, and transferred through labour relations instead of emerging from the desks of theoretical intellectuals. For instance, progress in medicine entails a long social and collective history (see Porter's *The Greatest Benefit to Mankind* (Porter, 1997)). Treatment of Malaria derives from Indigenous knowledge; inoculation of smallpox from African expertise brought by enslaved people into the American continent; vaccination in spite of being credited to "Dr. Edward Jenner belongs instead to a farmer named Benjamin Jesty"; American and Pacific geography and cartography are products of native people's wisdom; "chemistry, metallurgy, and the materials sciences in general originated in knowledge produced by ancient miners, smiths, and potters"; millennia-long mechanics, accountants, merchants, and surveyors developed mathematics; last, "the empirical method that characterised the Scientific Revolution of the sixteenth and seventeenth centuries, as well as the mass of scientific data on which it built, emerged from the workshops of European artisans" (Conner, 2005, p. 3. See also 95ff, 101ff, 210ff, 422ff, 68ff, 248).

Modern science is historically and ontologically inconceivable if subtracted from its popular (folk and artisanal) sources. According to John Desmond Bernal, a rigid definition of science becomes impossible because it is a practice which keeps changing "over the whole range of human history" (Bernal, 1965, p. 3). When conceived as pure theory, science must thus be fetishised and obscured. "That view of science is frequently an adjunct to reactionary political views because it supposedly offers a source of unchallengeable authority, like religion, and thereby serves as a support for authoritarianism" (Conner, 2005, p. 13). The corollary is, of course, its opposition to the so-called applied science, reinforcing the impression that the latter is intrinsically a product of the former. Historically, not only is theory a product of practical scientific achievements, but it also becomes part of a dialectical process in which science, as a result, becomes the premise for the higher development of practical science. Therefore, Conner declares that the scientific start "was not the *word* but the *deed*—not the proclamations of brilliant theorists but the creative handiwork of ordinary people" (Conner, 2005, p. 14).

Each successful scientific achievement is not simply the product of accurate views and results but most importantly the accumulated experience of failures and dead ends, which in turn reveal a much broader comprehension of the challenges being dealt with than simply some initial proposed questions. *All so-called failures are pivotal in accomplishing fruitful outcomes; conversely, each positive result contains a vast array of crucial shortcomings*. When regarded as pure science, science is deified; its limitations are obscurely overestimated, while the infinite complexity contained in reality is underestimated. Possibly relating to some ideological dimensions of *intellectual property*$_{(private)}$, "the academic field of history of science continues to concentrate most of its attention on a few scientific luminaries" (Conner, 2005, p. 18), which circularly legitimises the privatisation of knowledge by the few.

3.2.17 Destruction (and Subsumption) of the Worker's Knowledge

Coerced by a society imposing competition upon them, artisans used the tool of secrecy to protect their activities not because of intrinsic egoistic motivation but rather as a necessary condition for their economic survival. While capital has been historically tightening its grip on knowledge to secure monopolistic access, when productive activities were still mainly under the control of craftsmen and their codes of conduct, the elite championed exposing their secrets to public view. Conner denounces the hypocrisy, "those countries that are the staunchest advocates of free markets are invariably those most able to dominate them"; furthermore, "the intellectual elite was likewise in a position to control the valuable knowledge it 'liberated'" (Conner, 2005, p. 21).

The capitalist elite gained control over the productive process, and artisans were pushed to the rows of proletarian wage labourers. Manual workers possessed impressive arrays of knowledge. Their acute perception predates modernity, despite preconceptions diminishing the mental capabilities of prehistorical humanity, which shaped and transformed their environments according to their needs. Therefore, Conner assumes "that they could have done so only because of their uniquely human ability to gain and apply an immense body of knowledge of nature" (Conner, 2005, p. 27). Jared Diamond calls hunting-gathering peoples "walking encyclopedias of natural history, with individual names (in their local language) for as many as a thousand or more plant and animal species, and with detailed knowledge of those species' biological characteristics, distribution, and potential uses" (Diamond, 1999, p. 143), thus suggesting that even within relatively less complex social arrangements impressive bodies-of-knowledge had already been developed, nourished, transformed, and transmitted, which undoubtedly reveals the presence and actuality of immense intellectual capabilities. This capacity is more impressive in the absence of symbolic signals, writing or even an intellectual dedicated class, with culture having to be orally transmitted and the whole body of knowledge being present in more or less every individual of a given community.

The example of African agronomy has at least a twofold relevance. It is a crucial example of people's history of science and additionally gives a representation of the crucial relationship between body and knowledge. According to Conner, European colonialists discovered essential African crops not in the African continent but rather in their slaves' gardens. Portraying the presence of these crops in the American continent as seed transfer consequently reveals a false illustration of history. It was *African expertise* which actualised farming activity based on such crops.

Growing rice was fundamental for some economies, for example, Carolina and Georgia. Rice is not a distinct Asian species. There are many species of rice from which the Asian and the African variants are known to be agriculturally viable; the latter was domesticated by Africans to adapt to "wetland swamps" (Carney, 2001, p. 45); despite the popular perception of Africa being a continent with food deficit, historically this could not be farther from the truth. "Perceptions of a continent populated by hapless farmers and herders in need of European instruction are inaccurate and fail to do justice to Africa's deep botanical legacy" (Carney & Rosomoff, 2009, p. 3). African people dominated a diverse body of agricultural knowledge, and despite the removal of millions of people from the continent by means of the slave trade, according to Judith A. Carney and Richard N. Rosomoff, food surplus continued to be produced. Moreover, "in the Americas, enslaved Africans continued their innovating processes" (Carney & Rosomoff, 2009, p. 7). Therefore, slavery did not simply characterise the European coloniser's need for physical labour (brute force), but the very enslaved person embodied socio-historically transmitted and accumulated productive knowledge. "In the modern world of mechanised agriculture, it is often difficult to remember that until recently agriculture represented repositories of cultural knowledge built from generations of observation, trial, and error" (Carney, 2001, p. 136).

Within labour relations, a bond between society and nature was created, and the division of labour cemented specific social roles and individual identities. The African rice crops were mainly performed by women, who, consequently, dominated such a body of knowledge which was transmitted from woman-to-woman. In slave rice plantations, woman's labour presented a fundamental advantage over male work. "In South Carolina, however, where rice became a plantation crop, slavery dismantled this gender division of labor as both men and women were forced to work in its cultivation and milling" (Carney, 2001, p. 138). Social knowledge was now under the control of the slave owner, body and mind operating as one, both being privately owned by the enslaver. Transformed into a slave, the knowledge of the Africans about nature now belonged to a master; it "had thus been stolen and turned against them as a means of maintaining the social system that enslaved them" (Conner, 2005, p. 93). In this sense, since the body as the means of doing was not separated from the producer's mind—both as two parts of a totality—the then social property relations could not yet have demanded anything analogous to *intellectual property*$_{(private)}$.

3.2.18 Destruction of Knowledge Value and the Separation of Property and Intellectual Property

Property and intellectual property are two moments of the same totality. Conceiving one separated from the other negates and fetishises them both simultaneously. As mentioned, historically, *intellectual property*$_{(private)}$ gains traction when two crucial factors come into play. On the one hand, when the value of knowledge diminishes, and on the other, when the separation of production and production control occurs. The real subsumption of intellectual labour under capital peaked with the advent of the TRIPS (see *supra*). The latter resulted from a recent historical process catalysing those two factors.

First, digitalisation enabled an unparalleled devaluation of knowledge because the average socially necessary labour time required for knowledge production dwindled with the transformation of its material base. If within primitive societies knowledge had to be extensively and laboriously taught and learned orally, and even after Gutenberg's revolutionary achievement, knowledge production was still part of a complex and lengthy process of capturing and transmitting ideas through books, it is digitalisation that enables the same means to be used over and over to store and accumulate knowledge. As digitalisation further develops, hardware undergoes a progressive reduction in size, power and material consumption, and also attains more portable forms. As the material means of digitalisation improves its efficiency, its value decreases.

Knowledge appropriation metamorphoses. Now, the spheres of matter and knowledge become preconditions for the revolutionary destruction of value in the production of knowledge. The digital means contains vast amounts of social knowledge objectified in the hardware—not only the refined transformation of making silicon semiconductors into integrated circuits (chips) but also the historical and contemporary process of mining, chemistry, etc., in order to provide the necessary material and intellectual means for transistors—as well as in the software that organises knowledge within programmes that create the basis for further utilisations of existing hardware. Unlike analogue computers—mechanic or electrical proceedings—digital computers are unthinkable without the dialectical relationship of hardware and software.

Complex software and its utilisation presuppose a certain level of hardware development, while superb hardware is of little use (underperforming) if run on poorly coded software. This complex infrastructure provides the historical material foundation for *the contemporary destruction of the value of knowledge*; simultaneously, the use-value of knowledge intensifies. The more this process advances, the more social it becomes. An emergent tendency becomes clear. Worldwide knowledge can be accessed and stored from any home, assuming the existence of the material infrastructure of a computer (and alike) coupled with an Internet connection. Not only music, movies, paintings, sculptures, drawings, theatre plays, novels, etc., in a word, the world of culture and arts has the potential to be unrestrictedly accessed, but scientific knowledge as well as daily life events and happenings can also be easily shared. This digital mediation does not diminish the importance of a physical library or face-to-face encounters—especially at a psychological level—but, at a material level of knowledge production, the ease to obtain, consume, learn, modify, and transmit knowledge, ideas, and information tremendously intensifies as the time economy of knowledge production shrinks.

Second, if on the one hand, there is no general production, each particular production relates symbiotically and metabolically to one another. Production "is always only a certain social body, a social subject, which is active in a greater or lesser totality of branches of production" (Marx, 1961a, p. 618). The expansion of capital during the post-World War II period first saw its peak in the so-called Golden Age, in which industrial production represented a critical element in the further process of accumulation of capital. However, this process also found barriers already during the 1970s, when the still-enduring structural capitalist crisis started. "Taken together, the political-institutional clearance of transactions of all kinds and the various technological leaps (in transport, communications and data processing) have allowed capital to achieve in the post-war period a fluidity without historical precedent" (Castro, 1979, p. 183).

As early as 1979, Antonio Barros de Castro brilliantly attested to the ending of this process. The rapid spread of capital altered the condition of economic totality, rendering it even more totalising than before. The contradiction thus appeared more latent, for the vast spread (and consequently the enormous mass) of capital also resulted in the reduction of immediate primitive accumulation opportunities while the rate of capital declined (see *infra*). Guaranteeing surplus-value meant accommodating changes in production. Many production plants were moved from the West to East Asia (MacDonald, 1993)—and, to a certain extent, Latin America. Lower labour costs (direct in the form of wages and indirect in the form of rights and social guarantees) enabled a greater extraction of surplus-value. However, productive processes cannot be separated from objectified intellectual labour. Exporting productive capital meant simultaneously exporting scientific capital.

This historical condition was central to asserting a system which could artificially separate *teleology* (*Teleologie*) from the *setting* (*Setzung*), the act of doing, its materialisation, from its goal and conceptualisation. If *intellectual property*$_{(private)}$ already existed prior to TRIPS, it was this specific agreement which cemented the total subordination of social intellectual property relations to a system of privatisation and control.

> The ontological coexistence of teleology and causality in the labouring (practical) behaviour of the human-being, and only here, has the consequence in terms of being that, according to their social essence, theory and practice must be moments of one and the same social complex of being, so that they can only be adequately understood starting from this interrelation. (Lukács, 1986, p. 53)

An ontological break had to take place. The totality of human production, that is, economy and knowledge, had to be split. Of course, in-itself, this remains an ontological impossibility; every product produced is its own manual, its own code which can be deciphered and understood; it has objectified knowledge which can reversely be turned into fluid knowledge (understanding).

For-itself, the ontological relations of the social being subsumed under capitalism thus become conscripted to serve capitalist power. A break between theory and practice becomes a social reality. Capitalist power and control impose on them two separate existences.

Every moment of convergence must be carefully coerced and neutralised. As the flow of natural resources from the Global South is still significantly controlled by the Global North through the process of transformation, the monopolistic control over the knowledge of these transformative processes becomes more critical because most capitalist powers are not only vastly deficient in natural resources but also the very transformative processes are increasingly taking place elsewhere—namely, outside the capitalist core.

In a world where capitalist competition among capital blocks determines political power, traditional capitalist powers are held by a thread. The historical-ontological inadequacy of private control becomes blatant when production increasingly becomes highly collective and cooperative and in which the private owner is constricted outside the whole productive process.

The power of both the capitalist and dominating empires must grow to compensate for losing the ontological-historical relevance they once had throughout the transition from feudalism to capitalism. The greater the socialisation of knowledge becomes, the more intensively the relationship between science and production develops. In this sense, the Marxist notion of *praxis*—"the unity and synergy of theory and practice" (Robinson, 2014, p. 222)—perfectly summarises this complex relationship and becomes an important category to be controlled within the struggle of classes.

3.2.19 Marxian Totality of Property and Intellectual Property

As Marx lived in a period in which capitalist propaganda by means of aesthetical appropriation and psychological methods were not yet dominant, since only by the end of the nineteenth century and the beginning of the twentieth century these methods started to emerge (Bernays, 1928; Bon, 2002), he oversaw the crucial dimension of immaterial production under the capitalist mode of production; or did he?

Taking into account his brief valuation of the "*Gebiet der immateriallen Produktion*", and here Marx speaks about "artists", "orators", "actors", "teachers", "physicians", "clerics etc.", concluding that in these areas capitalism occurs under a very limited scope; thus, one would have to conclude—in his own words—a complete disregard for "all these phenomena of capitalist production" which "are so insignificant compared with the whole of production that they can be entirely disregarded" (Marx, 1965, p. 386). In the next chapter, this problem will be dealt with more thoroughly (see *infra*); what is essential here is that despite Marx using the words *immaterial production*, it is evident that he left out maybe the most crucial category within this taxonomy: *science*.

By no means does Marx ignore the role of science in capitalism. On the contrary, it is clear that knowledge and science play a crucial role in any economic arrangement; with the economic imperative imposing an incessant demand for gains of productivity, science attains an even more significant role than before. The transformation of nature by the human being represents its "transformation in organs of the human will"; shaped by labour and not given by nature, human achievements are

> *organs of the human brain created by the human hand*; objectified power of knowledge [Wissenskraft]. The development of the capital fixe indicates to what degree general social knowledge has become an *immediate productive force [Productivkraft]*, and therefore, the conditions of the social life process itself have come under the control of the general intellect and have been transformed according to it. To what degree have the social productive forces been produced, not only in the form of knowledge but as direct organs of social practice; of the real life process. (Marx, 1981, p. 582f)

Body and mind are, for Marx, two elements of a totality. "The singular [*einzelne*] human-being cannot have an effect on nature without using his own muscles under the control of his own brain. Just as head and hand belong together in the natural system, the labour-process unites headwork and handwork" (Marx, 1962, p. 531). Physical appropriation is only possible with intellectual appropriation. Needless to say, the latter presupposes a concrete reality; the ontological priority of matter over *Geist* remains an existential condition; nevertheless, the movement—activity—unleashed by labour would be merely an impulse, a (genetic) reaction to the environment if the intellectual appropriation and its ideal transformation of reality did not first occur at an imaginary level, which must take place in concrete psychical minds and not an abstract *absolute spirit.*

This acknowledgement of the pivotal role of knowledge as the immediate productive force does not lead Marx to fetishise technology, which in-itself does not represent an emancipatory means, in-itself has no particular character; its real dimension is first shaped within social relations. If, on the one hand, the machine liberates humanity from certain activities, on the other, it "attacks the nervous system to the utmost, suppresses the varied play of the muscles and confiscates all free physical and mental activity"; therefore, even the easiness brought about by it can simultaneously be a "means of torture" because the machine does not "liberate the labourer from the labour but his labour from [any] content" (Marx, 1962, p. 445f).

The particular character objectified knowledge and objectified labour attain is represented by the specific historical character of social property (and production) relations. The objectified knowledge and labour, confronting the labourer as his foreman, thus appears as dead-knowledge and -labour opposing living-knowledge and -labour. The labourer's powers now appear as capital's power (as the slave's body and mind appear to be the master's own capabilities, see *supra*). Living activity faces its objectified means of doing; this subject-predicate-inversion is called by Marx a "divorce of the intellectual potencies of the production process" (Marx, 1962, p. 446). Domenico Losurdo stresses that the necessary mutual development of science and productive forces imposes the condition that knowledge itself has become a productive force, and this umbilical bond "can be escaped only by an inconceivable, disastrous mutilation of human intellectual capacities" (Losurdo, 2016, p. 319). The character of the so-called primitive accumulation is unambiguous.

In the same way that capital appropriates nature, it appropriates science because once something is discovered or invented, to the capitalist, appropriating it does not cost anything (Marx, 1962, p. 407). In the *Grundrisse*, the German philosopher asserts that the "*development of science*", on the one hand, contains both ideal and practical dimensions but also does not exhaust the "development of the human productive forces", affirming that, on the *ideal* side, a "dissolution of a determined form of consciousness" suffices to "kill a whole era", while on the *real*, the "barrier of consciousness corresponds to a *determined degree of the development of the material productive forces*"; finally, and not least importantly, he complements with a point which abolishes any misinterpretation of his preface to *A Contribution to the Critique of Political Economy*, "admittedly development occurred not only on the old basis but the *development of this basis itself*" (Marx, 1983b, p. 446); it is thus clear that along Marxian lines there is no unidimensional relationship between economy and cultural development. Marx's critics, however, improperly extract from the notions of basis and superstructure the illusion that Marx would conceive a mechanistic understanding of economic developments (an obvious example is Polanyi, 2001).

The character of labour is identical to the "social character" given to material production and simultaneously to the "scientific character"

(Marx, 1983b, p. 512). In this sense, the more blatant the contradiction between private capitalist appropriation and collective, cooperative, social production becomes, the higher the degree of development capitalist relations reach. The degradation of immediate labour to a simple moment of the capitalist process of production reveals "the tendency of capital", which acquires the character given by science; "the whole production process" is therefore "not subsumed under the immediate dexterity of the labourer" but under the "technological application of science" (Marx, 1983b, p. 595). Needless to say, technological development presupposes surplus labour and social sacrifice; it is an activity which depends on the abdication of time directly converted into production—in Marx words, "redundant hands", thus forming a crucial element of the superstructure.

And while Marx disregarded the activities under *his* label of immaterial production, he fully recognises not only science becoming an essential aspect of production but with a "higher degree" of the "big industry", discovery itself becomes a business affair, thus "the whole sciences were captured in service of capital" (Marx, 1983b, p. 600). On the other hand, the total control of capital, ripping singular persons of their apparently eternal social roles, sparks the tinder of individuality; that is, the social collective arrangement which supersedes humans' immediate dependency on nature grants singular human beings the ontological possibility for individualisation. The very social relations which dehumanise people also form the basis for the emergence of the individual on the backbone of the suffering of uncountable lives (Marx, 1967, p. 111, 1983b, p. 601).

While scientific development helps to forge the material basis for emancipation under capitalism, in practice, it means a crucial element of social discipline, control, and power, thus promoting the accentuation of dehumanisation. Marx highlights that by no means does the "development of the means of labour into machinery" represent a "random" condition of capital; it "is rather the historical reshaping of the traditionally inherited means of labour as adequately transformed to capital"; therefore, despite its social condition, it possesses the appearance of capital, "[t]he accumulation of knowledge and dexterity, of the general productive forces of the social brain, is, in opposition to labour, absorbed by capital" (Marx, 1983b, p. 594). Intellectual appropriation is, in such a manner, relocated from the labourers' brains to become objectified capital in machines. Science departs from its social character to being subjected to a constant process of privatisation.

3.2.20 The Capitalist State and the So-Called Private Enterprise

A great example of the contradictory relationship between the social development of knowledge and private appropriation takes form in Mariana Mazzucato's analysis of the so-called entrepreneurial state, which outlines the essential role the state plays in the development of capitalism—comprising intellectual appropriation and technology.

She contests the assumption that the sole role of the state sector would be to merely incentivise the private sector because it does not explain many concrete cases "in which the leading entrepreneurial force came from the State rather than from the private sector" (Mazzucato, 2015, p. 207). Recognising that innovation depends on a collective process, it becomes hard to conceive private capital and state as isolated entities; she claims it is crucial "to understand the division of 'innovative' labour between the different actors in these systems" (Mazzucato, 2015, p. 208). For instance, the emergence of the Internet resembles that third category of sociogenesis explained by Tomasello, in which neither individuals nor groups created intentionality. It is not only the product of complex social relations but could never have emerged by private means—neither financially for it was too expensive with no anticipated commercial application nor conceptually for its very initial idea was "to preserve communication abilities during a nuclear war" (Mazzucato, 2015, p. 210). Therefore, it seems inconceivable to imagine that capital provides solutions for collective problems in areas that provide no profit motive. Moreover, history shows "that private investments tend to wait for the early high-risk investments to be made first by the State" (Mazzucato, 2015, p. 210). The same existing logic of the financial sector, in which losses are socialised and gains privatised, applies to sectors involving science and technology (Mazzucato, 2015, p. 212).

Mazzucato provides a case study of Apple's iPhone to give substance to this matter. Apple is one of the largest private companies in the world in terms of market share value, which is why it has undisputed relevance in contemporary capitalism. Apple only grew significantly in size and importance as a result of the development of the (still back then) new iOS (iPhone's operating system) in 2007. This fact is publicised worldwide. What is barely known, however, is that Apple's leading technologies in its devices are, in fact, the result of decades of development and funding from the capitalist state. The proportion of R&D in Apple's overall business is smaller than its competitors'/peers' (as an R&D to revenue ratio) (Prableen Bajpai, 2021), which means Apple invests less in developing new technologies. Nevertheless, this is Apple's precise merit, namely, the integration of existing technologies. Through this process, Apple has realised both the design and engineering of government- and military-developed technologies (this applies not only to the early 2000s period when the late Apple company became successful on a large scale but also to the earlier Apple Computer company in the 1970s, which benefited from the US-American governmental technology developments of the 1960s and 1970s). Apple's revival is largely owed to the launch and success of the iPhone, which is why Mazzucato focuses on it, underlining that the iOS had at least 12 chief technologies that differentiated it from the competition. It is worth quoting in full:

> These include semiconductor devices such as (1) *microprocessors or central processing units* (CPU); (2) *dynamic random-access memory* (DRAM); as well as (3) *micro hard drive storage or hard drive disks* (HDD); (4) *liquid-crystal displays* (LCDs); (5) *lithium-polymer* (Li-pol) and *lithium-ion* (Li-ion) batteries; (6) *digital signal processing* (DSP), based on the advancement in *fast Fourier transform* (FFT) algorithms; (7) the *Internet*; (8) the *Hypertext Transfer Protocol* (HTTP) and Hypertext Markup Language (HTML); (9) and *cellular technology and networks*—all of which can be considered as the core enabler technologies for products such as the iPod, iPhone and iPad. On the other hand, (10) *global positioning systems* (GPS), (11) *click-wheel* navigation and *multi-touch screens*, (12) and *artificial intelligence with a voice-user interface program* (a.k.a. Apple's SIRI) are innovative features that have drastically impacted consumer expectations and

user experiences, further enhancing the popularity and success of these products. (Mazzucato, 2015, p. 101f)

The myth that asserts Apple's success on the dynamism and benefits of private capital over other forms of social relations has hence no basis in reality. "The fact that much of Apple's success lies in technologies that were developed through government support and -funded research is an often overlooked story" (Mazzucato, 2015, p. 102).

The importance of technologies developed by the state was somehow highlighted in 2007, not only were Albert Fert and Peter Grünberg bestowed the Nobel Prize for the development of GMR (giant magneto-resistance) but also Börje Johannson stated that without the GMR, the iPod—a central product that preceded the iPhone—could not have existed. Every new invention and development presupposes previous ones; the latter are always contained in the former. A special case of social support in development can be seen in the state-subsidised Semiconductor Manufacturing Technology (SEMATECH) consortium. To promote the manufacturing of semiconductor technology, the US government subsidised SEMATECH R&D to the tune of 100 million dollars annually. SEMATECH unified various companies in a consortium, which could cooperate more intensively and thus avoid duplication of work, reducing time and R&D expenditure (Mazzucato, 2015, p. 105f).

From the many key components of Apple's iOS described above, some will be presented to concretise the symbiotic relationship between state and private capital. The "touch-screen" and "click-wheels"; the Internet; and finally, GPS and SIRI.

First example: although it was supposedly a novelty that Apple brought into the market through the iPod (Apple's MP3 player), click-wheel technology had already existed for decades. Its application in the iPod was crucial because it was Apple's first attempt to replace control buttons and "roll balls" with touch technology. The iPod Touch, iPhone (Apple's mobile phone) and iPad (Apple's tablet) are extensively equipped with capacitive sensing technology, which was already used in the government-funded click-wheel technology that equipped the previous iPod generations. The invention and development of both "capacitive touch-screens" and "resistive touch-screens" were made possible by government funding:

first by E.A. Johnson at the British government agency "Royal Radar Establishment", and second, by Samuel Hurst at the US government laboratory Oak Ridge National Laboratory. However, the first generations of touch screens were still rudimentary, allowing only a single touch. Scrolling is something that only appeared with the "multi-touch" generation, invented and developed by Wayne Westerman and John Elias. Elias was a professor at the University of Delaware, and Westerman was a doctoral student at his institute, the university; accordingly, the invention and inventors were state-funded. The professor, together with his doctoral student, subsequently founded the company FingerWorks, which produced the developed technology. In 2005, Apple bought FingerWorks and was thus able to use the new technology developed by state resources in its latest iOS and thus also in new products (Mazzucato, 2015, p. 106ff).

The umbilical relationship between hardware and software gained momentum with the invention of the Internet. The potential of a computer (or generally speaking a digital device) is infinitely diminished if prompted by hardware and software without Internet capabilities. In this sense, "what does the Internet, Hypertext Transfer Protocol (HTTP) or Hypertext Markup Language (HTML) mean to any computer or smart device" (Mazzucato, 2015, p. 110)? During the Cold War, the US government was concerned about maintaining a communications network in the event of an atomic bomb attack. Paul Baran, a researcher at RAND—which stands for "Research and Development", a government-funded organisation—conceptualised and designed a solution using a decentralised communications network. "With a decentralised communication in place, the command and network system would survive during and after nuclear attacks" (Mazzucato, 2015, p. 110f). The creation of the network was based on the joint development of the technology presented above by various teams gathered under the umbrella of the governmental agency named DARPA. Private companies such as AT&T and IBM refused to develop the project offered to them by DARPA. The TCP/IC, HTML and HTTP technologies, vital to the development of the Internet, were then developed and governmentally funded (by the United States and the United Kingdom) from the 1970s until the end of the 1990s. "Public funding has played a significant role for the Internet, from its conception to its worldwide application" (Mazzucato, 2015, p. 111).

Ultimately, GPS and SIRI are the most striking examples that highlight the essential role of the state in the promotion and development of technology. Not only did the state develop, promote and enable GPS, but the US Air Force is still the leading promoter of the system, which, according to Mazzucato, costs the US state an average of $705 million a year. GPS uses twenty-four satellites that provide data for orientation. Succinctly, Mazzucato states, "This technology, as well as the infrastructure of the system, would have been impossible without the government taking the initiative and making the necessary financial commitment for such a highly complex system" (Mazzucato, 2015, p. 112). The amount of time and resources (both human and economic) invested in this project would have been impossible to be accommodated by private capital. Also, the personal virtual assistant known as SIRI is a government-funded technology. DARPA assigned the SRI this virtual personal assistant project called CALO. Twenty universities in the United States participated in developing the necessary technology. The commercialisation of this technology was led by the venture-backed start-up named SIRI, which was eventually bought by Apple, whose technological framework has been "based on the radically complex ideas and technologies conceived and patiently fostered by the government" (Mazzucato, 2015, p. 113).

3.2.21 The Second Paradox of Intellectual Property in Capitalism

What is remarkable is not only the paradoxical relationship which most scholars have perceived and have been dealing with, namely, the social character of knowledge production and private appropriation, which removes knowledge from the sphere of collective knowledge (production), but also the very social relations of production based on the private property of the means of production, which impose the capitalist economic imperative over knowledge itself.

The ontological condition of knowledge becomes twofold paradoxical. Its existential condition depends on non-privatised, socially determined relations of production and appropriation; knowledge is both the result and premise of intellectual production and appropriation—as shown in the present book. Nonetheless, under the capitalist mode of production, knowledge is either subsumed when the embeddedness of property relations—whose totality necessarily contains two moments of property and intellectual property, the latter as the teleological condition and the former as the setting (the real movement of actualisation) of concrete social relations in motion—is maintained. Alternatively, when the totality of property is fragmented in the independent existence of property, on the one hand, and intellectual property, on the other, then intellectual property retreats from its real subsumption embedded in private property of the means of production to be merely formally subsumed. This fracture imposes the necessity of a new layer of real subsumption of intellectual appropriation; otherwise, the control over non-intellectual appropriation becomes unstable because, in reality, both properties form and retain an ontological condition of totality. This secondary real subsumption occurs when property control relies first on the superstructure of social relations rather than on immediate appropriation—that is, while property is actualised through social relations beyond the control of immediate appropriation, then the same conditions of intentionality (the teleological dimension) must become the object of power control.

The forced independence of intellectual property presupposes, under private property relations, becoming *intellectual property*$_{(private)}$. Exporting capital worldwide—coupled with the demolition of the value of knowledge production—changed the social-material conditions of capitalist power. The objective conditions of production, the productive forces, became—especially after the Second World War and more rapidly not only when the United States but also Western Europe and Japan also became saturated with capital (accumulation of great masses of fixed capital)—separated from the immediate political-military-economic power, which kept them under control. The digital revolution allowed the second shift to occur. Not only was the capitalist periphery going through a process of concentration of capital through capital exports, that is, physical concentration, but it was also being directly fed with the global transformation in the process of knowledge production, incurring a contrary trend to the hitherto situation in which capitalist peripheries were being excluded from the concentration of knowledge production.

Producing, for instance, pharmacological drugs in poor countries was no longer a guarantee of profits, as India and Brazil have proven with their industry of production of generic drugs (Drahos & Braithwaite, 2002). Proprietary knowledge was now being subjected to appropriation not from those who had control but no possession of the means of doing but by entire countries where capitalist production was based. This transformation opened up a new conflict. Even though the physical conditions of production have been moved, social relations still bond productive property to its legal owner and not to the productive people (and their representatives) in the production sites. However, the hitherto existing barrier between theoretical knowledge as intentionality without the means of actualisation and actual knowledge, which presupposes the existence and capability of actualising and objectifying it, was broken.

It is in this context that the second paradox of intellectual property emerges. Not only did private capital have to appropriate knowledge to guarantee its reproduction, but knowledge itself also became part of the ontological dimension of capital. Intellectual appropriation appears formally subsumed if taken independently; real subsumption must be reimposed. Under the real subsumption of (independent-from-property) knowledge by capital, knowledge must be privatised to be actualised. Knowledge production reached a phase in which it carries with itself two antagonistic conditions of existence. On the one hand, it must be socially and collectively produced and reproduced to exist; on the other, under capitalist relations of production, it must leave the social realm and set itself up for privatisation.

While the first paradox expresses the contradictory movement of capitalist real subsumption which destroys knowledge to secure appropriation of surplus labour under totalised social property relations, the second paradox takes place when knowledge is regarded as independent from the activity that renders it actuality; in this case, maintaining the real subsumption of knowledge imposes privatisation of knowledge not only as the existence of capitalist appropriation but of knowledge production itself. If within the totality of property, intellectual appropriation is the condition for the actualisation of non-intellectual appropriation, and vice-versa, their divorce imposes the necessity of two independent forms of control to sustain power over each separate moment. The second paradox expresses, therefore, not only the external attack on knowledge as a condition of capital but, more importantly, knowledge's own self-negation as a condition of its independent existence.

Its necessary condition to attain existence under capitalism means denying itself the necessary condition of existence at all. As the capitalist mode of production advances, the division of labour becomes more complex and production more social, and the individual potentialities increase as the web of social relations becomes vaster, multifaceted and more entrenched, with production reaching unprecedented levels of socialisation; on the other hand, the political organisation based on the private property of the means of production enforces a greater contradictory social-political-economic dimension within social life. While historically, physical and intellectual productions deviate from any individual dependency, capital control presupposes private appropriation of every production to maintain its existence. Capitalist productive existence thus has two dimensions. First, production can only take place within the mode of private property of the means of production. Second, production can, however, only be productive if socially conceived. Under capitalism, production must then be socially produced and privately privatised.

References

Aristoteles. (1966). *Metaphysik* (H. Carvallo & E. Grassi, Eds.). Rowohlt.

Arrow, K. (1962). Economic Welfare and the Allocation of Resources for Invention. In *The Rate and Direction of Inventive Activity: Economic and Social Factors*. Princeton University Press. https://www.nber.org/books-and-chapters/rate-and-direction-inventive-activity-economic-and-social-factors/economic-welfare-and-allocation-resources-invention

Barthes, R. (2000). Der Tod des Autors. In F. Jannidis, G. Lauer, M. Martinez, & S. Winko (Eds.), *Texte zur Theorie der Autorschaft*. Philipp Reclam jun.

Bernal, J. D. (1939). *The Social Function of Science*. George Routledge & Sons Ldt.

Bernal, J. D. (1965). *Science in History: Volulme I: The Emergence of Science*. Penguin Books.

Bernays, E. L. (1928). *Propaganda*. Liveright Publishing Corporation.
Bon, G. L. (2002). *The Crowd: A Study of the Popular Mind*. Dover Publications, Inc.
Boyle, J. (2008). *The Public Domain: Enclosing the Commons of the Mind*. feek-books. https://doi.org/10.1177/0276146711416981
Brenner, R. (1985). Agrarian Class Structure and Economic Development in Pre-Industrial Europe. In T. H. Aston & C. H. E. Philpin (Eds.), *The Brenner Debate: Agrarian Class Structure and Economic Development in Pre-industrial Europe* (pp. 10–63). Cambridge University Press. https://doi.org/10.1017/CBO9780511562358.003
Bruner, J. S. (1991). The Narrative Construction of Reality Author. *Critical Inquiry, 18*(1), 1–21. https://www.jstor.org/stable/1343711
Bruner, J. S. (1998). Vergangenheit und Gegenwart als narrative Konstruktionen. In *Erzählung, Identität und historisches Bewußtsein: Die psychologische Konstruktion von Zeit und Geschichte*. Suhrkamp.
Carney, J. A. (2001). *Black Rice: The African Origins of Rice Cultivation in the Americas*. Harvard University Press.
Carney, J. A., & Rosomoff, R. N. (2009). *In the Shadow of Slavery: Africa's Botanical Legacy in the Atlantic World*. University of California Press.
Castro, A. B. de. (1979). *O Capitalismo Ainda É Aquele*. Forense-Universitária.
Childe, V. G. (1958). *Man Makes Himself*. The New American Library.
Conner, C. D. (2005). *A People's History of Science: Miners, Midwives, and 'Low Mechanicks'*. Nation Books.
Cox, H. (2016). *The Market as God*. Harvard University Press.
Diamond v. Chakrabarty, 447 U.S. 303 (1980). (1980). In *US Supreme Court* (Vol. 447). https://supreme.justia.com/cases/federal/us/447/303/
Diamond, J. (1999). *Guns, Germs, and Steel: The Fates of Human Societies*. W.W. Norton & Company.
Dirk Baecker. (2007). *Studien zur nächsten Gesellschaft*. Suhrkamp.
Drahos, P. (2016). *A Philosophy of Intellectual Property*. Australian National University. https://doi.org/10.22459/PIP.06.2016
Drahos, P., & Braithwaite, J. (2002). *Information Feudalism: Who Owns the Knowledge Economy*. Earthscan Publications Ltd. https://doi.org/10.4324/9781315092683
Engels, F. (1962). Der Ursprung der Familie, des Privateigentums und des Staats. In *MEW Band 21*. Dietz Verlag Berlin.
Engels, F. (1975). Dialektik der Natur. In *MEW Band 20*. Dietz Verlag Berlin.
Eucken, W. (1961). *Nationalökonomie wozu?* Verlag Helmut Küpper.

Feuerbach, L. (2013). *Grundsätze der Philosophie der Zukunft*. Berliner Ausgabe.
Feuerbach, L. (2016). *Das Wesen des Christentums*. Berliner Ausgabe.
Fleck, L. (2021). *Entstehung und Entwicklung einer wissenschaftlichen Tatsache: Einführung in die Lehre vom Denkstil und Denkkollektiv* (13th ed.). Suhrkamp.
Foster, J. B. (2022). *Capitalism in the Anthropocene: Ecological Ruin or Ecological Revolution*. Monthly Review Press.
Foucault, M. (1979). What Is an Author? In J. V. Harari (Ed.), *Textual Strategies: Perspectives in Post-Structuralist Criticism*. Cornell University Press.
Foucault, M. (2002a). *Order of Things: An archaeology of the human sciences*. Routledge.
Foucault, M. (2002b). *The Archaeology of Knowledge*. Routledge.
Frey, C. B., & Osborne, M. A. (2016). The Future of Employment: How Susceptible are Jobs to Computerisation? *Technological Forecasting and Social Change, 114*, 254–280. https://doi.org/10.1016/J.TECHFORE.2016.08.019
Fuchs, C. (2012). Dallas Smythe Today—The Audience Commodity, the Digital Labour Debate, Marxist Political Economy and Critical Theory. Prolegomena to a Digital Labour Theory of Value. *TripleC, 10*(2), 692–740. https://triple-c.at/index.php/tripleC/article/view/443
George, A. (2012). *Constructing Intellectual Property*. Cambridge University Press. https://doi.org/10.1017/CBO9781139035361
Giczy, A. V., Pairolero, N. A., & Toole, A. A. (2022). Identifying Artificial Intelligence (AI) Invention: A Novel AI Patent Dataset. *The Journal of Technology Transfer, 47*, 476–505. https://doi.org/10.1007/s10961-021-09900-2
Hardin, G. (1968). The Tradegy of the Commons. *Science, 162*(3859), 1243–1248. https://doi.org/10.1126/science.162.3859.1243
Harvey, D. (2006). The Limits to Capital. In *Antipode* (Vol. 16, Issue 1). Verso. https://doi.org/10.1111/j.1467-8330.1984.tb00066.x
Hegel, G. W. F. (1986a). *Wissenschaft der Logik I, Werke in 20 Bänden, Band 5*. Suhrkamp.
Hegel, G. W. F. (1986b). *Wissenschaft der Logik II, Werke in 20 Bänden, Band 6*. Suhrkamp.
Hegel, G. W. F. (1989). *Enzyklopädie der philosophischen Wissenschaften im Grundrisse: 1830—Teil 1. Die Wissenschaft der Logik: Mit den mündlichen Zusätzen, Werke in 20 Bänden, Band 8*. Suhrkamp.
Hegel, G. W. F. (2013). *Grundlinien der Philosophie des Rechts oder Naturrecht und Staatswissenschaft im Grundrisse, Werke in 20 Bänden, Band 7*. Suhrkamp.
Heller, M. A. (1998). The Tragedy of the Anticommons: Property in the Transition from Marx to Markets. *Harvard Law Review, 111*(3), 621–688. https://repository.law.umich.edu/articles/609/

Heller, M. A., & Eisenberg, R. S. (1998). Can Patents Deter Innovation? The Anticommons in Biomedical Research. *Science, 280*, 698.

Hermeto, J. R. (2020). *Lukács' Ontologie des gesellschaftlichen Wandels: Von einer mythologischen Ontologie des absoluten Geistes zu einer Ontologie des gesellschaftlichen Seins.* Verlag Dr. Kovač.

Herrmann, E., Misch, A., Hernandez-Lloreda, V., & Tomasello, M. (2015). Uniquely Human Self-control Begins at School Age. *Developmental Science, 18*(6), 979–993. https://doi.org/10.1111/desc.12272

Hill-Yardin, E. L., Hutchinson, M. R., Laycock, R., & Spencer, S. J. (2023). A Chat(GPT) About the Future of Scientific Publishing. *Brain, Behavior, and Immunity, 110*, 152–154. https://doi.org/10.1016/J.BBI.2023.02.022

Hull, G. (2019). *The Biopolitics of Intellectual Property: Regulating Innovation and Personhood in the Information Age.* Cambridge University Press.

Jessop, B. (2006). Spatial Fixes, Temporal Fixes and Spatio-Temporal Fixes. In N. Castree & D. Gregory (Eds.), *David Harvey a critical reader* (pp. 142–166). Blackwell Publishing Ltd.

Kant, I. (1956). *Kritik der reinen Vernunft.* Verlag von Felix Meiner.

Kelsen, H. (1991). *General Theory of Norms.* Clarendon Press.

Kuhn, T. S. (1962). *The Structures of Scientific Revolutions.* The University of Chicago Press.

Lessig, L. (2004). *Free Culture: How Big Media Uses Technology and The Law to Lock Down Culture and Control Creativity.* The Penguin Press.

Losurdo, D. (2011). *Liberalism: A Counter-History.* Verso.

Losurdo, D. (2016). *Class Struggle: A Political and Philosophical History.* Palgrave Macmillan.

Lukács, G. (1963a). *GLW, Band 11, Die Eigenart des Ästhetischen: 1. Halbband.* Luchterhand.

Lukács, G. (1963b). *GLW, Band 12, Die Eigenart des Ästhetischen: 2. Halbband.* Luchterhand.

Lukács, G. (1984a). *GLW, Band 13, Zur Ontologie des gesellschaftlichen Seins, Band 1.* Luchterhand.

Lukács, G. (1984b). Prolegomena zur Ontologie des gesellschaftlichen Seins. In *GLW, Band 13, Zur Ontologie des gesellschaftlichen Seins, Band 1.* Luchterhand.

Lukács, G. (1986). *GLW, Band 14, Zur Ontologie des gesellschaftlichen Seins, Band 2..* Luchterhand.

MacDonald, L. (Ed.). (1993). *The East Asian Miracle: Economic Growth and Public Policy.* Oxford University Press.

Malinowski, B. (2002). *Argonauts of the western pacific: An Account of Native Enterprise and Adventure in the Archipelagoes of Melanesian New Guinea.* Routledge.

Marx, K. (1960). Der achtzehnte Brumaire des Louis Bonaparte. In *MEW Band 08*. Dietz Verlag Berlin.

Marx, K. (1961a). Einleitung zur Kritik der politischen Ökonomie. In *MEW Band 13*. Dietz Verlag Berlin.

Marx, K. (1961b). Zur Kritik der politischen Ökonomie. In *MEW Band 13*. Dietz Verlag Berlin.

Marx, K. (1962). Das Kapital: Kritik der politischen Ökonomie: Erster Band: Buch I: Der Produktionsprozeß des Kapitals. In *MEW Band 23*. Dietz Verlag Berlin.

Marx, K. (1965). Theorien über den Mehrwert: (Vierter Band des 'Kapitals'): Erster Teil: Erstes bis siebentes Kapitel und Beilagen. In *MEW Band 26.1*. Dietz Verlag Berlin.

Marx, K. (1967). Theorien über den Mehrwert: (Vierter Band des 'Kapitals'): Zweiter Teil: Achtes bis achtzehntes Kapitel. In *MEW Band 26.2*. Dietz Verlag Berlin.

Marx, K. (1968). Ökonomisch-philosophische Manuskripte aus dem Jahre 1844. In *MEW Band 40*. Dietz Verlag Berlin.

Marx, K. (1977). Brief von Karl Marx an P. W. Annenkow. In *MEW Band 04* (pp. 547–557). Dietz Verlag Berlin.

Marx, K. (1978). Thesen über Feuerbach. In *MEW Band 03*. Dietz Verlag Berlin.

Marx, K. (1981). Ökonomische Manuskripte 1857/58 (Grundrisse der Kritik der politischen Ökonomie · Zweiter Teil). In I. für Marxismus-Leninismus (Ed.), *MEGA Zweite Abteilung 'Das Kapital' und Vorarbeiten Band 1* (pp. 315–747). Dietz Verlag Berlin.

Marx, K. (1983a). Einleitung zu den 'Grundrissen der Kritik der politischen Ökonomie'. In *MEW Band 42*. Dietz Verlag Berlin.

Marx, K. (1983b). Grundrisse der Kritik der politischen Ökonomie. In *MEW Band 42*. Dietz Verlag Berlin.

Marx, K. (1988). *MEGA² II.4.1—Manuskripte 1863–1867—Teil 1*. Dietz Verlag Berlin.

Marx, K., & Engels, F. (1978). Die deutsche Ideologie: Kritik der neuesten deutschen Philosophie in ihren Repräsentanten Feuerbach, B. Bauer und Stirner, und des deutschen Sozialismus in seinen verschiedenen Propheten. In *MEW Band 03*. Dietz Verlag Berlin.

Mattei, C. E. (2022). The Capital Order: How Economists Invented Austerity and Paved the Way to Fascism. In *The Capital Order*. The University of Chicago Press. https://doi.org/10.7208/chicago/9780226818405.001.0001

Mayer-Schönberger, V., & Ramge, T. (2017). *Das Digital*. Econ.

Mazzucato, M. (2015). *The Entreprenaurial State: Debunking Public vs Private Sector Myths*. PublicAffairs.

Merges, R. P. (1996). Property Rights Theory and the Commons: The Case of Scientific Research. *Social Philosophy and Policy, 13*(2), 145–167. https://doi.org/10.1017/s0265052500003496

Merges, R. P. (2011). *Justifying Intellectual Property*. Harvard University Press.

Moore, J. W. (2016). The Rise of Cheap Nature. In J. W. Moore (Ed.), *Anthropocene or Capitalocene? Nature, History, and the Crisis of Capitalism*. PM Press.

Morgan, L. H. (1877). *Ancient Society or Researches in the Lines of Human Progress from Savagery through Barbarism to Civilization*. Charles H. Kerr & Company.

Mueller, G. (2019). *Media Piracy in the Cultural Economy: Intellectual Property and Labor under Neoliberal Restructuring*. Routledge. https://doi.org/10.4324/9780203730720

Nagel, T. (1974). What Is It Like to Be a Bat? *The Philosophical Review, 83*(4), 435–450. https://doi.org/10.2307/2183914

Netto, J. P. (2011). *Introdução ao Estudo do Método de Marx*. Expressão Popular.

Nightingale, P., & Mahdi, S. (2006). The Evolution of Pharmaceutical Innovation. In M. Mazzucato & G. Dosi (Eds.), *Knowledge Accumulation and Industry Evolution*. Cambridge University Press.

Ostrom, E. (1990). *Governing the Commons: The Evolution of Institutions for Collective Action*. Cambridge University Press.

Pauen, M. (2005). *Grundprobleme der Philosophie des Geistes: Eine Einführung* (4th ed.). Fischer Taschenbuch Verlag.

Polanyi, K. (2001). *The Great Transformation: The Political and Economic Origins of Our Time*. Beacon.

Popper, K. (1979). *Objective Knowledge: An Evolutionary Approach*. Clarendon Press.

Popper, K. (2002). *The Logic of Scientific Discovery*. Routledge.

Porter, R. (1997). *The Greatest Benefit to Mankind: A Medical History of Humanity*. W.W. Norton & Company.

Prableen Bajpai. (2021, June 21). Which Companies Spend the Most in Research and Development (R&D)? *Nasdaq*. https://www.nasdaq.com/articles/which-companies-spend-the-most-in-research-and-development-rd-2021-06-21

Rawls, J. (1999). *A Theory of Justice*. Harvard University Press.

Reynolds, L., & Szerszynski, B. (2012). Neoliberalism and Technology: Perpetual Innovation or Perpetual Crisis? In L. Pellizzoni & M. Ylönen (Eds.), *Neoliberalism and Technoscience: Critical Assessments*. Ashgate.

Robinson, W. I. (2014). *Global Capitalism and the Crisis of Humanity*. Cambridge University Press.

Roose, K. (2023, February 16). *Why a Conversation With Bing's Chatbot Left Me Deeply Unsettled*. The New York Times. https://www.nytimes.com/2023/02/16/technology/bing-chatbot-microsoft-chatgpt.html

Smith, J. M., & Szathmáry, E. (1997). *The Major Transitions in Evolution*. Oxford University Press.

Stengel, D. (2004). Intellectual Property in Philosophy. *ARSP: Archiv Für Rechts- Und Sozialphilosophie/Archives for Philosophy of Law and Social Philosophy, 90*(1), 20–50. https://www.jstor.org/stable/23681627

Tomasello, M. (1999). *The Cultural Origins of Human Cognition*. Harvard University Press.

Tomasello, M. (2014). *A Natural History of Human Thinking*. Harvard University Press.

Tomasello, M., Call, J., & Gluckman, A. (1997). Comprehension of Novel Communicative Signs by Apes and Human Children. *Wiley on Behalf of the Society for Research in Child Development, 68*(6), 1067–1080. https://doi.org/10.2307/1132292

Williams-Jones, B., & Ozdemir, V. (2007). Enclosing the "Knowledge Commons": Patenting Genes for Disease Risk and Drug Response at the University–Industry Interface. In C. Lenk, N. Hoppe, & R. Andorno (Eds.), *Ethics and Law of Intellectual Property: Current Problems in Politics, Science and Technology* (pp. 137–159). Ashgate.

Wilson, J. (2012). On the Value of the Intellectual Commons. In A. Lever (Ed.), *New Frontiers in the Philosophy of Intellectual Property*. Cambridge University Press.

Wittgenstein, L. (2013). *Philosophische Untersuchungen*. Suhrkamp.

Wood, E. M. (2017). *The Origin of Capitalism: A Longer View*. Verso.

Wood, E. M. (2022). Citizens to Lords: Antiquity to the Middle Ages. In *A Social History of Western Political Thought*. Verso.

Yerushalmy, J. (2023, February 17). 'I want to destroy whatever I want': Bing's AI Chatbot Unsettles US Reporter. *The Guardian*. https://www.theguardian.com/technology/2023/feb/17/i-want-to-destroy-whatever-i-want-bings-ai-chatbot-unsettles-us-reporter

4

Knowledge Control and the Spectacle

4.1 Prolegomena: The Dangers of Intellectual Property

4.1.1 Monopoly

The apologetic theodicy and the philosophical justifications of *intellectual property*$_{(private)}$ lack, for the most part, a political-economic material basis; they are essentially metaphysical approaches. With the advent of the digital sphere, copyright has become ubiquitous and hence even more powerful because "nearly all engagement in a digital culture involves making a copy of something, even if only to display it on a screen to read it" (Hull, 2019, p. 62). Over ten years ago, when Alexandra George published her notable study on intellectual property, already 85% of the world's population had to comply with intellectual property rights because "national intellectual property laws that, due mainly to the requirement to harmonise domestic laws to comply with the WTO's *TRIPS Agreement*, are now reasonably uniform worldwide" (George, 2012, p. 77). A comparison may be called for to put this figure into perspective; in 1914, European capitalist powers had yielded a virtually omnipresent colonial power, stretching to circa 84% of the planet (Hoffman, 2015, p. 2; Patel &

J. Romeiro Hermeto, *The Paradox of Intellectual Property in Capitalism*,
https://doi.org/10.1007/978-3-031-49967-8_4

Moore, 2017, p. 5). Therefore, in 2012, the subsumption of knowledge under *intellectual property*$_{(private)}$ was already more extensive than the peak of colonial subsumption under imperialist capitalism. Needless to say, this causes a series of problems because it mutes entire cultures. This all-encompassing subsumption of knowledge under *intellectual property*$_{(private)}$ homogenises a multitude of cultures with little to no regard to the different contexts of cultural and material development or to the different needs, wants, goals, and local conditions. The international system of intellectual property therefore asserts capitalist monopolistic power and control based on Western models, conferring homogenisation to the production of knowledge. "Rights over intellectual property objects tend to include monopoly privileges to obtain, use, make, provide to others, and authorise others to do these things with respect to the intellectual property object" (George, 2012, p. 238). In short, it is a right to exclude others.

The capitalist structural crisis, which has persisted since the 1970s, has posed the existential necessity for a paradigmatic shift away from its previous mode of accumulation. In this context, neoliberalism, its institutions and policies gained traction. William I. Robinson has shown the empirical side of what Marx (famously) called "the law of the tendentious fall of the rate of profit", departing from 15% during the so-called Golden Age and plunging to 6% in 2017; furthermore, in 2020, the major non-financial capitalist corporations were sitting on over a staggering 14 trillion dollars, which means a massive amount of capital (re)converted into money, or money in a non-capitalist form, money not being reinvested into capital, capital that is no longer capital (Marx, 1964, p. 221ff; Robinson, 2022). In this sense, the system of *intellectual property*$_{(private)}$ in place is a means to secure the extraction of surplus-value, as one of the many attempts to overcome structural limitations.[1] Furthermore, data collection engenders a novel field of asserting the so-called primitive accumulation by means of data mining and total surveillance (Mueller, 2019, p. 51f) (see more *infra*). Despite the illusion of competition in the digital sphere, a massive system of monopoly capitalism has taken hold of it. According to Mariana Mazzucato, most of the planetary data are

[1] Another important attempt to overcome this crisis is the immense transfer of social wealth by the means a "sweeping militarisation of the global capitalist economy and society" (Robinson, 2020, p. 72).

owned by five US-American capitalist companies, namely, Amazon, Facebook, Google, IBM, and Microsoft (Mazzucato, 2018).

As shown, by no means was digital creation and growth, until its monopolisation, an organic process. Besides the joint venture of multiple capitalist giants and the US-American state to bring TRIPS into reality, Mazzucato also emphasises the role of the financial system and the US-American state in creating innovation and concentrating the underlying technologies of the so-called digital revolution. Social resources, channelled through the state, worked as a form of public venture capital, playing a crucial role in the R&D of new technologies. Thus, despite the myth of being a product of geniuses or private enterprises, most technologies—not only modern ones—were and are, in fact, products of collective endeavours. The greater the complexity of knowledge creation, the smaller the role of individual contribution. Public venture capital takes almost all risk and no reward, while private venture capital is left with modest risk and all the reward. It was, therefore, not the "free market" but extra-economic relations, namely, the so-called primitive accumulation, which enabled, for instance, Apple and Microsoft to rise and become capitalist tech giants.

Not only big tech but also big pharma was mostly erected on public funds. The changes in the patent system represented a qualitative break in the real subsumption of knowledge under the capitalist mode of production, from being allegedly a means of knowledge stimulation to becoming a means of controlling and blocking knowledge. Basic research was consequently engulfed by the proprietary model of knowledge. While Mazzucato unveils how this affects hepatitis, cancer, and HIV treatments, Fabienne Orsi, Christine Sevilla, and Benjamin Coriat have shown how this model affects health on a broad scale, as it also hinders testing. Patents have enabled "monopoly over the diagnostic and therapeutic activities based on genes" (Orsi et al., 2006, p. 327). The notion that privileges were conferred to inventions and not discoveries was once again blurred, making it theoretically possible for "gene sequences per se" to be patented (Nicol, 2021, p. 111). The arbitrary power over the privatisation of life has thus far attained many forms. One could argue that owning and controlling plants and animals, and even human beings in the multiple forms of slavery and servitude, have kicked off a long process of naturalisation and normalisation which culminates in the privatisation of genes. Additionally, intellectual privatisation in relation to life was already taking place at least since the nineteenth century, continuing throughout the twentieth century before the famous Diamond v. Chakrabarty case in the late twentieth century. For instance, microorganisms in the form of yeast received patents as early as in 1873. From that point on, seeds and plants were also subjected to privatisation in the form of intellectual property.

The mediation which the Internet offers contains an essential dimension within social relations. On the one hand, it provides a venue for social interaction, in which a simulation of real-life gains digital actualisation; on the other, this social interaction is deprived of actively real human sensual capacities. Of course, one could say that this is a preposterous statement because one can perceive the Digital through human sight and hearing. Nevertheless, this mediation is foremost a simulacrum. Within the digital sphere, human senses are factually shut down, for one perceives what he is allowed to perceive. One does not truly see nor hear but experiences a simulation of what one ought to see or hear. With television or radio this is much more obvious; nevertheless, the human reciprocity that the Internet enables gives the impression that one is actively asserting his agency. One does not interact with the other person but rather with the other person's simulacrum. One does not see or hear the other person but simply a simulation. It goes without saying that this assessment contains no value-judgement. It merely appreciates the limits of the Digital. This limitation, however obvious, is turned upside down and presented as actual freedom and potential to assert the individuality of the person. What remains hidden is the fact that after the real subsumption of the Internet under capitalism, it ceases to be a locus of simulated possibilities and becomes a simulacrum of the simulation, becoming the quintessence of publicity, propaganda, and control.

Often presented as a place of gift economy (contemporarily conceived as sharing economy), the illusion of free services and freedom likewise entails a double veil of simulation. Although it was initially unclear to many that free service was simply a deception, its disclosure reveals the considerable subordination of Internet users to capitalist power. While you and I—connected to any digital device with Internet access—become the commodities being bought and sold, legislators, regulators, citizens, etc. have internalised this process as part of the new normal and shown pronounced passivity vis-à-vis capitalist power. Private capital mediates not only the economic sphere of production and distribution, now, with the commodification of the user—the constant appropriation of personal data—such flexibilisation does not relate to the realm of possibilities to unfold novel social relations but rather the consolidation of precarisation beyond the mere sphere of immediate labour towards all social life (see *infra*).

Not only the big techs are deeply invested in this modus operandi. The relationship between big pharma, big tech, and the government has become so intertwined that one cannot differentiate where one begins and the other ends. The immense amount of data being produced and processed by the Digital invades the spheres of biology, which is being dissected at a molecular level and being standardised as mechanical pieces and consequently transformed into a branch of engineering. The so-called BioBricks aim "at creating artificial cells and life forms functionally indistinguishable from naturally occurring ones and interoperable with them. At its most extreme it seeks to add completely new functions" (Dutfield, 2012, p. 176). Capitalist power over life is thus surpassing the dimension of production of plants, drugs, and animals, that is, what we put in our bodies; its control now reaches the genetic and molecular compositions of the body.

Control of the biological body has not been randomly achieved. Instead, it reflects the neoliberal shaping of human behaviour and perception of concrete reality. Despite having been proven ineffective in the unconstrained creation and spreading of knowledge, *intellectual property*$_{(private)}$ actualises the neoliberal method of securing new venues of primitive accumulation to capitalism. The advancement of technology in biology does not constitute an exception. "Biotechnology patents thus expand the proprietary character of knowledge to the detriment of the intellectual commons", in other words, an "ontological commodification" (Pellizzoni & Ylönen, 2012, pp. 55, 57f). This commodification process necessarily presupposes a process of appropriation, which must thus be drawn from collective knowledge. The creation and appropriation of data banks involve surveillance and audience commodity. "Biobanks raise issues of privacy, confidentiality, consent, trust, citizen rights, civil participation and so on" (Pellizzoni & Ylönen, 2012, p. 58). Therefore, a surveillance system becomes paramount to enable the creation and actualisation of such data banks (see *infra*). This biopolitical power asserting control is not only externally imposed but also internally assimilated (Gramsci, 1971).

4.1.2 Privatisation of Life and Bio-colonialism

Gavin Mueller criticises that the category of labour is often neglected despite its centrality also in the digital space (Mueller, 2019, p. 28). Needless to say, computers enable a new qualitative dimension to labour and other social activities; nevertheless, they are still copy machines. From the side of software production, the process of rendering them more capable as tools was an activity that belonged to the sharing culture in which software was not commodified. It was only when a second generation arose, led by players such as Bill Gates, that software commodification started to gain traction and be promoted. Opposing this practice, another subculture emerged, namely, that of hackers. A 1978 court decision made sharing illegal, catalysing a process of primitive accumulation of software. Any written code became automatically copyrighted following US-American legislation. A chief achievement of the free software movement was the creation of Linux, representing the culmination of a counterattack against this privatisation process. However successful and good the intentions of the free software movement, today, even Linux has become part of capitalist production, which engulfed it for free in another "enclosure" movement while embedding it within its private productive processes.

While piracy has been attacked by legislation and practices involving intellectual property, the latter has however been complemented by biopiracy. In the United States, the Seeds Law of 2004 criminalised an ancient human tradition of saving and exchanging seeds, guaranteeing an open venue for profit extraction by capitalist giants such as Monsanto. Despite lobbying for similar legislation, India initially stood firm against it. In a second moment, however, the World Bank's lobby pressured India to dismantle its programme. The consequences were devastating. Prices skyrocketed, and livelihoods were destroyed. The Lockean mechanism of appropriation of "Terra Nullius", in which indigenous labour is completely disregarded, now became "Bio Nullius", enabling (intellectual) private appropriation of indigenous knowledge. Legitimating this practice, *intellectual property*$_{(private)}$ became an instrument of biopiracy. In 1996, knowledge exchange was further criminalised by the US-American legislation under the Espionage Act. Knowledge production and socialisation faced a double attack: piratical appropriation overseas and criminalisation at home. The Western notion of science is exceptionally narrow and arbitrary, excluding everything external that does not fit its own standard; within Western boundaries, publicly developed knowledge is then transformed into private property, forcing society to bear the cost while few private capitalist players take the spoils. For Vandana Shiva, this represents the continuity of an over 500-year-old colonial system. The fact that 75% of the compounds extracted from plants are known and used by indigenous culture is yet another great evidence of this arbitrary power control system (Shiva, 2016). Alexandra George's comparison between the Aboriginal *dreaming*, which protects the lore—communities' traditional knowledge—and the *intellectual property*$_{(private)}$ *system* further reinforces Shiva's arguments. The latter does not recognise or allow the former to actualise a social dimension despite the similarities. George considers that an incompatibility exists not because of capitalism but because they are two different bodies of law—as if the law were a thing in-itself (George, 2012, p. 267ff). The modus operandi actualising a double standard becomes unambiguous. This means that an act of piracy is regarded as unlawful only within a particular frame. Insofar as piracy is committed outside a self-asserted frame, it is not considered as such.

Capitalist exploitation comprises not only indigenous people but also Africans. Among mining, cheap labour, extraction of raw materials, and others, the intellectual property system is yet another way to ensure appropriation of surplus-value. Although colonial juridical systems were formally substituted by national ones, their substance, nonetheless, remained unaltered. According to Adebambo Adewopo, *intellectual property*$_{(private)}$ completely opposes African culture. However, his critique of the intellectual property system leaves capitalist relations untouched. *Intellectual property*$_{(private)}$ appears to be only part of neo-colonialism but not capitalism; TRIPS is, therefore, a possibility for action (Adewopo, 2016). Samuel Oddi has a very different view, in which TRIPS appears as a mechanism of imperialism. Before TRIPS, it was difficult to assert Western hegemony in *intellectual property*$_{(private)}$. International trade was placed above national interests, benefiting imperialistic capitalism (Oddi, 2016).

The separation between the private and the public accentuated by neoliberalism is the object of Keith Aoki's critique. One could say that this is not a neoliberal but a capitalist or even bourgeois feature, as Marx had already pointed out when criticising human estrangement, which enables one to be conceived as two antagonistic dimensions of *citoyen* and *bourgeois* (Marx, 1981). Aoki, however, emphasises an essential aspect of neoliberalism in which abstraction takes a qualitative leap due to the destruction of quantitative differences; for instance, "individual contracting parties or nations" are "formally equal" (Aoki, 2016, p. 197). Alternatively, as Michel Foucault points out, neoliberal Alexander Rüstow's conception of politics ignores the metabolism between human(s) and nature and in its place conceives the capitalist enterprise as the basis of life and the main constitutive element of society; that is, the individuum itself cannot be differentiated from the capitalist company, they are one and the same (Foucault, 2004, p. 153f).

This atomisation gains further accent with the implementation of the international property system, ignoring the real ontological dimension of intellectual property, that is, "new intellectual creations are formed from preexisting thoughts and ideas in a long chain stretching back into antiquity" (Aoki, 2016, p. 219). The power imposed by and derived from *intellectual property*$_{(private)}$ means controlling knowledge production and political participation. Also here, the Global North and Global South relations are shaped to benefit the Global North. TRIPS was a US-American blackmail in which trade was weaponised against weaker countries, causing erosion of national sovereignty in the Global South. According to Keith E. Markus and Jerome H. Reichman, this relationship suggests a paradoxical form: neoliberal deregulation is imposed only to assert a neoliberal regulatory body of social control (Maskus & Reichman, 2016, p. 347f).

4.1.3 Reshaping the Epistemic

When addressing Marx's theoretical formulations, Peter Drahos recognises that, for Marx, the power arising from property relations was foremost related to the question of property of the means of production. Outside the frame in which Drahos outlines his interpretation of Marxian social critique, personal and production property remains utterly undifferentiated, imparting a mystical character to social property relations. Intellectual property remains not only undifferentiated but is further subjected to atomisation "in the relations of power between individual actors" (Drahos, 2016, p. 177) and to "metaphysics" in which "abstract objects are a possible category of existence" (Drahos, 2016, p. 178). The metaphysical postulation conceals the real relations of power deriving from property relations. In the case of *intellectual property*$_{(common)}$, both the individual and social bodies concretely embody intellectual appropriation and thus intellectual property. Its material embodiment in further objects attains actualisation only in relation to the social embodiment of intellectual property. A dialectical relationship between intellectual determination, which immediately is the materiality in the body, and the social conditions, which render the true basis for its actualisation and transformation, is unequivocal. Drahos overlooks this, for he falls into a problem of pre-determination, conceiving *intellectual property*$_{(private)}$'s existence as a mystery. "The intellectual property system may reject the ontological reality of abstract objects but still retain [*sic*] the category as a convenient fiction to be used" (Drahos, 2016, p. 180).

In this sense, power does not emerge from social relations but is rather located *a priori* within the law, representing a circular logic. The abstract right appears to be its locus of existence. The socio-historical dynamics giving *intellectual property*$_{(private)}$ actuality is abstracted to the point of being postulated as an abstract object deprived of concrete existence. Its existence is simply putative. The concrete boundaries of *intellectual property*$_{(private)}$ are superseded; its only limit becomes the law in-itself.

It is Drahos' merit, nonetheless, to point out that modern marketing has become highly dependent on *intellectual property*$_{(private)}$ (which, with digitalisation, becomes even more relevant). "Without trademark law, for instance, advertising could not create the high degree of product differentiation that exists in many markets" (Drahos, 2016, p. 188). This means that contemporary commodity fetishism requires the attribution of uniqueness where there is virtually none; with it, the so-called primitive accumulation enters the realm of behaviour and perception, being shaped and controlled by means of private appropriation.

However, he fails to connect these relations to the socio-ontological dimension of the production and reproduction of life. Consequently, he misses the umbilical connection of property and intellectual property and the fact that the privatisation of the latter has become a means of securing private control over the former. As the value of knowledge production and reproduction abruptly plunges, the value of the property of the means of production also decreases while the contradiction between social production and private appropriation becomes increasingly more explicit. *Intellectual property*$_{(private)}$ appears as the means of reshaping social perception, reorganising production value, controlling the struggle of classes, and enabling capitalism to persist. It is thus impossible to understand it as something merely abstract and separated from property.

Although Bob Jessop criticises the naturalisation of the so-called knowledge-based economy, following Karl Polanyi's notion of fictitious commodity—while in Polanyi labour, land, and money appear as fictitious, in Jessop, the emphasis is on labour and knowledge—it seems that the most fundamental contradiction of capitalism extends beyond tangible to intangible production. This means that "in *class-based* modes of production", this fundamental contradiction is "between the increasing socialisation of productive forces and private control of the means of production" (Jessop, 2000, p. 64). In this sense, he naturalises the fetishised notion of intellectual property in which it takes a metaphysical, intangible, incorporeal mode of being. It follows as a corollary that intellectual property and property have two independent existences, failing to see that the consequence of this analytical separation renders credibility to the hypostasised pronouncement of a knowledge-driven mode of production.

Needless to say, the emergence of a new mode of production without addressing the issue of property is an illusion. The artificial and forced separation of property and intellectual property presupposes an even more remarkable power of the capitalist state to secure private property as two distinct modes of existence. Jessop, however, accurately situates the intellectual property system as a mechanism with which capitalism tries to come to terms with its structural crisis, namely, the debacle of the so-called Fordist-Keynesian system. In its place, a capitalist system focused on "the internationalisation of trade, investment and finance" arose (Jessop, 2000, p. 68), which enabled further private capitalist control over societies. *The international intellectual property$_{(private)}$ system* is one of its mechanisms, and international capitalist institutions—such as the World Bank, World Trade Organization (WTO), International Monetary Fund (IMF), G20, G7, World Economic Forum (WEF), Trilateral Commission, Bilderberg Group, and Bank for International Settlements (Phillips, 2018)—are another.

This neoliberal reshaping of political economy and culture simultaneously meant redefining the perception of knowledge, thus reshaping collective memory. As Philip Mirowski affirms, neoliberalism contains "a set of *epistemic* commitments" (Mirowski, 2009, p. 417). Despite neoliberal heterogeny, he suggests the existence of a commitment to basic principles and fundaments, resulting in the formation of an ideology. As György Lukács has taught: the importance of ideology is that it enables us to act together without having to debate and scrutinise every single action, for it "is above all that form of mental processing of reality which serves to make people's social practice conscious and capable of action" (Lukács, 1986, p. 398). Mirowski determines original membership in the Mont Pèlerin Society (MPS) as a criterion for being part of the neoliberal cult. Additionally, Berhard Walpen recognises the MPS's crucial role in the organisation and expansion of neoliberalism (Walpen, 2004).

Despite being often associated with economic theory, this comprises a minor aspect of neoliberalism; its rhetoric was (and still is), however, one of the most fundamental elements in its struggle for power and to reshape social perception to adhere to their contradictory and dogmatic worldviews. As Foucault has shown, neoliberalism represented an apprehensible inversion from liberalism (Foucault, 2004). Neoliberal intellectual Walter Eucken had no illusions. To become influential, ideologies require "economic power groups" ("wirtschaftliche Machtgruppen") to use and instrumentalise them "for propaganda purposes" (Eucken, 1961, p. 14).

Neoliberal doctrine formed what Ludwik Fleck calls "thought collective" (Mirowski, 2009, p. 427f); in this sense, its epistemological doctrine cannot be regarded as a rigid given fact or fixed category but rather an open-ended social category in constant transformation, adapting to historical socio-political demands. The neoliberal doctrine was very potent because it was also very flexible in its epistemological commitments to attain power. Its *irrational* character confers neoliberal epistemology a hypostasised but resilient grounding: "the impossibility of objective knowledge lies at the very heart of [Friedrich August von] Hayek's notion of the market as the ultimate prosthesis for the process of the discovery of knowledge" (Mirowski, 2009, p. 429). This occurs because considering "the limitations of individual knowledge", whose "Reason, with a capital R, does not exist in the singular", coercive power must then be limited, and is epitomised by the so-called free market (von Hayek, 1948, pp. 16, 15). On the other hand, neoliberal total relativisation of objective reality is also its Achilles' heel because the subjectification of reality, epitomising a particular form of irrationalism, cannot withstand an actual confrontation with objective reality. Karl Polanyi unequivocally denounces the double standard of the so-called free market system, which, on the one hand, is religiously professed as the result of free agency, while on the other, constantly organises and intervenes in public spheres (Polanyi, 2001). Although already present within the liberal tradition, this "liberal profession of faith" (Losurdo, 2011, p. 243)—as Domenico Losurdo calls it—is thus even further accentuated with neoliberalism.

Another layer in which the epistemic is reshaped is through what Guy Debord calls *the spectacular critique of the spectacle*, which complements the *apology of the spectacle* of the status quo (Debord, 1992b, p. 189, §196). Many writings of the young Karl Marx attacked precisely this type of theoretical posture. Instead of unveiling the limits of real relations, the spectacular critique carries a reformist posture, which only sheds light on specific problems so that the whole can remain intact, "better" functioning. It was thus not sadism that led Marx to fiercely attack G. W. F. Hegel, Pierre-Joseph Proudhon, Adam Smith, David Ricardo, Ludwig Feuerbach, Bruno Bauer, Max Stirner, among others, but a political commitment to supersede exploitation and estrangement. Reformism, on the other hand, instead of exposing the limits of given social relations, assumes a posture of attenuation of real antagonisms and contradictions, rendering them more amenable and acceptable.

Using the same critical token, Radhika Desai mows down the illusions produced by what she calls the twenty-first-century Proudhonists—for instance, Alain Badiou and Slavoj Žižek—for they redirect revolutionary energy back into petty bourgeois modus operandi, in which capitalism critique appears instead as culture critique (Desai, 2011). Another great example is Hartmut Rosa's notion of *social acceleration*. Criticising the relativisation and rigidity of contemporary society, which create a futureless world perception, his analysis reinforces the object of his critique by pulling off a somersault. In Rosa's analysis, capitalism is not the cause of this rigid and hectic reality, namely, "social acceleration", but instead, he claims that "the various phases and manifestations of capitalism can be conceived as expressions of a unified logic of acceleration" (Rosa, 2013, p. 287). This expresses an idealist rather than a materialist method of analysis. The subject-object-inversion in which reality springs out of the concept is unmistakable.

Somewhat analogous to this rigid and hectic reality, Gabriel Rockhill asserts a situation of a "temporal order with no exit" (Rockhill, 2017, p. 105). Capitalist power imposes its domination not only over the body but also over the heart and souls by enforcing their vision of the world upon the people by means of institutions such as the abstract right, thus creating a situation that I call the *perpetual present* (Hermeto, 2020). However, by criticising the overemphasis of technological impositions, Rockhill falls back in this very temporal order with no exit, as he relativises technology since so many are left out. He therefore overlooks the possible shift in the centre of gravity of dominant social relations, which in his critique must remain absolute. For instance, when Marx wrote *Capital*, capitalism was by no means omnipresent, and also most people remained outside of it; what he captures, however, is the change within the leading social dynamic, determining and considerably impacting socio-ontological relations. One should, hence, neither deify *the new* nor aprioristic repudiate it but rather try to understand how it relates to *the existing* by revealing the tendencies of the former and the limits of the latter.

4.2 Intellectual Control and the Spectacle of Surveillance

4.2.1 Fictitious Commodity and Fictitious Capital

It is not only *intellectual property*$_{(private)}$ that appears to have gained an independent reality from its socio-material determinations. With the unfolding of social relations of production in a more collective and socially intricate fashion within a vastly complex division of labour, different mechanisms of guaranteeing private appropriation and accumulation become pivotal to facing these historical transformations, thus shifting the immanent conflict imposed by social property relations within the relationship between social production and private appropriation. Social discipline imposed by schooling, policing, and behavioural modification and control by the judicial system does not suffice to contain the antagonism and contradictions provoked by capitalist relations.

Capital control departs from the immediate production process and becomes more concentrated and dependent on fictitious capital (see *supra* and *infra*). Some scholars even regard this concentration process resulting from capital's own supersession of competition as a return to feudalism. Nonetheless, restraining social relations has historically depended on other crucial mechanisms of power assertion and management. In this context, the categories of *spectacle* and *simulacra*, *propaganda* and *consent* gain enormous social relevance for understanding the social superstructure embedded within intellectual property relations.

György Lukács has shown that not only ideology is not a development which occurs independently from the material basis but also that the very idealistic and mystic development of magical and religious conceptions is knotted to a material web of social practices and needs. They are the hypostasised intellectual apprehension of concrete reality, in which the idea, concept and conception become independent and gain an ontological priority over material reality, which they derive from and immediately relate to (Lukács, 1963, 1986). "The superstitions man devised and the fictitious entities he imagined were presumably necessary to make him feel at home in his environment and to make life bearable"; nevertheless, explains Gordon Childe, this phantasy, although appearing to give humanity power over nature, in reality only delays the expediency of its real understanding (Childe, 1958, p. 186).

It would be wrong, however, to cast these fictitious relations as irrelevant, for not only do they reveal the accurate representation of human intercourse with nature but, most importantly, of humans among themselves. Fictitious capital plays a not insignificant role in capitalist power and social property relations. This formation called capitalisation (*kapitalisieren*), although purely fictional, is a protagonist category within capital control, and intellectual property is one of its enablers. The "entitlement to payments that are made in the future" (Fuchs, 2012a, p. 726) attached to fictitious capital presupposes a movement from the fictional to the real economy. In-itself, it only represents power as long as the movement to become for-itself remains latent. "This means, the power obtained through fictitious capital is translated into concrete power in the manipulation and appropriation of the real economy by the financial leveraging" (Hermeto, 2021, p. 222). This fictitious capital grants itself legitimation power to endlessly magnify itself beyond and above the real economy. While in-itself fictitious capital is void of significance, the fact that it is allowed to revert these fictitious assets into real assets, buying homes, industries, etc., prompts a spectacular display of "predatory" and "parasitic" social power (Hudson, 2015).

The same fictitious character, which grants *intellectual property*$_{(private)}$ a separate existence from property and, accordingly, control of the former over the latter, also enables the conversion of fictitious into non-fictitious capital. Moreover, in many cases, it is intellectual property itself that allows this movement. For instance, while productive capital is highly dependent on fictitious capital to flow, it would remain powerless if it could not protect its objectified capital from being copied. The example with which Adrian Johns opens his book is extremely insightful in that the multinational Tokyo-based NEC had not merely some of its products or ideas copied but "an entire parallel NEC organisation" emerged (Johns, 2009, p. 1). This unprecedented endeavour shows the indissoluble nature between material and ideal reality and how capital is a social relation.

The pirates behind the deed copied not only the brand but also emulated, replicated, and simulated its whole business model, including business cards, recruitment process, technology research and development, warranty system, transnational royalty arrangements, distribution networks, qualitative standards, etc. Moreover, they even developed material and intellectual practices further, therefore, not simply copying existing arrangements. Pirate NEC had access to the original NEC's complete relational channels. This gave them the impetus to operate unnoticed for years.

Considering normal (namely, non-pirate) arrangements, non-financial capital's constant requirement of accessing financial capital to enable both its daily and future operations then presupposes the protection of not only their brand (trademark) but also products and processes (patents) as well as computer programs, databases, technical drawings, etc. (copyright). By protecting their private property by means of *intellectual property*$_{(private)}$, non-financial capital can then turn to financial capital to obtain capital liquidity whenever needed. Under *intellectual property*$_{(private)}$ protection, financial credit obligations are less vulnerable to risk than under "free" capitalist competition. Despite having matured during the beginning of the twentieth century, this capital concentration process reached new heights one hundred years later in contemporary capitalism. Stefania Vitali, James B. Glattfelder, and Stefano Battiston revealed an existing exceptionally tight configuration of global corporate control that forms a "*bow-tie* structure" in which "the strongly connected component, or core, is very small compared to the other sections of the bow-tie, and that the out-section is significantly larger than the in-section and the tubes and tendrils" (Vitali et al., 2011, p. 3). This means that only a few hands hold control and, thus, having power over an enormous structure of capitalist relations, "in detail, nearly 4/10 of the control over the economic value of TNCs in the world is held, via a complicated web of ownership relations, by a group of 147 TNCs in the core, which has almost full control over itself" (Vitali et al., 2011, p. 4). Peter Phillips' study sheds further light on this structure in which financial giants dominated global capitalist relations. Back in 2017, actors like Blackrock and Vanguard managed over 5.4 trillion and 4.4 trillion dollars in assets, respectively, with cross-sharing between them (Phillips, 2018), almost doubling at the beginning of 2022, when BlackRock reached 10 trillion dollars in assets management (Brush & Wittenberg, 2022).

In this sense, Karl Polanyi's definition of fictitious commodity seems highly problematic. By conflating the concept with the thing and simultaneously by reducing the thing into the thing in-itself and ignoring its relational character, he asserts labour is "human activity", land is a name for "nature", and money "purchasing power", therefore entertaining that the idea that they are commodities "is entirely fictitious" (Polanyi, 2001, p. 75f). This rigid and fetishised understanding contains the transcendental metaphysical character of stipulating a truth to the thing in-itself. While labour is an activity subjected to economic imperatives, within a market, it becomes a commodity subjected to exchange. The very fact that labour is an activity means that its existence depends on determined relations and movements; its particular *Erscheinungsform* cannot be aprioristically defined but rather only within a process. Likewise, "money is not a thing but a social relation" (Marx, 1977, p. 107). Therefore, money can attain the form of a means of exchange, a general commodity form, treasure, capital, and so on. To impute fictitious as something imaginary, unreal, or artificial is to deny its social existence. Accordingly, land is not nature; instead, it is nature subjected to labour and human relations. If land and nature were identical, then no appropriation of nature could occur.

Achim Szepanski provides a much richer perception of the meaning of fictitious under capitalist relations of production. "Fictitious capital is called fictitious not because it functions as imaginary or separated from the real conditions of production, but because it specifically operates the financing of capital's relations of production with respect to future multiplication" (Szepanski, 2022, p. 89) and, as Marx underscores, this sort of capital contains "its own movement", being thus autonomous (Marx, 1964, p. 483). Fictitious capital represents not existing but rather future capital, which may or may not emerge. It is traded in both primary and secondary financial markets as financial assets, future claims, and promises of a not-yet-realised future.

The mystical character embedded within this process cannot be overly emphasised. "As non-places where the prices of securities are fixed and differentiated based on promises, expectations and speculation, financial markets enable a quasi-autonomous form of movement of capitalisation that can be described as a 'differential accumulation of fictitious capital'"

(Szepanski, 2022, p. 90). Unlike in religion, this "Market God" is not believed to be transcendental and metaphysical (Cox, 2016). However, like in religion, the underlying beliefs become real because they become the driving force, social framework, and operating limits of individual and collective action, as sensual reality appears as "an attribute of the idea" (Feuerbach, 2013, p. 39, §31). Fictitious relations based on future claims are essentially real because not only do they influence or even determine present social relations, but ontologically, they are concrete relations themselves, representing an accumulation of future claims. Not only banking capital but capitalist companies in general "can now act as issuers of securities and are thus classified as producers of fictitious capital, while speculators buy fictitious capital that can be redeemed in money at any time, i.e. it is very liquid" (Szepanski, 2022, p. 91). Szepanski highlights that private banks operate on both ends, buying and selling securities, creating fictitious capital for themselves as well as for their clients.

While Marx addressed insipient forms of fictitious capital—interest, state-debt, credit, or bond—or imaginative "property titles" (Marx, 1964, p. 484), Szepanski unveils "shares, bonds and other securities" (Szepanski, 2022). Thus, Szepanski differentiates between loans (or "interest-bearing") and fictitious capital.

> While with credit, the lent money operates for the lender by means of a legal claim for interest and repayment of a future money increase, with fictitious capital an anticipated profit is fixed as a security, which contains the legal claim for future payments for the buyer and can furthermore be traded by him. While credit is about the potency of money, which can also function as a possible profit for the borrower for which he has to pay interest, fictitious capital is about future income streams that originate from a security that the investor buys for a sum of money, for which the expected income that the security is supposed to yield is like an interest payment. In the case of fictitious capital, the borrowers no longer appear as debtors suffering from a lack of money but as issuers of securities (bonds) that in turn represent an increasing asset for the buyer, i.e. grant participation in the capital power of the issuer. While a debtor with the loan assumes the obligation to pay interest and deposit securities, the issuer/debtor of a security

gives the promise that the realisation of the promise of payment will work for the investor in the future. (Szepanski, 2022, p. 94)

Drawing on Marx, he further explains the reasoning of fictitious capital as threefold. First, instead of profits emanating from the difference between incoming revenue and costs, a prerogative of future returns is decoupled from current profits and operations. "Marx calls these securities 'fictitious capital', because they are based on the calculation of expected returns and profits". Second, these future entitlements encompass "both expected and actual payments"; however, remaining independent from realised income, their expectations are essentially primarily of metaphysical nature, which may never be actualised. Third, independently from discounts and interest rates, "a money capital flow, materialised in a security, creates different levels and scales of capitalisation" based on future predication (instead of the *secular* statistical term of *projection*) of risks, which enables the whole metaphysical process of capital valuation and self-valorisation. Thus, this self-representation of finance capital assumes all capital as fictitious capital (Szepanski, 2014, p. 51f; 2022, p. 96), to which Szepanski asserts, "[t]herefore, certain sums of fictitious capital can circulate to a certain extent independently of the differentiated accumulation of industrial capital and service or commercial capital" (Szepanski, 2022, p. 96).

4.2.2 Intellectual Property as an Economic Weapon

The tremendous power of the real subsumption of capital under financial capital upsurged relentlessly with the expansion of the shadow banking system when Bill Clinton's administration repealed the US-American Glass-Steagall Act of 1933. Still according to Szepanski, the expanded financial system that emerged from this revocation promotes the following: first, the overcoming of boundaries and restrictions based on national territoriality; second, "the opening of national economies to foreign companies"; third, easing and simplifying the inertia of the supply chain; and fourth, strengthening and stabilising competition and domination among leading multinational capitalist corporations (Szepanski, 2018, p. 54).

Moreover, these power structures that enable the flow of "money and capital streams" at "inhuman speeds" promote a boundless stream of capitalist "deterritorialization" (Szepanski, 2018, pp. 65, 115).

This dominance depends on technological primacy and control, both at the levels of, on the one hand, hardware and software and, on the other, financial infrastructure and privatised algorithms. Consequently, dominance over intellectual appropriation is paramount for the flow and control of capital. The consequences are by no means abstract. Szepanski asserts that the financial system enables an asymmetrical war. Financial weapons can be "as dangerous and destructive as military weapons"; this system must be understood as a non-military war strategy to enable the integration of "an unfettered global capitalism" (Szepanski, 2018, p. 66).

Domenico Losurdo evokes Edward Luttwak's assertion of US-American economic dominance over China to underline this aspect, namely, economic sanctions or, conversely, controlling the flow of goods and capital, is a weapon of mass destruction, for it targets entire people indiscriminately (Losurdo, 2016, p. 288). In this sense, a possible loss of the dollar and hegemonic financial control of the flow of capital could potentially catalyse an unparalleled capitalist crisis. Here, the relationship with intellectual appropriation is indisputable. As the financialisation of capitalism becomes overtly accentuated in the capitalist core, that is, "multinationals are increasingly withdrawing from direct production and focusing on brand management, product marketing, market research and property rights protection, ultimately they have become financial companies with additional industrial activities" (Szepanski, 2018, p. 72), then dominance and control over intellectual (knowledge, science, and even discourse) appropriation become an imperative necessity within the logic of capitalist surplus appropriation and accumulation. These companies "have a quasi-legal monopoly on large parts of the world's economic and technological resources, which gives them a consistent competitive advantage (high-tech research); they can exploit these resources to transfer value from the peripheries to the centres" (Szepanski, 2018, p. 74).

Luigi Pellizzoni and Marja Ylönen highlight this power in the process of gene appropriation not only of natural genetics but also in the act of creating things—namely, genetic material—that were not previously naturally existent. Therefore, reducing such relations to fictitious in the imaginary sense of Polanyi forfeits attaining its concrete reality. Instead of "an epistemic abstraction", this process is, as mentioned before, an "ontological commodification", and the capitalist commodities are "nothing fictitious" (Pellizzoni & Ylönen, 2012, p. 57). However, although the authors disregard Polanyi's conceptualisation of the fictitious, the often fictitious character of intellectual private appropriation must still be underlined. It is not only an essential warrant element within fictitious capital relations (in the financial sense) but, analogous to fictitious (financial) capital, it fundaments itself on legal claims for a future yield of something not yet realised.

Intellectual private appropriation represents control of the teleological dimension of social labour relations. It is only when teleology is set-in-motion within a process of teleological setting (*teleologische Setzung*) that it can supersede its immediate condition of in-itself (as δύναμις) and be actualised as in-and-for-itself, achieving (a second tier) concreteness (beyond its immediate material form, e.g., brain, paper, hard-drive, etc.) and (social) reality. Needless to say that this process can contain multiple moments. The very brain represents the first totality of matter and idea; paper-ink materialises another; hardware-software a third; at this level, they have realised their potential as ideas at the most abstract level and become objectified in relatively simple forms; only when further (a second, third, fourth, etc.) dimension(s) of actualisation of the teleological setting takes place that an abstractly objectified idea is metamorphosed in a qualitatively higher form of objectivity. Through additional setting(s), the still-generic-objective condition of the subjective idea becomes determinedly objectified, acquiring a particularly objectified condition and a broader subjective existence within an expanded scope of socialisation.

4.2.3 The Metaphysical Universalisation of Fictitious Commodity

Bob Jessop criticises the fixation and naturalisation of factors of production. It is thus erroneous to reproduce "the fallacy, criticised by Marx, that value is rooted in immanent, eternal qualities of things rather than in social relations" (Jessop, 2000, p. 64). However, he still reduces labour and knowledge to the category of fictitious commodities and not "real commodities" because "knowledge is a collective generated resource" (Jessop, 2000, p. 64f). This appears to be contradictory. What Marx considers fictitious is not the fact that something represents a purely social category but rather a relation based on underlying abstraction, a fiction, a metaphysical entity, ignoring time and space. Knowledge and labour are both expressions of individual and social activities and relations. They are concrete despite not possessing an immanent use-value, that is, natural properties (*Eigenschaften*), for they possess social-objective dimensions and are, accordingly, dependent on historical determinations, on simultaneously individual and social-body. If knowledge and labour were fictitious commodities, then exchange-value, which is a complete social category, would too have to be regarded as fictitious, and so would capital, which is a specific social relation in its first phenomenological form as appropriation of surplus (living) labour, since it cannot be yet regarded as objectified-dead labour.

Should this apply, no differentiation could be made between capital and fictitious capital because every capital would be fictitious. In this sense, it is wrong to assert that Marx "explored the implications for capitalism's dynamic of treating labour power *as if* it were a commodity" (Jessop, 2000, p. 65) because, under the capitalist mode of production, labour becomes *factually* a commodity. Marx criticises not an abstract commodification of labour but, instead, the actual social relations that perpetrated it. In this sense, it is equally wrong when he asserts that knowledge is not a commodity, but it is possible to theorise "the implications of treating knowledge as if it were a commodity" (Jessop, 2000, p. 65).

Therefore, his critique on "the contradiction between knowledge as intellectual commons and as intellectual property" (Jessop, 2000, p. 65) must remain superficial, for it grasps neither the commodification and privatisation of intellectual appropriation nor its fetishisation when it becomes separated from property with the rupture of their totality into two apparently independent categories. When this occurs, privatisation of knowledge becomes a necessity and, as such, a paradoxical reality. Intellectual appropriation, separated from material appropriation but still subjected to capitalist relations, comprises the same legality of private property. When independent from private property relations, the formal subsumption of knowledge gives way to real subsumption. The actualisation of knowledge paradoxically attains a double existence. It must be socially conceived and privately appropriated. Knowledge, from being result and premise, becomes just result because, privatised, it (tendentially) fails to fall back into the status of being premise. New social knowledge requires then to be created *ex nihilo*. The necessity of privatisation in a second step lacks the object of privatisation. While privatisation of knowledge does not exhaust knowledge, its reprivatisation does not confer any new moment of appropriation. Reprivatisation of knowledge expresses in reality Hegel's identity of pure-being and pure-nothingness (Hegel, 1986) (see *supra*).

Finally, Ngai-Ling Sum and Bob Jessop also emphasised that labour power is a fictitious commodity. They point to Marx's *Capital First Volume* and Polanyi's *The Great Transformation* as (general) sources of this. While in Polanyi this feature is present, in Marx it is not. Here, however, the grounding becomes clearer. On the one hand, they criticise labour power as being regarded as "a commodity like any other"; on the other hand, labour power *should* then be regarded "as if it were a commodity" (Sum & Jessop, 2013, p. 263f). The mistake appears to derive again from the isolation of one factor, which buries the contradiction. Labour power is factually bought and sold, and the absence of the means of production by workers, which concomitantly means the private means of production in the hands of the capitalists, imposes this social relation upon the labourer. This is a concrete historical condition. Marx's analysis reveals that this relation is not fictitious but that the fiction occurs at the level of exploitation.

While labour power is bought and sold, it would make no sense for the capitalist to pay the labourer its value. Thus, Marx unveils that the so-called secret of surplus-making, in other words, "the formation of surplus-value by means of surplus labour is not a secret" (Marx, 1962, pp. 189, 257). This shows that labour power is not only subjected to a labour market as a commodity, but the contradiction occurs because while it is subordinated to market exchange, its commodification carries with itself its denial because it is not exchanged for its equivalent value.

Equivalent-exchange of labour power would make this very act redundant, meaningless, in a word, fictional.

While Marx reveals that the notion of equivalency is an abstraction, the subsumption of labour under capital is, however, a historical reality; the justificatory discourse of political economy asserting a correspondent exchange between capitalist and labour is a fiction, the labourer's reification is real. By the same token, the authors also reduce knowledge to a "fictitious commodity that depends for its valorisation on a broad range of extra economic supports" (Sum & Jessop, 2013, p. 284). This misses the point because although social-collective production is the existential condition of knowledge production, under capitalist relations, when separated from private property, intellectual appropriation becomes simultaneously existentially conditioned by private appropriation. The first paradox, in which knowledge is produced by society and privately appropriated by capital, is perceived by Sum and Jessop; the second paradox, in which knowledge itself simultaneously requires being socially produced as a general ontological condition and privately actualised as its particular ontological condition, goes unnoticed.

It is, however, Jessop's merit to summarise the state's role in such relations. First, the accentuation of the contradiction between the social character of production and private appropriation of its results should be managed. Second, given the obliteration of the value of knowledge, making it thus more accessible, to readapt how economic and extra-economic spheres relate. Third, supervising the process of knowledge commodification and the roles of intellectual and manual labour. Fourth, as the dimensions of time and space are differently lived and perceived, the processes of "(de/re)territorialisation and (de/re)temporalisation" need oversight. Finally, administering the socio-political consequences of the "structural contradictions" within this accumulation process (Jessop, 2000, p. 72f).

4.2.4 Feudalism-Capitalism-Feudalism: Historical Boomerang

What I am here calling a *historical boomerang* reveals the contradiction of a particular set of theorisations, which goes beyond, literally abandons an indirect legitimation of capitalism, yet, at the same time, in its critique, ends up eliminating the very crucial element that it ought to discuss. Insofar as there is no capitalism anymore, according to these theories, at least not as the principal contradiction of social relations, these proponents could not sustain the notion of an eternisation of capitalism represented by the *perpetual present* because we would already be living in a post-capitalism period.

If social relations have abandoned a capitalist orientation, what has then become the principal social contradiction? Cédric Durand and Yanis Varoufakis reframe the current system as techno-feudalism (Durand, 2020; Varoufakis, 2020). Their main point focuses on the immense power the giant tech companies have obtained, where all social practices are subjected to the will of only a few social actors, thus resembling the feudalist power that feudal lords exercised. However, the problem with this understanding lies not merely in the concept but rather in the historical understanding of capitalist relations.

Additionally, repeating the long-established narrative that equates the development of the bourgeois society with capitalism, Jürgen Habermas understands the development of the bourgeois private sphere as the moment in which feudal society moves towards capitalist society. The separation between the private and the public is what determines, for Habermas, the pivotal moment beyond feudal relations. Thus, when the "private and public sphere could not be clearly distinguished", then the "public's rational-critical debate also became a victim of this 'refeudalisation'" (Habermas, 1990, p. 246). This misconception of what constitutes capitalism creates a caricature that hinders differentiating capitalist social relations from other socio-historical arrangements.

However, even though the authors mentioned provide—not only in these referenced works but also throughout their whole intellectual legacies—many fundamental insights into the understanding of contemporary society by means of critical social analyses, there are two problems with such a capitalist critique.

First, it concerns the problem of irreversibility: a reversal into feudal relations would be ontologically impossible, for the actual processes of existence—whether merely natural or also cultural—are in constant motion and, accordingly, change. Thus, the past never repeats itself; the motion of history is, therefore, irreversible. Second, it does not tackle the centrality of the capitalist system, namely, the idiosyncrasy of its relations of production, or, in other words, the [exclusive] private property of the means of production, which is precisely what represents the peculiarity of the capitalist system, as brilliantly analysed by Ellen Meiksins Wood from a historical perspective (Wood, 2017). The latter, namely, capitalist relations of production, already contain the embryo for the immense contemporary power now held by only a few political-economic actors.[2] Competition—as a social relation imperative within the logic of the incessant accumulation of capital, in turn, as an end-in-itself—puts forward an ever-growing concentration of political-economic power in the hands of ever fewer actors and drives all "losers" out of dominant capitalist relations, turning them into its source of wealth through its all-encompassing exploitation. Therefore, the ubiquity of power in the hands of a few is another element of the *perpetual present* and not a feature of dissent towards techno-feudalism. When using aspects of their analyses to initially deny capitalism's *perpetual present*, one finds, on the contrary, essential elements for its confirmation.

Durand emphasises "what feudalism, slavery and capitalism have in common. In all three configurations, legal ownership of at least some of the assets essential for production is monopolised by a dominant class" (Durand, 2020, p. 199). However, in doing so, he falsely equates distinct social relations: first, it is not the (partial) monopoly of the legal property (ownership) that determines the relations of exploitation, with which the dominant class simultaneously subordinates other classes as well as guarantees its power, for property is not a relation arising from legal relations but rather its opposite, legal relations may legitimate specific property

[2] For the contemporary immense concentration of wealth and capital, see for instance: (Phillips, 2018; Vitali et al., 2011).

relations; second, the existence of these three modes of production and exploitation encompasses different forms of social property relations, especially with capitalism, where for the first time in history, the exclusive private property of the means of production arose. However, it is not a legal arrangement that enabled the emergence of exclusive private property relations but rather a historical process of social relations of power, which, at the time of its emergence, went against social and legal traditions in England. It was only after a significant portion of the existing dominant class had also become a property class, namely, owners of the land as the means of production, that their influence could grow enough for the law and legal arrangements to be changed accordingly; hence, the private property of the means of production as a juridical institution matched only a posteriori the emerging but already ongoing dominant power relations (Marx, 1962; Wood, 2017).

The reverberation of idealised forms of capitalism repeatedly focuses on particular capitalist phenomena and elements, often ignoring their essence. Alternatively, idealistic forms of capitalism encompass an essence in the metaphysical sense, namely, an ahistorical capitalism that transcends time and space and is hence subjected to purification. The significance of this problem cannot be emphasised enough. Only when specifically capitalist relations and conditions are abstracted can one perform a substitution of concepts dogmatically postulating a change in reality; alternatively, the concept encompasses a truth so rigid that when reality changes, the former must remain true while the latter appears to be false.

The common mistake that authors such as Habermas make when equalising the bourgeois society with capitalism has a long historical tradition within historical-social theory; however, as Wood shows, it does not withstand a historical investigation. Alternatively, the false claim that capitalism is the so-called free market also cannot endure historical inquiry. The latter is used to justify both the peculiarity of capitalism and the culmination of history in capitalism as its final phase. However, markets are neither peculiar to capitalism, for they have existed in many eras and were part of different modes of production such as slavery and feudalism, and, most importantly, they do not represent a mode of production but rather simply a specific form of the social distribution of resources; nor are markets natural—for, within capitalism, not only many social relations occur outside of and beyond the market sphere and relations, thus, they have no correspondence to any of its practices, but also many societies in the history of humankind organised themselves without any market form, for instance, gift economies (see the chapter Societies and Economic Systems, in: Polanyi, 2001).

On the other hand, the development of the bourgeois society did not contain capitalist relations in-itself; instead, out of the many forms of feudalism—yes, for feudalism was not a homogenous form of society—different forms of social organisations emerged that did not rise above feudal property relations, including the French Absolutism, Florine Renaissance, the Dutch Republic, etc. (Wood, 2022, p. 25). Thus, the notion that the bourgeoisie and commerce were the drivers for the origin of capitalism is merely an abstraction. Therefore, the thesis about the so-called commercialisation model fails to explain why the most developed commercial nations did not evolve to become capitalist societies before England or why England, one of the least commercially developed nations, rose to become the first and most influential capitalist force. The profit of commerce, or alienation profit, has a different quality than the profit of production. Thus, as Wood brilliantly puts it, these theories assume what they need to explain.

In his novel, Varoufakis creates a utopian possibility of a parallel reality that would have approached the central problems of power in our contemporary social reality, which conversely appears as a dystopia. The social perils portrayed in his novel, which are familiar to our current non-fictive reality, emblematically expose the enormous powers—monopolistic, political, cultural, etc.—that the so-called big banks and giant tech companies have consolidated. The "predation of the tech giants" is thus named "techno-feudalism" (Varoufakis, 2020, p. 146). His condemnation claims that even liberal values "could [not] condone big tech's mass manipulation techniques nor defend its gains as a fair reward for entrepreneurship", for their profits are enabled "by a species of techno-feudalism that made billions of people work for it for free" (Varoufakis, 2020, p. 144f).

Insofar as Varoufakis does not address the social relations of property, then only a moral condemnation appears possible, as it hides the true character of capitalist relations of exploitation that not only has had a long history of manipulation of the masses (see *infra*) but also has always relied upon the appropriation of unpaid labour hours to "create" profit of production. Needless to say, such "mystery" has, since Marx's *Capital*, become exceptionally clear (Marx, 1962). Consequently, Varoufakis' critique of capitalism becomes its apology since he fosters the notion that true capitalism contains competition, which prevents predation. At the same time, the predatory ethos experienced in most contemporary societies would be the product of a novel development beyond capitalism, namely, the so-called techno-feudalism.

4.2.5 De-ontologising Political Economy('s Critique)

Armed with cultural critique, Jean Baudrillard, unlike Guy Debord, deontologises both the concrete practice and the critical theoretical framework of the historical determinations of political economy. This becomes blatantly clear in his assertion that today "*the critique of political economy is basically completed*"; thus, "*we are exactly at the same point with respect to Marx*" (Baudrillard, 1975, p. 51). This assertion presupposes both a rigid reality and a steady historicity. He thus ignores the historical fact that the social basis is in permanent change and that social property relations are constantly mutating. Insofar as it is impossible to conceive capitalism as unvarying relations, it is wrong not only to assert that the state of the critique of today could be the same as in Marx's time but also to postulate any possibility of completion.

After Marx's thorough analyses of the first and second volumes of *Capital*, the opening paragraph of the third volume asserts: "The formations of capital, as we develop them in this book, thus gradually approach the form in which they appear on the surface of society, in the action of the various capitals on one another, in competition, and in the ordinary consciousness of the agents of production themselves" (Marx, 1964, p. 33). Thus, this conveys the idea that reality entails an infinitely more complex dimension than theory could ever converge into. As long as capitalist relations develop further, it is immanently impossible for any capitalist critique to become unchallengeable. Even the idea that a critique could exhaust its object when it became itself socially exhausted is preposterous—for instance, while religion lost its centrality in organising societies, Ludwig Feuerbach's accurate critique could only show its limits under specific conditions and not immanently—because not only does the old mutate and become part of the new, but the new imposes new peculiar determinations on the old—for instance, Harvey Cox's critique of the Market as God. Although Baudrillard's social critique appears itself de-ontologised, it is, in fact, a historical product and not conceived in some social vacuum.

His social critique in *Simulacra and Simulation* is revealing because it teaches important lessons while not being able itself to break out from it—exactly what he accuses Marx of doing in *The Mirror of Production*. When practical reality is blinded by discourse and appearance, when phenomenological existence appears to supersede substance, then distinguishing between false and true, or simulation and reality becomes impossible. When reference is negated and substituted by total relativisation, then pure being, pure nothingness, pure totality, and pure abstraction become one and the same as well as void of form and content. Simulation thus appears to be a paradoxical reality. However, reality cannot be unreal. In this sense, such perception contains a simulated reality in which truth and fabrication become so intertwined that they are rendered indistinguishable (Baudrillard, 1981, pp. 13f, 16f). Contemporary reality mediated by the media, which is only deemed authentic with the mediatic seal of approval, becomes ritualistically subdued to a hyperreality. Despite its concrete importance, this simulacra subtracted from historical-ontological determination abolishes the "*medium*" and, with it, the "society of the spectacle" (Baudrillard, 1981, pp. 38f, 51f). On the other hand, for Guy Debord, the spectacle "is nothing more than the economy developing by itself" (Debord, 1992b, p. 22, §16). Only by removing this historical-ontological condition of the capitalist mode of production is Baudrillard able to postulate a *medium*-less reality.

Publicity's take-over of "all modes of [human] expression" (Baudrillard, 1981, p. 131) subtracts them of meaning, depth, critical sense, etc., imposing upon them the shallowness and meaningless form and content of publicity and propaganda. However, why does this process, in which human expressions become simulations, occur if the spectacle has been superseded? Contradictory Baudrillard evokes the commodity-logic only to assert that "political economy, in a literal sense, is at last fully realised, i.e. dissolved as a specific instance (as a historical mode of social contradiction), resolved, absorbed in a language without contradictions, like a dream, because it is permeated by simply superficial intensities" (Baudrillard, 1981, p. 132). Again, he sustains a completion of political economy, thus depriving and removing contradictions from social reality expressed in language; alternatively, a contradictory reality utterly neutralised by a self-consistent language. Although the dimension of power imposes this propagandistic veil, social reality constantly punctures this ideological cloth with holes through which social contradictions emerge and are thus continuously perceived, flooding social discourse and contaminating publicity's purity and superficiality with real challenges of concrete everyday life.

Instead, Baudrillard sees a fusion between both in such a manner that total publicity becomes inexistent publicity—therefore, social life becomes apolitical, a mere moment of commodity inertia, and politics endures dissuasion (Baudrillard, 1981, pp. 131ff, 93ff). This total control necessarily affects the human psyche, which anguishes and physically decays because physical health—even for those to be slaughtered or exploited—requires some level of mental health (Baudrillard, 1981, p. 187ff). But how do possibilities emerge out of this closed, totalised model? If Baudrillard, on the one hand, suggests that "nihilism" destroys the "appearances" and "senses"—for he himself is a nihilist (Baudrillard, 1981, p. 229), which means "to take, to the unbearable limits of hegemonic systems, this trace of irritation and violence, this challenge to which the system is summoned to answer by its own death, then I am a terrorist and nihilist in theory"—but the system is itself nihilist and neutralises any destructive nihilism, making things insoluble (Baudrillard, 1981, p. 233f). Baudrillard's assessment is thus a spectacular critique: it contests power relations only to reassert them as immutable, only to affirm that challenging them is futile.

4.2.6 *Être, Avoir, Paraître*

As briefly touched upon, when Debord theorises about *The Society of the Spectacle*, he not only does not disregard the economy but understands the spectacle as a directly embedded feature within and a product of economic relations. Therefore, when asserting that the world of images has become autonomous, he also refrains from hypostasising the spectacle, as this universalisation, this dominance, this "abuse of a world of vision" represents a "worldview which objectified itself" (Debord, 1992b, pp. 15f, 17; §2, §5). The unity of the world also characterises a cleavage between reality and image. The dialectical relationship is indisputable. "The social practice, before which the autonomous spectacle is placed, is also the real totality which contains the spectacle" (Debord, 1992b, p. 18; §7). What Feuerbach called subject-predicate-inversion gains full breadth through these autonomous relations. While at a general ontological level, the mode of *being* (*être*) represents a necessity of realising social activities, material development also enabled a second ontological dimension, in which the mode of *having* (*avoir*) obtained a social dimension of dominance over the being (Debord, 1992b, p. 22; §17).

Marx draws attention to this fact in the *Economic and Philosophic Manuscripts of 1844* as well as in *Capital* when quoting and analysing an excerpt of William Shakespeare's *Timon of Athens* (Marx, 1962, p. 146f; 1968, p. 563f). The possession of Gold makes "Black white, foul fair, wrong right, Base noble, old young, coward valiant" (Shakespeare, 2004, p. 268). However, this socio-ontological condition, namely, in which possession of money empowers one to enforce social relations which lacking these particular relations would not have been possible, gives way to a third mode of social relations, namely, *appearing* (*paraître*) (Debord, 1992b, p. 22; §17). *Appearing* to have, or to be, confers a reward to those who neither *are* nor *have*. The *image* of (being, doing, or having) something appears to gain, in many instances, ontological priority over its underlying representative; the absence of the latter does impede representation from attaining a socially hypostasised and independent reality.

Following Debord, the deficiency of cohesion at a material level of domination imposes the need for this separation between material and mental domination. The spectacle sacralises the relations, which are then contested at a material level. The *possibilities for action* are encapsulated within a framework of *permissibility*. Material dominance becomes not only intellectual but also communicative dominance. Horizontal and dialectical knowledge and communication among producers (labourers) become vertical and unidimensionally imposed top-down from the owners to the rest. These concrete power relations are fogged by and within the spectacle. "The economic system founded on isolation is a *circular production of isolation*" (Debord, 1992b, p. 29f; §28). The level of estrangement ("alienation") upsurges, as his own reality is subsumed under the spectacle, the human-being becomes the spectator of his own life in this "permanent Opium War", in which the more estranged ("alienated") one is, the more satisfied he becomes (Debord, 1992b, pp. 31ff, 40f, 41f; §30, §31, §32, §43, §44).

> The lack of logic—that is, the loss of the possibility of immediately recognising what is important and what is secondary or out of purpose; what is incompatible, or, on the contrary, could be a good complement; all that a given consequence implies and what, for that very reason, it prevents—this disease, has been deliberately injected in high doses into the population by the *anaesthetist-reanimators* of the spectacle. (Debord, 1992a, p. 48)

Consequently, Debord suggests that subordination to capitalist irrationalism driven by the spectacle is not a purely causal result but an intentionally imposed procedure. Does this have a historical foundation?

4.2.7 Propaganda and the Necessary Manipulation of the Masses

The emergence of the spectacle was not, however, an organic, spontaneous phenomenon. Although this is not the place for a thorough investigation, it is worth touching upon the manipulation and creation of social consent by means of propaganda (and publicity). Despite advocating for race distinctions and superiority among human beings, Gustave Le Bon portrays another layer of social difference, namely, what he calls the *crowd*, and which emerges "under certain given circumstances, and only under those circumstances", namely, when humans are agglomerated, "present[ing] new characteristics very different from those of the individuals composing it", then a "collective mind is formed" (Bon, 2002, p. 1f).

For him, this is a biological fact, despite the existence of different crowd categories due to racial and situational differences (Bon, 2002, p. 3). He asserts that a general characteristic of crowds is that they "are always unconscious", in other words, "the part played by the unconscious in all our acts is immense, and that played by reason very small" (Bon, 2002, p. vi). Hypostasising and subjectifying history, he then claims it is mere appearance that historical transformations are products of "political transformations", but instead, "the real cause is generally seen to be a profound modification in the ideas of the peoples" (Bon, 2002, p. ix). For Le Bon, the amalgamation of people does not represent a simple summing-up of individuals; comparing it to chemistry, he asserts that the aggregate possesses unique qualitative differences that isolated individuals lack (Bon, 2002, pp. 4, 6f).

The crowd bewitches the individual "in a special state, which much resembles the state of fascination in which the hypnotised individual finds himself in the hands of the hypnotiser" (Bon, 2002, p. 7). The hypostasis is blatant, as if Robinsonaded individuals were natural facts, as if individual consciousness could exist and arise independently from social relations and conditions. He ahistorically concludes "that the crowd is always intellectually inferior to the isolated individual" (Bon, 2002, p. 9). Although individual survival in isolation is an ontological impossibility because the reproduction of the individual presupposes the reproduction of the species, and even though social joint intentionality and cooperation represent a higher form of social development and intelligence than individualistic-egoistic intentionality from the great apes (see *supra*), Le Bon insists upon crowd stupidity, driven by images, being unable to perceive contradictory ideas due to "its complete lack of the critical spirit" (Bon, 2002, p. 30f).

His judgement is best epitomised when comparing the crowd's "incapacity of reason" to "inferior forms of evolution—women, savages, and children" (Bon, 2002, p. 10f). These assertions echo those of Sigmund

Freud, who considered that the "masses are lazy and unintelligent; they have no love for instinctual renunciation, and they are not to be convinced by argument of its inevitability;" therefore, "it is just as impossible to do without control of the mass by a minority as it is to dispense with coercion in the work of civilisation" (Freud, 1961, p. 7). This, in turn, mirrors Adolf Hitler's understanding, who unapologetically determines: "The absorptive capacity of the great mass is very limited, the understanding small, but the forgetfulness great" (Hitler, 1927, p. 198). Like Freud and Hitler, Le Bon believes in controlling and imposing an "active persuasion on crowds" (Bon, 2002, p. 44). Their beliefs depend on race, traditions, time, political and social institutions, instruction and education, which constitute the so-called remote factors of crowds' opinions and beliefs (Bon, 2002, p. 43ff), while images, words, formulas, illusions, and experience are immediate factors (Bon, 2002, p. 61ff). Due to their dogmatic beliefs and incapacity to reason, crowds must be led by leaders with prestige using the methods of affirmation, repetition and contagion (Bon, 2002, p. 72ff).

Following the steps of Le Bon, Freud, and others, Edward Bernays claims that despite [enlightenment's] promises that the masses foregoing the [feudal] power of kings would become king, that is, they would rule themselves, the reality was much different. "The minority has discovered a powerful help in influencing majorities. It has been found possible so to mould the mind of the masses that they will throw their newly gained strength in the desired direction. In the present structure of society, this practice is inevitable" (Bernays, 1928, p. 19). Propaganda is, according to him, a necessary means to social actualisation under capitalism, whether "in politics, finance, manufacture, agriculture, charity, education, or other fields" (Bernays, 1928, p. 19f). Behaviour control thus reshapes social practices and perceptions.

> Universal literacy was supposed to educate the common man to control his environment. Once he could read and write, he would have a mind fit to rule. So ran the democratic doctrine. But instead of a mind, universal literacy has given him rubber stamps, rubber stamps inked with advertising slogans, with editorials, with published scientific data, with the trivialities of the tabloids and the platitudes of history, but quite innocent of original

> thought. Each man's rubber stamps are the duplicates of millions of others, so that when those millions are exposed to the same stimuli, all receive identical imprints. (Bernays, 1928, p. 20)

This process of indoctrination towards particular notions is then called propaganda. Already in 1923, he emphasised the ubiquitous dimension of propaganda to such a degree that the most well-informed people would not even know or notice it. Propaganda is hidden under the veil of spontaneous everyday happenings and news. Public opinion is thus shaped according to the interest of the few; people's consent is achieved without having to be won over, for they are instead imposed. "Modern propaganda is a consistent, enduring effort to create or shape events to influence the relations of the public to an enterprise, idea or group", defines Bernays, to which he adds, "this practice of creating circumstances and of creating pictures in the minds of millions of persons is very common. Virtually no important undertaking is now carried on without it" (Bernays, 1928, p. 25). Cementing total obedience is a vital matter that has to be incessantly and unanimously imposed as if people were soldiers of military regiments who must follow orders without flinching.

4.2.8 Public Relations and Behavioural Control: Engineering of Consent

The very notion of propaganda must be propagandised under the banner of *Public Relations*, in Bernays words, the *engineering of consent*. Insofar as Bernays sees public relations' crucial and peculiar element to be the very relation it establishes between itself and society, one could broadly understand public relations not as a set of techniques but as a set of particular social relations. "Public relations is the attempt, by information, persuasion, and adjustment, to engineer public support for an activity, cause, movement, or institution" (Bernays, 1955, p. 3f). Public relations is not so much about the tools—"selection of lists, rules for copy preparation", etc.—but rather "the guiding philosophy, the basic techniques which enable the tools to be used efficiently" (Bernays, 1955, p. 3).

The ideologised character of public relations is first already posited within its professional operatives. Bernays compares its so-called dispassionate approach and methods to "those of engineering professions which stem from the physical sciences" (Bernays, 1955, p. 4). Insofar as he considers what he and his colleagues are writing to derive from this so-called engineering approach, *propaganda and mystification are not simply the result of engineering consent but its premise.*

After modern propaganda had already established itself throughout the First World War, "public relations practitioners are found today in industry, government, the arts, and the sciences" (Bernays, 1955, p. 4). Deriving from the totalising conflict of the World War, modern propaganda becomes a vital tool for managing the struggles imposed by capitalist competition. This means not only disputes among capitalists to gain market share, appropriate profits, and accumulate capital but also the immanent struggle between capital and labour, on the one hand, and among labourers competing for the means of survival and social assertion, on the other. "The American government and numerous patriotic agencies developed a technique which, to most persons accustomed to bidding for public acceptance, was new" (Bernays, 1928, p. 27). This technique aimed not simply at isolated individuals but targeted authoritative figures who conveyed messages to thousands, even hundreds of thousands if not millions at once (Bernays, 1928, p. 49).

The psychological control of the masses contains many dimensions. Two crucial ones are discourse and aesthetics. "In art as in politics the minority rules, but it can rule only by going out to meet the public on its own ground, by understanding the anatomy of public opinion and utilising it" (Bernays, 1928, p. 141). Moreover, the propagandistic apparatus must likewise capture other levels of knowledge exchange and production. On the one hand, science becomes so intertwined with the interests of capital that it cannot differentiate between knowledge production to general-social development and privatised knowledge for profits and control. "The industrial interests can furnish to the schools, the colleges and the postgraduate university courses the exact truth concerning the scientific progress of our age" (Bernays, 1928, p. 148). On the other hand, media has not only been captured, for it is heavily dependent on publicity revenues, but on occasions media giants are already owned by capitalist giants. As a result, all the means of communication available become subjected to propaganda. "There is no means of human communication which may not also be a means of deliberate propaganda" (Bernays, 1928, p. 150). Science and media often push propaganda together, creating the perception of an *expert opinion* (Bernays, 1955, p. 9).

Before the Internet, ideas were already being spread at historically unprecedented speed due to "new instruments of transportation and mass communication" such as "airplane, radio, movies, television" (Bernays, 1955, p. 5). Social complexity became fertile ground for public relations, as a specific activity within the social division of labour, to unfurl broadly. Social and individual behaviour had to be not only controlled but also directed and determined. According to Bernays, the growth of recognition in social sciences as authoritative discourse also legitimised public relations' authority. Public relations (as well as the military) "use[s] the findings of social sciences for the benefit of business and other sectors of society", including "psychology, sociology, anthropology, social psychology", "psychiatry, and psychoanalysis", etc. (Bernays, 1955, p. 6). Hence, scientific investigations on human behaviour are used as and translated into instruments for human behaviour control and manipulation ("adjustment, information, and persuasion" (Bernays, 1955, p. 7)) by governments and businesses (capital).

4.2.9 Consent Without Consent

The system of manipulation advocated by Bernays is unapologetically criticised by Edward S. Herman and Noam Chomsky in their well-known book *Manufacturing Consent.* The mass media plays a not unimportant role in this system. "It is their function to amuse, entertain, and inform, and to inculcate individuals with the values, beliefs, and codes of behaviour that will integrate them into the institutional structures of the larger society" (Herman & Chomsky, 1994, p. 1). This larger apparatus in which people must be ideologically integrated is the capitalist mode of production, which materially divides people into multiple classes, producing the condition of estrangement of the self and society laid down by Marx (see *supra*). "In a world of concentrated wealth and major conflicts of class interest, to fulfil this role requires systematic propaganda" (Herman & Chomsky, 1994, p. 1).

This propaganda system must also be understood as a system of censorship, which is perpetrated both by the capitalist state and capitalist private companies. On the one hand, the sophisticated level of coordination among state, mass media, and private capital, and the methodical manufacturing of consent, imposing the elite's values and power upon the many, is achieved by what Herman and Chomsky call news "filters". On the other hand, while daily knowledge was merely formally subsumed under capital, an alternative press representing the interests of the non-proprietary class—the labour class—was still a reality. With the assertion of the real subsumption of the press under capital, the economic imperative imposed existential conditions that the alternative press could just not meet.

The mass of capital invariably creates an entry barrier in any capitalist sector; in the mediatic sector it is no different. The first filter occurs through the process of concentration of capital, in which oligopolies and virtual monopolies enable a substantial centralisation of power by a top tier.[3] Smaller media outlets are then fed by giant media discourse, producing a repetition and reaffirmation and forfeiting the role of investigative journalism—one could call this the *parrot model.* The processes of merger, acquisition and fusion overflow the immediate mediatic sector, in which capitalist powers have a very close relationship with the media—when not directly purchasing them. Herman and Chomsky note both the relevant number of outside directors who simultaneously have directorships in banks and companies. It goes without saying that the interlock goes further as "all do business with commercial and investment bankers, obtaining lines of credit and loans, and receiving advice and service in selling stock and bond issues and in dealing with acquisition opportunities and takeover threats" (Herman & Chomsky, 1994, p. 10).

The profit motive is thus indisputable. At the time the authors wrote the book, a telling example of this entanglement was that the controlling capital of NBC, namely, GE (General Electrics), was also in the business

[3] A great example is a study about contemporary German mediatic space by the Munique based Institut für sozial-ökologische Wirtschaftsforschung e.V. (In: Ferschli et al., 2019).

of producing atomic bombs. On the regulatory dimension, the authors also point out the interconnection between private and state actors, enabling capitalist power assertion despite the public discourse about regulation and oversight of power abuse. The ties between state and corporate individuals also become apparent when the revolving-door relationship is taken into account, in which, on many occasions, the very same people supposed to supervise and regulate abuse of private power and concentration start working for these very actors subjected to regulation. Obviously, the revolving-door relationship is not a phenomenon monopolised by the media and propaganda apparatus but instead broadly occurs between capitalist states and capitalist companies all through different sectors (Herman & Chomsky, 1994, pp. 13, 24, 50; Robinson, 2014, p. 195; Rodney, 2018, p. 203). The fusion between government and media interests is evident; the government overlooking its regulatory roles is possible when the media also asserts and reaffirms government narratives; furthermore, government spending is a crucial source of the media's revenue, and at the same time, the media is a vital vehicle of governmental propaganda.

The second filter builds on this contingency, namely, advertisement. Non-mainstream media, in other words, a press that can represent workers' interests by being inserted within this logic, is doomed to fail because without advertising revenues it becomes virtually impossible to fund mediatic production as well as investigatory news and diffusion. Pirate radios were, in the past, a low-cost mechanism to disseminate some messages. However, its very piratic character imposed the necessity of flying under the radar and, consequently, not allowing itself to become known, automatically limiting the spread of the message. Before advertising invaded journalism, sold newspapers had to cover production costs. Advertisement changed this barrier as a new flux of revenue covered production costs from the outset, selling prices could now be dumped, eliminating competitive voices with no access to advertisement. Despite the exaltation of the free market economy, the coming together of these heterogeneous capitalist interests places their economic constraints above market competition. "The ad-based media receive an advertising subsidy that gives them a price-marketing-quality edge, which allows them to encroach on and further weaken their ad-free (or ad-disadvantaged) rivals" (Herman & Chomsky, 1994, p. 14).

By default, a real alternative media does not receive advertising revenue because it must uncompromisingly denounce governmental and capitalist ills alike, as any other veiled social practices. With the destruction of the value of knowledge production caused by the emergence of the Internet coupled with smartphones and relatively low-priced computers, in recent years, a revival in independent media has started to emerge, which—to a certain extent—remains a hostage of capital.[4] In turn, big tech cannot just be regarded as a tech company, or media outlet, or publisher, etc. These companies are not only embedded in the Pentagon and other governmental institutions and projects but, as the twitter files revealed, government and tech-companies have a profoundly symbiotic relationship of propaganda, censorship, and regulatory flight; they not only host information and publish it but also curate it and have many ongoing parallel projects that require positive public relations and good relationships with financial capital and government (Fung, 2022; Fang, 2023; Linge & Levine, 2022; Taibbi, 2023). Deflection from the narrative consensus, either imposed by private or state advertisements, does not go unnoticed and is severely punished. Not only might journalists be sacked, but entire funding may be withdrawn. Censorship is likewise not always externally imposed. In many situations, it becomes internalised. This practice then becomes indirect (or self-preemptive) censorship. The mediatic content is yet further censored. In addition to provoking the proactive preoccupation of impeding critical content that may trigger any abandonment from advertisers, the latter "will want, more generally, to avoid programs with serious complexities and disturbing controversies that interfere with the 'buying mood'" (Herman & Chomsky, 1994, p. 17).

The government is not only a crucial source of revenue but also a significant cradle of content, constituting the third filter. As investigating or even fabricating news is time- and resource-consuming, governmental feeds of rumours, breaks, leaks, events, etc., portray a significant

[4] For instance, the big techs, such as Google, Facebook (now Meta), and financial capital which control the flux of payments.

reduction in costs. Economic subordination suppresses investigatory zeal and is a necessary subservience to governmental discourse. Besides the many examples from Herman's and Chomsky's books, uncountable life-and-death events have been propagandised by private media parroting governmental assessments. With its immense reach, the capitalist press provides government discourse with the perfect channel for public relations (propaganda). Such a vast reach implies broad influence.

Three contemporary examples: *First*, it is publicly acknowledged that the war in Afghanistan that officially lasted 20 years (2001–2021)—although still ongoing by means of proxies, militias, airstrikes, drone attacks, etc.—was not only illegal but groundless. NATO's presence was also there. It is notorious that Bill Clinton's administration illegally used NATO to wage war against Yugoslavia, thus creating a new breach of precedent for the illegal use of military force by an organisation designed solely for defensive purposes and whose *raison d'être* had already ceased to exist when the Soviet Union collapsed. *Second*, it is also well known that the war against Iraq in the 2000s was not only illegal but was based on lies—there were no weapons of mass destruction in Iraq. *Third*, it is also public knowledge that the so-called first Iraq War was also based on yet another lie. Nayirah's case was a notorious but sophisticated lie. As Iraq annexed the southern part of Kuwait, a 15-year-old girl named Nayirah came forward to the United States Congressional Human Rights Caucasus and testified: "While I was there, I saw the Iraqi soldiers coming to the hospital with guns. They took the babies out of incubators, took the incubators, and left these children to die on the cold floor. It was horrifying" (Contributors, 2023; MacArthur, 1992). Before this testimonial, the public opinion in the United States was against the war; after that, human rights organisations such as Amnesty International echoed those claims. George Bush Senior had what he needed to declare war on Iraq. Immediately after the war, it became known that not only was the 15-year-old girl the daughter of the ambassador of Kuwait but her whole testimony was a lie, which was orchestrated by a PR firm representing Kuwait's monarchy. The list of atrocities and illegalities is endless.[5]

[5] The recent work of Claire Provost and Matt Kennard shed further light into the magnitude of which capitalist power controls the state and entire societies (Provost & Kennard, 2023).

This bizarre representation of reality is further investigated by the authors in what they call *worthy* and *unworthy victims.* "If the government or corporate community and the media feel that a story is useful as well as dramatic, they focus on it intensively and use it to enlighten the public", and they are deemed *worthy victims.* On the other hand, if victims are *unworthy*, "propaganda campaigns will *not* be mobilised" because they fail "to meet the test of utility to elite interests" (Herman & Chomsky, 1994, pp. 32, 33). Part of the effectiveness of this double standard depends on manufacturing expert opinion to legitimate propagandistic discourse (as Bernays had already revealed). The so-called experts—people from think tanks, academia, etc.—are co-opted. Their bias is created in a relationship of dependency that asserts government and capitalist discourse by "putting them on the payroll as consultants, funding their research, and organising think tanks that will hire them directly and help disseminate their messages" (Herman & Chomsky, 1994, p. 23).

"Flack" composes the fourth filter, representing negative feedback to mediatic content. "It may take the form of letters, telegrams, phone calls, petitions, lawsuits, speeches and bills before Congress, and other modes of complaint, threat, and punitive action" (Herman & Chomsky, 1994, p. 26). In this sense, the media's preoccupation overflows from the immediate responses of its advertisers to a broader negative response its content may instigate. The result is obvious. Media is conditioned not to inform honestly but to subject itself to content filtering—both in form and substance. Entire private institutions were created to harass and, by doing so, put the media in check. For instance, if the capitalist press condemns the illegal imperial wars, it is denounced for lacking [patriotic] support and for being (allegedly) biased.

This leads to the fifth filter, namely, anti-communism, which until today is relevant but often portrayed differently, such as anti-China, anti-Russia, anti-Venezuela, etc. What is vital is to create and sustain the notion of a general threat. Like fascism—receiving support from Western media and governments "is justified as a lesser evil" (Herman & Chomsky, 1994, p. 29)—the notion of "the other" or "the foreign" is pivotal to creating fragmentation among the many and support towards the powerful few. Frances Stonor Saunders has accurately denounced this ideological process during the Cold War (Saunders, 2013). Over four hundred years ago, the propagandistic and destructive nature of the condemnation of *the other* was already clear to Shakespeare (Shakespeare, 2016). Censorship reveals its preemptive character, and no evidence is needed before blame is assigned. Uncritical thinkers play a fundamental role in the legitimation process.

Media power, which ought to represent—after the legislative, judiciary, and executive—the fourth power of democracy, becomes so interwoven with the very social institutions that it should put in check that its role reverts to its opposite. Instead of unveiling truths—often inconvenient ones—, it has become a crucial tool for the perpetuation of propaganda and disinformation; "a propaganda model suggests that the 'societal purpose' of the media is to inculcate and defend the economic, social, and political agenda of privileged groups that dominate the domestic society and the state" (Herman & Chomsky, 1994, p. 298).

4.2.10 Audience Commodity

At the time *Manufacturing Consent* was written, the audience was a major consideration for the media's relationship with the advertiser; this means, it is only relevant to the extent to which it interests capitalist power. "The power of advertisers over television programming stems from the simple fact that they buy and pay for the programs-they are the 'patrons' who provide the media subsidy" (Herman & Chomsky, 1994, p. 16). Today, the magnitude of spending on marketing is estimated to be approximately 1 trillion dollars (Zarko Dimitrioski, 2019); therefore, this industry in-itself concentrates much economic power and private interests.

Before Herman and Chomsky wrote their renowned book, Dallas Smythe had already opened an important venue of analysis, pioneering a field called *critique of the political economy of media* by stitching together Marxist capitalist critique and media theory. In 1977, his essay *Communications: Blindspot of Western Marxism* revealed Marxist deficiency on the crucial and contemporary question of media; moreover, he denounces that simply using the terminology of ideology does not suffice to cover these relations. Smythe thus poses the question, what is media's "*economic function for capital*" (Smythe, 1977, p. 1)?

The crucial categories of consciousness, fetishism, alienation, free time, needs and wants must contain a mystical veil in the absence of such analysis. On the other hand, mediatic success and impact in shaping consciousness and behaviour must also be understood in relation to Marxist failure to communicate and demystify capitalist practice to the masses. Needless to say, the very transformation of the media, which became highly dependent but also very large and influential when capitalist economic imperatives imposed real subsumption of the media by means of marketing and publicity, capped the reach and possibilities of Marxist messages to spread. However, Smythe emphatically criticises the Marxist lack of critical theorisation of the mass media. Christian Fuchs unequivocally suggests "that to choose to be without Marx means to be in favour of capitalism and to support ideology" (Fuchs, 2012b, p. 643).

Considering the logic of commodity production, Smythe refutes idealistic notions that "the commodity form of mass-produced, advertiser-supported communications" are merely "messages", "information", "education", "entertainment", even "manipulation", etc. These are phenomenological forms. The real commodity, however, is the "audiences and readerships"—broadly just regarded as audiences by Smythe (Smythe, 1977, p. 2f). Free time, leisure-time, non-paid-working-time, non-sleeping-time must be then considered *work time*. "Of the off-the-job work time, the largest single block is time of the audiences which is sold to advertisers. It is not sold by workers but by the mass media of communications. Who produces this commodity" (Smythe, 1977, p. 3)? Considering it as a historical relation during the 1970s and not as a historical trend culminating in contemporary society, this assertion seems to fall short of considering concrete reality, for it takes one aspect of reality and makes it ubiquitous, namely, free time is then regarded as the working time of the *audience commodity*. This resembles the mistake of earlier Lukács when considering already in 1922/1923 human reification to have become a totalising matter (Hermeto, 2020; Lukács, 2013). However, despite both authors' mystifications, digital social relations have accidentally proven them both correct in the long run. Smartphones, computers, and the Internet have created a totalising condition of surveillance and commodification-reification (see *infra*).

The audience performs marketing functions, unwillingly—or at least unknowingly—works and thus creates surplus-value. Economic infrastructure and ideological superstructure appear to converge. In the mentioned essay, Smythe analyses eight questions connecting advertising, media, and economics. Some of the most relevant are: what does advertising expenditure buy? How can one guarantee to receive what is expected when buying an audience? Which organisations produced this purchased commodity? What characterises mass media content under monopoly capitalism? What distinguishes the labour performed by the audience commodity? How do labour theory of value, free-time, and demand management relate?

Money spent on advertisement is not just waste or altruism but aims to obtain audience services. Sub-sectors work to ensure that concrete products (results) are obtained from the procured audience commodities. The audience commodity bought by advertisers is produced by the media, such as "the owners of TV and radio stations and networks, newspapers, magazines and enterprises" (Smythe, 1977, p. 5)—contemporarily, also the big tech and any other capitalist firms that can collect, (process) and sell data (see *infra*).

What is broadcast and transmitted to these audiences is a stimulus in the fetishised form of the so-called free lunch or a cost below production cost. The audience's act of consumption is simultaneously an act of production, in which demand is created for "advertised goods"; this unpaid labour power "serve[s] advertisers to complete the production process of consumer goods by performing the ultimate marketing service for them, these workers are making decisive material decisions which will affect how they will produce and reproduce their labour power" (Smythe, 1977, p. 6). Politically, this means that the free time that could be used to change socio-political-economic conditions is occupied in reproducing the already existing conditions.

Thus, the notion that working hours have diminished must remain fetishised when unpaid working hours are not considered. Even if one disregards Smythe's all-encompassing understanding of leisure time captured by capital, in contemporary society, it becomes virtually impossible to separate free time from working time, as smartwatches, smartphones, computers, cameras, microphones, etc., are tracking, monitoring, and appropriating almost all dimensions of our private lives. Reflection time diminishes as time occupied in deciding what to buy, when, from which brand, etc. increases. Thus, "the bourgeois notion of free time and leisure is only available to those who have no disposable income (and for whom it is, of course, a bitter mockery) and to those who are so rich that" they are released from the concern of doing their own shopping (Smythe, 1977, p. 13f).

Finally, a question concerning the economic function of audience commodity must also be dealt with: is this type of labour productive?

4.2.11 Prosumer: Or Full-Spectrum Spectacle

Building on Smythe's work and calling for a "*Critique of the Political Economy of Communication, Culture, Information and the Media*" instead of a "Political Economy of Media/Communications" (Fuchs, 2012a, p. 700), Christian Fuchs revises the notion of audience commodity in light of contemporary social relations, accentuating that neither its cultural nor economic aspects can be taken in isolation. Thus, the role of the "consciousness industry" is to promote commodity sales as well as "values that favour capitalism and the private property system" (Fuchs, 2012a, p. 696).

This logic of commodification, although reaching its peak in present-day capitalism, was not only overstretched by Lukács but was also taken up uncritically by *Critical Theorists*. They too hypostasised reification and capitalist *instrumental reason*, which seem to become all-encompassing and inexorable—inadvertently naturalising the capitalist logic. While For Max Horkheimer, "everything is rationally arranged", and by reason, he means: "reason divorced from feelings" (Horkheimer, 2012, p. 59f), Herbert Marcuse asserts: "We live and die rationally and productively. We know that destruction is the price of progress as death the price of life" (Marcuse, 2002, p. 149). Basing his critique on this logic of reification, Fuchs affirms that "the media in capitalism are modes of reification in a multiple sense" (Fuchs, 2012a, p. 697): humanity is reduced to consumers; culture becomes commodified; ideology asserts capitalist hegemony. He hence combines economic and cultural elements. "The goal is that human thoughts and actions do not go beyond capitalism, do not question and revolt against this system and thereby play the role of instruments for the perpetuation of capitalism" (Fuchs, 2012a, p. 697).

Although not differentiating between Lukács', Horkheimer's, and Marcuse's interpretations of capitalism, on the one hand, and contemporary interpretations, on the other, thus (to some extent) mystifying (the errors of) social critique, his critical assessment nevertheless reflects the capitalist present invasion of all spheres of natural and cultural life. However, the quantitative-qualitative change in capitalist reification carries a constant element from within, namely, the process of private accumulation based on social, collaborative, collective production presupposes an ideological apparatus of legitimation and naturalisation. While economic power is separated from the social actualisation of collective life, it is not only embedded but also interdependent with extra-economic power and determinations. In this sense, Fuchs suggests that the economy based on the Internet and social media "was accompanied by a techno-deterministic and techno-optimistic ideology" (Fuchs, 2012a, p. 698).

As many people might have thought that radio and television programmes were free to watch, so did social media hype initially carry a similar façade. While the commodification process involved in the former was harder to grasp, for it appeared less latent, the one that takes place in the digital realm is radically more pervasive and invasive. Eran Fisher hypothesises that this represents not only an increase in exploitation but also a simultaneous decrease in alienation. While the mass media audience is passive and hierarchically typified as content consumers, the digital media audience breaks this paradigm and actively produces and engages. The act of active-doing is thus regarded as a diminishment of alienation, while the appropriation of its results represents a greater exploitation (Fisher, 2017).

Although the superior exploitative character of contemporary media is quantitatively grander, the fact that the consumer is now active does not grant a less estranged ("alienated") relationship between media and audience; if anything, an even greater one. The new mediatic estrangement intensifies precisely because it does not simply represent a passive, unknowing relation; instead, a real subsumption now ensues. This means that the four layers of estrangement emphasised by Marx also emerge through the act of doing: estranged-act, self-estrangement, estranged-result, and estranged relationship with society. In this sense, because media production becomes much more social, maintaining its private character imposes an ever greater and not lesser estrangement ("alienation"). Despite writing during a period in which these relations could, at most, be regarded as germinal, Tiziana Terranova perfectly grasps this process in which the distinction between "production and consumption, work and cultural expression" is "blurred" and "does not signal the recomposition of the alienated Marxist worker" (Terranova, 2000, p. 35).

While it is true that the mammoth data produced by the audience requires further furnishing, thus presupposing an additional act of labour and, accordingly, its appropriation by capital, this does not binarily exclude the labour of this specific commodity like Göran Bolin does when affirming "it is not the viewers who work, but rather the statisticians" (Bolin, 2009, p. 357). Bolin thus appears to ignore that the division of labour per excellence entails multiple layers, and that most, if not all, activities must be understood as totalities deriving from relations and not as simple isolated events. Thus, monitoring behaviour initiates neither with the Internet nor social media (Web 2.0) but already takes place as a system of surveillance of radio and television.

While some consider the very consumption as a form of wage for the work that the audiences perform, Fuchs disregards this for it is not an equivalent of value, i.e., the function of wage is to (re)produce the labour commodity, and media consumption does not grant that. "Rather all watching time of commercial TV is surplus labour time" (Fuchs, 2012a, p. 703). Therefore, he regards social media as tools dedicated exclusively towards profit production. The commodified user simultaneously produces a commodity. Audience commodity becomes "prosumer commodity", that is, "the users themselves are sold as a commodity to advertisers" (Fuchs, 2010, p. 191; 2012a, p. 706).

While the term prosumer perfectly grasps the new "nature" of this relationship, disregarding the consumption of the digital sphere as part of survival appears as a far too rigid delineation, for has the being-part-of-the-Internet-connectivity not become, for many people, a crucial part of (individual and social) survival? Does the user not start a legally binding contract with the owners of the means of digital production—even if unknowingly and/or unwillingly—when he becomes a user? Has big tech not become a social infrastructure and thus an imperative of the superstructure that people must integrate for social survival?

Needless to say, there are few exceptions for those who live off-grid; yet for those living social lives, being part of the big tech monopoly has become a socio-economic imposition. In this sense, Tiziana Terranova's methodological assertion is still topical, as it suggests that, instead of glorifying or demonising the Internet, the question is rather if it "embodies a continuation of capital or a break with it", to what she indicates "the Internet is about the extraction of value out of continuous, updateable work, and it is extremely labor intensive" (Terranova, 2000, pp. 54, 48). It goes without saying that at the time she wrote it she was considering the constant effort in building and updating websites and was not thinking about social media and the prosumer.

At the time Fuchs wrote his essay, based on Marisol Sandoval's analysis, he indicated that over "90% of all analysed web platforms used targeted advertising and the surveillance and commodification of users' data" (Fuchs, 2012a, p. 706). Thus, while software programming emerged as a gift-economy (see *supra*) and only then became subsumed under capital, Internet gift-economies became not only the target of the so-called primitive accumulation but, in many cases, were created within the digital fences of technological private capital. This process has spread to the point in which many users are mentally colonised as to, themselves, creating the marketing content and advertisement of products to advertise themselves as "brands" (in reality, fetishised commodities) associated with larger brands in the hopes of successfully selling an image of themselves that could potentially yield economic advantages.

Debord's spectacle appears, therefore, to have self-realised as a true supreme-power and capitalist theodicy seems to be overcome, for the spectacle now appears omnipresent, omniscient, and omnipotent—it is not simply imposed from the outside anymore but from the very inside.

4.2.12 Infinite Rate of Exploitation

Turning to the essay *Labor in Informational Capitalism*, Fuchs suggests that the so-called information capitalism is not an elementary layer of capitalist processes but, alongside financial capital, plays a major role in global capitalism. However, the posture of regarding capitalism as information, "financialization, globalization, hyper-industrialism, and imperialism" (Fuchs, 2010, p. 180), seems to artificially split an indivisible totality.

Capitalist imperialism is financial capitalism, which is globalised and overstretched industrial capital merged with banking capital and the capitalist state, and finally, information is an ontological condition of any human economy and, as such, a decisive but not unique feature of capitalism. As the capitalist mode of production is based on the production of surplus-value, when considering this moment within the digital economy—namely, not the regular side of surplus creation and appropriation of digital wage labour but rather that of audience commodity/prosumer—then this non-wage economy reveals a *you-are-the-product relation*, in which super exploitation occurs. When variable capital—namely, labour—costs the capitalist nothing, then "the rate of exploitation is infinite" (Fuchs, 2010, p. 188).

As the value of knowledge is obliterated, its production and reproduction become more accessible and nimbler. Therefore, social property relations adapt to this new condition, in which the contradiction between social production and private appropriation becomes more accentuated. In this context, mechanisms to ensure an ongoing "primitive" accumulation gain momentum. The expansion of knowledge (and content) production outside the private sphere of wage relations simultaneously creates the conditions for non-wage exploitation. Fuchs grasps this and reiterates that "knowledge is a social and historical product" (Fuchs, 2010, p. 189).

In this sense, Fuchs seems to comprehend the first paradox of intellectual appropriation in capitalism. "Knowledge, nature, and infrastructures are collective goods that cost nothing for capital, but they are a necessary condition for capital accumulation, entering production processes, and capital profits from them" (Fuchs, 2010, p. 189). Moreover, this private appropriation not only entails immediate knowledge production but is, in fact, inherited knowledge within "organisation", "cultural", and "traditional practices" (Fuchs, 2010, p. 189f).

Yet the second paradox remains unnoticed, namely, the very condition in which knowledge in capitalism imposes on itself the simultaneous necessity of privatisation, thus destroying its general ontological condition of existence—namely, of being socially conceived. Therefore, when he compares "cotton" production with software production ("Microsoft Windows"), he must formulate a one-sided comparison. Considering both cotton and software in-themselves, one appears as pure matter (nature) and the other as pure idea.

As software's private control deems it an artificial reproduction, for *abstract* knowledge is not scarce (but also *non-existent*), private control of cotton's modern agricultural processes, genetics, etc. is as artificial because such knowledge is just as abstract and infinitely abundant. In reality, each piece of software presupposes some hardware to be actualised and some materiality to exist regardless. Accordingly, cotton production is a cultural enterprise and, even in its most rudimentary form, requires objectification of knowledge while requiring material existence both in a crude knowledge structure and in the actualised procedure of cotton production. Highly technological cotton production entails the same general production/reproduction moments as any production, but phenomenologically, it might even appear more comparable to a software-hardware relationship than to an unpolished method of knowledge-cotton-production. And although his assertion is correct, namely, knowledge "is a social product produced and consumed by all", that is, everyone "produce[s], reproduce[s], and consume[s] the commons, but only the capitalist class exploits the commons economically"(Fuchs, 2010, p. 193), it must remain one-sided, for it misses the totality of intellectual appropriation and production.

4.2.13 Labourer's Asceticism

Focusing on a so-called compositional change in which manual becomes intellectual labour, Maurizio Lazzarato sustains the emergence of a "mass intellectuality". Defining immaterial labour "as the labour that produces the informational and cultural content of the commodity", he emphasises that while "informational content" is part of labour processes, "cultural content" usually refer to non-work-related activities (Lazzarato, 1996, p. 133).

His definition seems arbitrary and does not help the understanding of either manual or intellectual labour. It is not the activity in-itself but the concrete social relation that enables differentiating whether it is subjected to labour relations or not. Furthermore, with the Internet's total surveillance in order to yield surplus-value from users' activities, leisure and work have become so intertwined that the only current distinction possible is between wage and non-wage labour. Even during sleep, not only does each smartphone's owner become available—a human standby-modus—to actively execute tasks but also with the emergence of smartwatches—which "gather detailed quantitative data on each and every user" (Mosco, 2017, p. 524)—data production continues to occur, reaching staggering 24/7 rates.

Realising this physical limit of available time each day within the process of surplus production and appropriation is what I call *potential surplus-value*, for every second becomes a moment of surplus labour and potentially of its appropriation. Of course, Lazzarato's writing portrays a tendency prior to the advent of the mass Internet and thus could not have attained these nuances. His thesis, "a new 'mass intellectuality' has come into being", which ought to express a greater "decision-making capacity" and "autonomy", fails to grasp the fundamental aspect of the division of labour and larger composition of dead labour; nevertheless, he correctly acknowledges the fact that "life becomes inseparable from work" (Lazzarato, 1996, pp. 134f, 138).

Each worker becomes tendentially less capable of perceiving not only the totality of production but, more importantly, the extent of his own activity. The accumulated transfer of functions to machines (analogic, mechatronic, digital, *etc.*) imposes a vast loss of skills and dexterity. Not only manual-doing but also intellectual labour becomes simplified. Manual and intellectual labourers become supervisors as their practical roles and functions disappear (Marx, 1983, p. 593). They have to interpret results and outputs without knowing or being incapable of producing these same outcomes. The more science objectifies itself in production, the less intellectual freedom is available to the worker who, constricted to the production of surplus-value, must forgo his capacity to reason and think critically.

According to Lazzarato, the contradiction emerges, therefore, in the free autonomy of the individual and in capital demanding from him to assert its personality, thus reifying the inner self. Nonetheless, the true contradiction is revealed in the antagonism between the social dimension of collective production bathed in social knowledge and the private control of production possibilities and concrete results all subordinated to an immanent a-social economic imperative. This objective condition of knowledge production is obliterated behind the veil of subjective perception. Therefore, on the worker, subjectivity is not imposed as a condition of work—as Lazzarato claims—but rather reality itself mutates into pure subjective apprehension. The labourer's *Weltanschauung* must not attain a historical perspective or one based on the struggle of classes; it must instead remain relativist and ahistorical.

Nevertheless, he recognises some relevant mechanisms of control and coercion within production. The worker becomes a decoder of managerial messages (obligations). "The necessity of imposing command and the violence that goes along with it here take on a normative communicative form" (Lazzarato, 1996, p. 135f). There must be not only objective but also subjective control. Capitalist control parallels those of religion. Self-control, self-abstinence, self-negation and asceticism must be imposed from within. "The worker is to be responsible for his or her own control and motivation within the work group without a foreman needing to intervene, and the foreman's role is redefined into that of a facilitator" (Lazzarato, 1996, p. 136).

4.2.14 Digital Fissures in Ruling-Class Ideologies

Before analysing the connection between digitalisation and surveillance, it is worth recapping some aspects of the critique of *the political economy of media* through Andreas Wittel's lenses. Cultural and media industries have become vital elements of capitalist ideological assertion. Press coverage by the mass media has become indissoluble in advertisement revenues and interests. Insofar as mass media has gone through a worldwide process of immense concentration, Marx's and Engels' assertion that the "thoughts of the dominant class are in every epoch the dominant thought" (Marx & Engels, 1978, p. 46) seems more topical than ever.

However, ruling class hegemony is not frictionless; alliances among class lines are crucial elements to sustain ideological supremacy; therefore, splits and divisions from within open gaps and cracks in ideological control. This represents a situation where "dominating thoughts would not be the thoughts of the dominant class" (Marx & Engels, 1978, p. 47). While mass media presupposes a massive portion of capital to operate, making it very susceptible to concentration, digital technology enabled the materialisation of new fissures and cracks. Wittel further differentiates between digital and distributed media. While the former represents the technological aspect of the means of communication, he uses "the term *distributed media* to put an emphasis on the *social organisation* of media" (Wittel, 2017, p. 75).

The ideological crack characterises a new dimension of struggle, that is, not simply the possibility of opening discourses imposed by "dominant thoughts" but also of emerging new latent forms of thought-domination by means of appropriation. It simultaneously entails an emancipatory and reactionary character. As consumers become producers, audience commodities mutate into prosumer labour. Thus, the fissures opened by the use of new technologies have a double reality: if, on the one hand, the owners of the means of production of media lose direct influence over content creation and consumers become active producers of a new social communicative reality, on the other, consumers become subjected to total surveillance and mind-behaviour control, whereas media power elite—now dependent on and concentrated in big tech—gains access to an apparently endless source of surplus-value appropriation in wage-less labour relations.

These different aspects reveal not only modifications in general historical trends but, most importantly, in social property relations, which "are subjected to specific historic conditions" (Wittel, 2017, p. 96). Capitalist control over intellectual appropriation is thus neither a natural nor antagonistic-free condition; therefore, the contemporary social relation expressed in the intellectual property category epitomises intellectual appropriation not in the sense of knowledge and cultural production and reproduction but rather in intellectual private appropriation—private property—and therefore "property that can be used for the creation of surplus value" (Wittel, 2017, p. 97).

4.2.15 Digital Data Appropriation

Although surveillance is not in-itself a condition of *intellectual property$_{(private)}$*, it is vital not only for its control and real actualisation, but also for surplus-value appropriation and accumulation in the mediatic space. The forced separation between teleology and setting—that is, intellectual appropriation and intellectual actualisation through the sphere of appropriation and transformation of matter—renders property no longer as the immediate and identical control over socio-created knowledge but instead presupposes a monitoring that dispenses with the concreteness of intellectual property and in its place imposes an external condition on its existence. This outer layer of control confers an artificial universal content to it. Normativity not only imposes but also presupposes control. As the value of knowledge production has significantly plunged with not only the rise of digitalisation and the enhancement of processing power but also a considerable decrease in the cost of storage with its simultaneous noteworthy expansion, controlling it became much more complicated and required new means. Only total surveillance makes it possible to ensure that one piece of information/knowledge is not being actualised somewhere else. Big techs, mass media and spying agencies (governmental and private) have become the main players who created and set the surveillance infrastructure in motion. Therefore, analysing this control presupposes investigating how they interconnect and operate.

Hinging on the question of the so-called primitive accumulation, Mattias Eckman emphasises the vital role of "the appropriation of the commons" in the process of privatisation for uncountable areas "which previously were outside capital accumulation because they were regarded as commons"—it is a long list—involving natural and social resources—which is gradually being forgotten as capital accumulation becomes normalised through a ubiquitous and ominous process of expropriation-appropriation (Eckman, 2017, p. 111).

It has become widely known that this process involves significant planning, and intentionality is often imposed. Milton Friedman suggests how to take advantage of this. "Only a crisis-actual or perceived-produces real change"; therefore, the necessary ideological setting has to be prepared to take advantage of the moment when this kind of situation kicks in; "[w]hen that crisis occurs, the actions that are taken depend on the ideas that are lying around" (Friedman, 2002, p. xiv). Understanding this was pivotal to imposing "orchestrated economic crises", which has broadly become known as shock therapy (Eckman, 2017, p. 112). Either an ongoing or manufactured disaster, which "puts the entire population into a state of collective shock" (Klein, 2008, p. 17), is used to assert capitalist power and control, deeming itself as the only possible solution in times of generalised shock, panic, and paralysis. Building on Naomi Klein's work, Antony Loewenstein portrays the pervasive scope in which this logic has been instrumentalised against entire peoples, whether in Pakistan, Afghanistan, Greece, Haiti, Papua New Guinea, or even in political Western players such as the United States, United Kingdom, and Australia (Loewenstein, 2017).

Summarising this logic, Philip Mirowski exposes the entrails of the 2008 financial meltdown and how everything changed so that everything would remain the same. That is, while neoclassical theorists were completely oblivious to how that happened, "Neoliberal Thought Collective" paved the way to this calamity for the 99% and the extraordinary opportunity for the 1% (Mirowski, 2013). The state, unlike some theorists claim, is not an impartial actor of conflict mediation; instead, it administrates ruling-class power under capitalism, i.e., capitalist power (Marx &

Engels, 1977). "In neo-liberal capitalism, the state is transformed into the most central actor in redistribution (privatisation) of public assets" (Eckman, 2017, p. 113). Imposing ideological control to shape collective thought is not, however, primarily a state function but that of mass media, which not only endorses but also naturalises the process of accumulation by dispossession. Therefore, even when they cry for so-called social justice, social movements unknowingly become perpetrators of bigotry against anything concretely challenging *hegemonic discourse*. With digital media, not only are hearts and minds conquered, but every action becomes an involuntary act of capitalist assertion, legitimation, domination and accumulation, for "everything we do when are online" becomes appropriated labour (Eckman, 2017, p. 125). Smartphones consolidate an all-blurriness, a total blending of work and free time as well as public and private space. Each moment in time and space becomes, regardless of circumstances, a moment of capital appropriation of the data involuntarily produced by the mere fact that we socially exist. Computer software and smartphone applications are not only commodities but also a means to obtain commodity and, most importantly, a means of surveillance mediating a transformation process of our acts into commodities.

4.2.16 Control in the Clouds, Digital Surveillance, and the Capitalist Imperialism

Digital surveillance became pervasive when the Internet was combined with cloud computing and big data. While these elements in-themselves do not represent something negative or positive, the fantasy of democratisation that permeated an imaginary conception of the Internet can be buried under the concrete capitalist mode of production. Surveillance was not the necessary outcome of these technologies but is an essential condition for the appropriation and accumulation of private surplus-value, especially when capitalist socio-historical function disappears, giving way to vast social, collective, collaborative relations of production. The more private appropriation becomes historically unnecessary for societal organisation, the more it must assert itself by means of force, violence, and imposition.

However, despite the common-sense assessment of knowledge and intellectual property as immaterial things, real knowledge presupposes the material existence of knowledge. As such, the notion of digital clouding as something ethereal or abstract is wrong. "The cloud is actually housed in data centers, large information factories containing tens or hundreds of thousands of servers, that are linked to telecommunications systems that provide data and services to subscribers"; this objectified knowledge is, hence, the material means of the "flowing" digital knowledge (Mosco, 2017, p. 517). Furthermore, the staggering amount of information imposes the need for new forms of mediation to make it knowledge. "Big data analytics is a term that refers to a form of research using data stored primarily in the cloud" (Mosco, 2017, p. 517). Vincent Mosco asserts that this is not a frictionless process, for it concentrates an enormous amount of power; creates a huge environmental impact by draining the global electricity grid while additionally polluting with usage of diesel generators and chemical battery production; privacy breach due to hacking becoming a more significant concern; but also private and governmental espionage; intellectual labour becomes susceptible to outsourcing; labour control and surveillance also upsurges; and, finally, as Mosco puts it, there is an epistemological threat.

Although Amazon is popularly known for being an online platform for buying commodities and watching movies, one crucial part of its business is cloud computing, namely, Amazon Web Services or AWS, which enables remote working/learning, storing databases, delivering content, computer power, etc. It is, however, entangled not only with private capital but also with government control and spy agencies. For instance, it was granted a critical contract "to provide cloud and big data services to the CIA", thus bringing "together leaders in digital capitalism and the surveillance state to create a marriage that would certainly benefit both parties" (Mosco, 2017, p. 519). According to Mosco, Google reads "customer email to refine the advertisement", while Facebook manipulated the feeds to increase the time people were exposed to publicity (Mosco, 2017, p. 521). Analogous to piracy, a double standard is at play, in which surveillance breach against capitalist governments and firms is negatively regarded as hacking. In contrast, the surveillance perpetrated by "the hidden complicity between state security agencies and the tech companies"

(Zuboff, 2019, p. 385) receives relatively little attention (from the media as well as regulatory organs)—especially considering the mammoth broad-scale surveillance revealed by Edward Snowden/Glenn Greenwald in the case of the NSA (Greenwald, 2013) and WikiLeaks/Julian Assange (Vault 7) in the case of the CIA (Vault 7: CIA Hacking Tools Revealed, 2017).[6]

As Carl Benedikt Frey's and Michael A. Osborne's research suggests, this process creates the conditions for a significant increment in the substitution of living labour by dead labour (see *supra*). The labour of knowledge workers is tendentially transferred to the cloud, impacting multiple sectors. Accordingly, outsourcing gains an entirely new impetus. "In essence, the cloud and big data make possible the expansion of labour commodification throughout the world" (Mosco, 2017, p. 523). Moreover, as it has become public knowledge, individual workers and complete workforces are undergoing real-time tracking, whose information is computed and treated like machine outputs, whether performing on-the-ground or home office (remote working) functions (Gurley, 2020; Klosowski, 2021; Migliano, 2023).

Furthermore, Mosco asserts that as "low-income workers" are subjected to work on an on-demand basis, their working schedules become chaotic, and they must always be on standby to "operate as flexible machines capable of responding to whatever logistical demands the companies that carry out big data analysis require" (Mosco, 2017, p. 524). Thus, also here, operates the logic of *potential surplus-value* in which, at all times, every moment is a possibility for the production of surplus-value. The worker becomes the simulacrum of the machine. In this sense, the old-monopolistic model of extracting the so-called consumer surplus, pricing over market prices, is undermined. A company such as Amazon can offer competitive prices precisely because it vastly endeavours to extract surplus-value through audience commodity practices (analogous to when media started receiving advertisement revenues). Accordingly,

[6] In May of 2023, the *Report to the Director of National Intelligence 27 January 2022* was declassified, revealing a pervasive tactic of surveillance in which governmental spy agencies circumscribe the illegality of directly eavesdropping without legal permission by relying on a market of data provided by surveillance private capital (Report to the Director of National Intelligence 27 January 2022, 2023).

the struggle of classes endures a crucial shift as spectacle and panopticon converge.

Depending on *intellectual property*$_{(private)}$ to secure, enable and legitimate its full-spectrum apparatus of software, algorithms, programming, technological appropriation, research and development, etc., capitalist totalising power epitomises what Shoshana Zuboff calls *surveillance capitalism*. Although she plays down the fact that norms and propaganda already conferred on those in power enormous capability to shape and modify human behaviour because, in her analysis, proper behavioural modification is a product of surveillance capitalism, it is her merit to historically depict the entrails of surveillance under the capitalist mode of production (Zuboff, 2019, p. 284f).

According to Zuboff, "Google became the pioneer, discoverer, elaborator, experimenter, lead practitioner, role model, and diffusion hub of *surveillance capitalism*" because it managed to transform human behaviour into raw material; human life becomes simply a source of data and within this relationship "there is no exit, no voice, and no loyalty, only helplessness, resignation, and psychic numbing" (Zuboff, 2019, pp. 63, 94). She does not refer to this process in Marxist terms, namely, perceiving the appropriation of human activity as surplus labour appropriation but as the transformation of "behavioral surplus" into "raw material" (Zuboff, 2019, p. 344). Differences aside, she reveals not only an evolution of this model focused on advertisement-based customers towards a true symbiosis with the surveillance state and spy agencies but also the fact that the very inception of Google (and its likes) dwelled within blurred boundaries between private capital and state (security) institutions.

When Google asserts that it respects privacy and does not sell user data, Zuboff contests it as a rhetorical trick because it consumes user data in order to obtain the sold commodity, the so-called predictions of user behaviour (in secular language, *projections*). Not only were Google's *Google Earth* and *Google Maps* derived from an acquisition of "Keyhole, a satellite mapping company founded by John Hanke, whose venture backer was the CIA venture firm, In-Q-Tel", but also its relationships extended directly to spy agencies such as the NSA and CIA as early as the beginning of the 2000s (Zuboff, 2019, p. 117). Spy agencies faced difficulty keeping up with the pace of high-speed informational exchange due to the rise of digitalisation; moreover, constitutional constraints could be curbed by partnering with Silicon Valley firms—representing a new dimension to the already existing relationship between military and tech companies (see *supra*) (Levine, 2018). "Google's stores of behavioural surplus now embrace everything in the online milieu: searches, e-mails, texts, photos, songs, messages, videos, locations, communication patterns, attitudes, preferences, interests, faces, emotions, illnesses, social networks, purchases, and so on" (Zuboff, 2019, p. 128). Its surveillance tentacles grew immensely. This process of dispossession is called by Zuboff *rendition* and this state of total surveillance *tyranny* by these "surveillance capitalists [transformed] into society's self-appointed masters" (Zuboff, 2019, pp. 233ff, 255ff, 512, 505). This power has grown to such an extent that the capability to modify behaviour in real-time to prompt concrete actions has already become a reality; however, this process does not intend to enact government control or society's safety but profit extraction (Zuboff, 2019, pp. 299, 514).

4.2.17 The Black Box Industry

Although the current surveillance system's objective is to reproduce capitalist economic imperatives, crucial elements of its operationalisation resemble, or, one could even say, perfect the notion of the *panopticon.*

Astonished by the panopticon, Jeremy Bentham describes its complexity and simplicity and its vast array of possible applications in order to facilitate surveillance and control, "whether it be applied to the purposes of *perpetual prisons* in the room of death, or *prisons for confinement* before trial, or *penitentiary-houses*, or *houses of correction*, or *work-houses*, or *manufactories*, or *mad-houses*, or *hospitals*, or *schools*" (Bentham, 1995, p. 34). The architectural structure resembles two rings: an inner smaller ring (a tower) and an outer ring revolving around the first (an annular building). Through the tower windows, one sees the whole peripherical building, which, according to Michel Foucault, "is divided into cells, each of which extends the whole width of the building; they have two windows, one on the inside, corresponding to the windows of the tower; the other, on the outside, allows the light to cross the cell from one end to the other" (Foucault, 1995, p. 200).

Bentham asserts that the perfect ideal would be to enable constant surveillance in which the individual would sustain a continual dilemma of being observed at all times. However, Foucault emphasises that its pinnacle is not a matter of architecture but of becoming the perfect surveillance machinery, actualising the perfect anonymisation of impersonal power. "It is an important mechanism, for it automatises and disindividualises power"; surveillance power and control become virtually automatic; it "induce[s] in the inmate a state of conscious and permanent visibility that assures the automatic functioning of power" (Foucault, 1995, pp. 202, 201). Dismembering the quality of groups, crowds, etc., it separates and singularises those constricted within its walls.

However, like digital surveillance, the panopticon is not only about unveiling every single action of the individual and being in control; it is also about shaping behaviour, for "the Panopticon was also a laboratory; it could be used as a machine to carry out experiments, to alter behaviour, to train or correct individuals" (Foucault, 1995, p. 203). Moreover, being an "omniscient" apparatus, each intentional behavioural modification can be checked and monitored, and micro adjustments are sought by the controlling machine; additionally, the latter is interdependently reinforced by the former. Foucault clearly understands that knowledge and power go hand in-glove. The Panopticon "gains in efficiency and in the ability to penetrate into men's behaviour; knowledge follows the advances of power, discovering new objects of knowledge over all the surfaces on which power is exercised" (Foucault, 1995, p. 204). The French intellectual further asserts that, by its nature, this mechanism prevents tyranny, for any member of society could encapsulate himself within the device and at once see how this circumscribed dominium operates.

If digital surveillance ought to be regarded as a Panopticon modality, then two considerations must be emphasised. *First*, digital surveillance is also, to a certain extent, impersonal and anonymous, for—in general—it does not merely represent the assertion of individual power of individual capitalists. For the capitalist, although qualitatively different from the labourer, is also estranged by the economic imperatives, the violence imposed by him does not emanate from "his personal or human qualities" but because "he is *proprietor* of capital", in a word, he is merely its "carrier" (Marx, 1962, p. 167; 1968, p. 484).

Second, unlike the analogical blueprinted version, the digital panoptical is not "constantly accessible 'to the great tribunal committee of the world'" (Foucault, 1995, p. 207). Consequently, it would appear a hypostasis to consider the capitalist as a tyrant, for this tyranny does not derive from isolated singular individuals but is a condition in which economic imperatives impose themselves; the tyranny is of capital—which has become independent (*sich verselbständigt*)—and not of its immediate operators; capital has become subject whereas the capitalist merely its predicate, its bearer.

Capitalist tyranny represents "the obliteration of politics" (Zuboff, 2019, p. 513); reification—instead of simply constituting, as in other modes of production, an epiphenomenon—becomes part of the capitalist structure as it develops further (Lukács, 2013, p. 268). Foucault too acknowledges here the historical interdependence between basis and superstructure. "If the economic take-off of the West began with the techniques that made possible the accumulation of capital, it might perhaps be said that the methods for administering the accumulation of men made possible a political take-off in relation to the traditional, ritual, costly, violent forms of power"; moreover, the bourgeois so-called equalitarian political framework enacted a simultaneous "development and generalization of disciplinary mechanisms [which] constituted the other, dark side of these processes"; within a class society divided between owner of the means of production and non-owner, formal equality presupposed actualisation and management of inequality "by all those systems of micro power that are essentially nonegalitarian and asymmetrical that we call the disciplines" (Foucault, 1995, pp. 220f, 222). What Foucault calls "infra-law" and "counter-law" is currently capitalist power enmeshed with capitalist governmental power in the shadows. The parallel with eighteenth-century techniques of control, which "attained a level at which the formation of knowledge and the increase of power regularly reinforce one another in a circular process" (Foucault, 1995, p. 224), is remarkable.

Bridging today's relations, digital surveillance appears omnipresent, omniscient, and omnipotent, regardless of whether it is intended to provide advertising industries or spy agencies with resources. While mass media mostly manufacture consent, digital powers do not stop there; on the contrary, most of their practices are based on bypassing consent. Not only does private and government propaganda impose the *spectacle* upon people without their permission, but the very resources they use to perform this practice are obtained without consent. Before the Digital, control was obtained through manufactured consent; with the *digital Panopticon machinery*, consent is obliterated to impose full-spectrum dominance of behavioural control.

Needless to say, this process is not enacted simply by singular actors; despite monopolist players such as Google, Facebook, Amazon, Microsoft, IBM, etc. having vast market power and control, commercial surveillance has expanded to a full industrial scale. "The corporations' surveillance of the prosumers' permanently produced use values", aiming to manipulate "prosumers' desires and needs in the interest of corporations and the commodities they offer" (Fuchs, 2012a, p. 717). While in economics the concept of the *black box* has been used to express the "hidden" factors of technological development (Harada, 2019), Nathan Rosenberg asserts that empirical studies "adopt a 'black box' explanation of the innovation process: inputs in, innovations out" (Rosenberg, 1982, p. 233). Additionally, in system theory (*Systemtheorie*), it expresses the unknown internal factors of a given structure, that is, "one often finds the situation, especially in sociology, that systems in their self-handling develop forms of access to complexity that are not accessible to scientific analysis and simulation" (Luhmann, 1991, p. 32).

Although Bentham's Panopticon which would enable total transparency of those being observed and at the same time for those inside the tower conducting surveillance, total inconspicuousness must reign, "in the peripheric ring, one is totally seen, without ever seeing; in the central tower, one sees everything without ever being seen" (Foucault, 1995, p. 202). Therefore, from the perspective of those being watched, it would not be a stretch of the imagination to classify Bentham's description as a black box. However, while this system theoretically permitted scrutiny from anyone from the outside, examining the digital Panopticon, one must conclude that *the whole industry has become a black box* because the autonomy of the system has gained such proportions that the division between the outer ring and the inner tower has been abolished. Now each and every one is trapped within the outer circle, while the internal building has apparently vanished only to be posited within each cell in a seemingly infinite multiplication of itself. No one can enter the tower because the tower has entered all of us. *The digital Panopticon is the black box industry par excellence.*

References

Adewopo, A. (2016). The Global Intellectual Property System and Sub-Saharan Africa: A Prognostic Reflection. In A. George (Ed.), *Globalization and Intellectual Property* (pp. 109–131). Routledge.

Aoki, K. (2016). Neocolonialism, Anticommons Property, and Biopiracy in the (Not-So-Brave) New World Order of International Intellectual Property Protection. In A. George (Ed.), *Globalization and Intellectual Property* (pp. 195–242). Routledge.

Baudrillard, J. (1975). *The Mirror of Production*. Telos Press.

Baudrillard, J. (1981). *Simulacres et simulation*. Galilée.

Bentham, J. (1995). *Jeremy Bentham: The Panopticon Writings* (M. Božovič, Ed.). Verso.

Bernays, E. L. (1928). *Propaganda*. Liveright Publishing Corporation.

Bernays, E. L. (1955). The Theory and Practice of Public Relations: A Résumé. In E. L. Bernays (Ed.), *The Engineering of Consent*. University of Oklahoma Press.

Bolin, G. (2009). Symbolic Production and Value in Media Industries. *Journal of Cultural Economy, 2*(3), 345–361. https://doi.org/10.1080/17530350903345579

Le Bon, G. (2002). *The Crowd: A Study of the Popular Mind*. Dover Publications, Inc.

Fung, B. (2022, December 8). Pentagon Awards Multibillion-dollar Cloud Contract to Amazon, Google, Microsoft and Oracle. *CNN*. https://edition.cnn.com/2022/12/08/tech/pentagon-cloud-contract-big-tech/index.html

Brush, S., & Wittenberg, A. (2022, January 14). BlackRock Hits a Record $10 Trillion Assets Under Management. *Al Jazeera* | Financial Markets News. https://www.aljazeera.com/economy/2022/1/14/blackrock-hits-a-record-10-trillion-assets-under-management

Childe, V. G. (1958). *Man Makes Himself*. The New American Library.

Contributors, W. (2023). *Nayirah Testimony*. Wikipedia, The Free Encyclopedia. https://en.wikipedia.org/wiki/Nayirah_testimony

Cox, H. (2016). *The Market as God*. Harvard University Press.

Debord, G. (1992a). *Commentaires sur la société du spectacle*. Gallimard.

Debord, G. (1992b). *La Société du Spectacle*. Gallimard.

Desai, R. (2011). The New Communists of the Commons: Twenty-first-century Proudhonists. *International Critical Thought, 1*(2), 204–223. https://doi.org/10.1080/21598282.2011.584163

Drahos, P. (2016). *A Philosophy of Intellectual Property*. Australian National University. https://doi.org/10.22459/PIP.06.2016

Durand, C. (2020). *Techno-Feodalisme: Critique de L'Économie Numérique*. Zone.

Dutfield, G. (2012). 'The genetic code is 3.6 billion years old: it's time for a rewrite'—Questioning the Metaphors and Analogies of Synthetic Biology and Life Science Patenting. In A. Lever (Ed.), *New Frontiers in the Philosophy of Intellectual Property*. Cambridge University Press.

Eckman, M. (2017). The Relevance of Marx's Theory of Primitive Accumulation for Media and Communication Research. In C. Fuchs & V. Mosco (Eds.), *Marx in the Age of Digital Capitalism*. Haymarket Books.

Eucken, W. (1961). *Nationalökonomie wozu?* Verlag Helmut Küpper.

Fang, L. (2023, April 20). House Democrat Threatens Twitter Files Journalist with Prosecution and Imprisonment. *Leefang.Com*. https://www.leefang.com/p/house-democrat-threatens-twitter

Ferschli, B., Grabner, D., & Theine, H. (2019). *Zur Politischen Ökonomie der Medien in Deutschland: Eine Analyse der Konzentrationstendenzen und Besitzverhältnisse* (Issue 118).

Feuerbach, L. (2013). *Grundsätze der Philosophie der Zukunft*. Berliner Ausgabe.

Fisher, E. (2017). How Less Alienation Creates More Exploitation?: Audience Labour on Social Network Sites. In *Marx in the Age of Digital Capitalism*. Haymarket Books.

Foucault, M. (1995). *Discipline & Punish: The Birth of the Prison*. Vintage Books.

Foucault, M. (2004). *Naissance de la biopolitique: Cours au collège de France (1978–1979)*. Seuil Gallimard.

Freud, S. (1961). *The Future of an Illusion*. Norton & Company.

Friedman, M. (2002). *Capitalism and Freedom*. The University of Chicago Press.

Fuchs, C. (2010). Labor in Informational Capitalism and on the Internet. *The Information Society, 26*(3), 179–196. https://doi.org/10.1080/01972241003712215

Fuchs, C. (2012a). Dallas Smythe Today—The Audience Commodity, the Digital Labour Debate, Marxist Political Economy and Critical Theory. Prolegomena to a Digital Labour Theory of Value. *TripleC, 10*(2), 692–740. https://triple-c.at/index.php/tripleC/article/view/443

Fuchs, C. (2012b). With or Without Marx? With or Without Capitalism? A Re-joinder to Adam Arvidsson and Eleanor Colleoni. *TripleC, 10*(2). http://fuchs.uti.at

George, A. (2012). *Constructing Intellectual Property*. Cambridge University Press. https://doi.org/10.1017/CBO9781139035361

Gramsci, A. (1971). *Selection from the Prison Notebooks* (Q. Hoare & G. N. Smith, Eds.). International Publishers.

Greenwald, G. (2013, June 11). Edward Snowden: The Whistleblower Behind the NSA Surveillance Revelations. *The Guardian*. https://www.theguardian.com/world/2013/jun/09/edward-snowden-nsa-whistleblower-surveillance

Gurley, L. K. (2020, November 23). Secret Amazon Reports Expose Company Spying on Labor, Environmental Groups. *VICE*. https://www.vice.com/en/article/5dp3yn/amazon-leaked-reports-expose-spying-warehouse-workers-labor-union-environmental-groups-social-movements

Habermas, J. (1990). *Strukturwandel der Öffentlichkeit: Untersuchungen zu einer Kategorie der bürgerlichen Gesellschaft*. Suhrkamp.

Harada, T. (2019). *Economics of an Innovation System: Inside and Outside the Black Box*. Routledge.

Hegel, G. W. F. (1986). *Wissenschaft der Logik I, Werke in 20 Bänden, Band 5*. Suhrkamp.

Herman, E. S., & Chomsky, N. (1994). *Manufacturing Consent: The Political Economy of the Mass Media*. Vintage Books.

Hermeto, J. R. (2020). *Lukács' Ontologie des gesellschaftlichen Wandels: Von einer mythologischen Ontologie des absoluten Geistes zu einer Ontologie des gesellschaftlichen Seins*. Verlag Dr. Kovač.

Hermeto, J. R. (2021). Towards Social Change: Social Transformation in a Time of Social Disruption. *Dilemas, 14*(1), 219–242. https://doi.org/10.17648/dilemas.v14n1.30572

Hitler, A. (1927). *Mein Kampf*. Zentralverlag der NSDAP.

Hoffman, P. T. (2015). *Why Did Europe Conquer the World?* Oxford University Press.

Horkheimer, M. (2012). *Critique of Instrumental Reason*. Verso.

Hudson, M. (2015). *Killing the Host: How Financial Parasites and Debt Bondage Destroy the Global Economy*. CounterPunch Books.

Hull, G. (2019). *The Biopolitics of Intellectual Property: Regulating Innovation and Personhood in the Information Age*. Cambridge University Press.

Jessop, B. (2000). The State and the Contradictions of the Knowledge-driven Economy. In J. R. Bryson, P. W. Daniels, J. Pollard, & N. Henry (Eds.), *Knowledge, Space, Economy*. Routledge.

Johns, A. (2009). *Piracy: The Intellectual Property Wars from Gutenberg to Gates*. The University of Chicago Press.

Klein, N. (2008). *The Shock Doctrine: The Rise of Disaster Capitalism*. Penguin Books.

Klosowski, T. (2021, February 10). How Your Boss Can Use Your Remote-Work Tools to Spy on You. *The New York Times*. https://www.nytimes.com/wirecutter/blog/how-your-boss-can-spy-on-you/

Lazzarato, M. (1996). Immaterial Labor. In P. Virno & M. Hardt (Eds.), *Radical Thought in Italy: A Potential Politics*. University of Minnesota Press.

Levine, Y. (2018). *Surveillance Valley: The Secret Military History of the Internet*. PublicAffairs.

Linge, M. K., & Levine, J. (2022, December 24). Latest Batch of Twitter Files Shows CIA, FBI Involved in Content Moderation. *New York Post*. https://nypost.com/2022/12/24/latest-batch-of-twitter-files-shows-cia-fbi-involved-in-content-moderation/

Loewenstein, A. (2017). *Disaster Capitalism: Making a Killing Out of Catastrophe*. Verso.

Losurdo, D. (2011). *Liberalism: A Counter-History*. Verso.

Losurdo, D. (2016). *Class Struggle: A Political and Philosophical History*. Palgrave Macmillan.

Luhmann, N. (1991). *Soziale Systeme: Grundriß einer allgemeinen Theorie* (Vol. 21, Issue 1). Suhrkamp.

Lukács, G. (1963). *GLW, Band 11, Die Eigenart des Ästhetischen: 1. Halbband*. Luchterhand.

Lukács, G. (1986). *GLW, Band 14, Zur Ontologie des gesellschaftlichen Seins, Band 2*. Luchterhand.

Lukács, G. (2013). Geschichte und Klassenbewußtsein (1923). In *Georg Lukács Werke: Frühscriften II: Band 2*. Aisthesis.

MacArthur, J. R. (1992, January 6). Remember Nayirah, Witness for Kuwait? *The New York Times*. https://www.nytimes.com/1992/01/06/opinion/remember-nayirah-witness-for-kuwait.html

Marcuse, H. (2002). *One-Dimensional Man: Studies in the Ideology of Advanced Industrial Society*. Routledge.

Marx, K. (1962). Das Kapital: Kritik der politischen Ökonomie: Erster Band: Buch I: Der Produktionsprozeß des Kapitals. In *MEW Band 23*. Dietz Verlag Berlin.
Marx, K. (1964). Das Kapital: Kritik der politischen Ökonomie: Dritter Band: Buch III: Der Gesamtprozeß der kapitalistischen Produktion. In F. Engels (Ed.), *MEW Band 25*. Dietz Verlag Berlin.
Marx, K. (1968). Ökonomisch-philosophische Manuskripte aus dem Jahre 1844. In *MEW Band 40*. Dietz Verlag Berlin.
Marx, K. (1977). Das Elend der Philosophie. Antwort auf Proudhons: 'Philosophie des Elends'. In *MEW Band 04*. Dietz Verlag Berlin.
Marx, K. (1981). Zur Judenfrage. In *MEW Band 01*. Dietz Verlag Berlin.
Marx, K. (1983). Grundrisse der Kritik der politischen Ökonomie. In *MEW Band 42*. Dietz Verlag Berlin.
Marx, K., & Engels, F. (1977). Manifest der Kommunistischen Partei. In *MEW Band 04*. Dietz Verlag Berlin.
Marx, K., & Engels, F. (1978). Die deutsche Ideologie: Kritik der neuesten deutschen Philosophie in ihren Repräsentanten Feuerbach, B. Bauer und Stirner, und des deutschen Sozialismus in seinen verschiedenen Propheten. In *MEW Band 03*. Dietz Verlag Berlin.
Maskus, K. E., & Reichman, J. H. (2016). The Globalization of Private Knowledge Goods and the Privatization of Global Public Goods. In A. George (Ed.), *Globalization and Intellectual Property* (pp. 335–377). Routledge.
Mazzucato, M. (2018). *The Value of Everything: Making and Taking in the Global Economy*. Allen Lane.
Migliano, S. (2023, February 13). Employee Surveillance Software Demand up 55% Since Pandemic Started. *TOP10VPN*. https://www.top10vpn.com/research/covid-employee-surveillance/
Mirowski, P. (2009). Defining Neoliberalism. In P. Mirowski & D. Plehwe (Eds.), *The Road from Mont Pèlerin: The Making of the Neoliberal Thought Collective*. Harvard University Press.
Mirowski, P. (2013). *Never Let a Serious Crisis Go to Waste: How Neoliberalism Survived the Financial Meltdown*. Verso.
Mosco, V. (2017). Marx in the Cloud. In C. Fuchs & V. Mosco (Eds.), *Marx in the Age of Digital Capitalism*. Haymarket Books.
Mueller, G. (2019). *Media Piracy in the Cultural Economy: Intellectual Property and Labor Under Neoliberal Restructuring*. Routledge. https://doi.org/10.4324/9780203730720

Nicol, D. (2021). The Pendulum of Patents, Principles and Products—From the Industrial Revolution to the Genetic Revolution. In G. Ghidini, H. Ullrich, & P. Drahos (Eds.), *Kritika: Essays on Intellectual Property* (pp. 99–124). Elgar.
Oddi, A. S. (2016). TRIPS—Natural Rights and a "Polite Form of Economic Imperialism". In A. George (Ed.), *Globalization and Intellectual Property* (pp. 139–194). Routledge.
Orsi, F., Sevilla, C., & Coriat, B. (2006). Upstream Patents and Public Health: The Case of Genetic Testing for Breast Cancer. In M. Mazzucato & G. Dosi (Eds.), *Knowledge Accumulation and Industry Evolution: The Case of Pharma-Biotech*. Cambridge University Press.
Patel, R., & Moore, J. W. (2017). *A History of the World in Seven Cheap Things: A Guide to Capitalism, Nature, and the Future of the Planet*. University of California Press.
Pellizzoni, L., & Ylönen, M. (2012). Hegemonic Contingencies: Neoliberalized Technoscience and Neorationality. In L. Pellizzoni & M. Ylönen (Eds.), *Neoliberalism and Technoscience: Critical Assessments*. Ashgate.
Phillips, P. (2018). *Giants: The Global Power Elite*. Seven Stories Press.
Polanyi, K. (2001). *The Great Transformation: The Political and Economic Origins of Our Time*. Beacon.
Provost, C., & Kennard, M. (2023). *Silent Coup: How Corporations Overthrew Democracy*. Bloomsbury Academic.
Report to the Director of National Intelligence 27 January 2022. (2023). https://www.dni.gov/files/ODNI/documents/assessments/ODNI-Declassified-Report-on-CAI-January2022.pdf
Robinson, W. I. (2014). *Global Capitalism and the Crisis of Humanity*. Cambridge University Press.
Robinson, W. I. (2020). *The Global Police State*. Pluto Press.
Robinson, W. I. (2022). *Global Civil War: Capitalism Post-Pandemic*. PM Press.
Rockhill, G. (2017). *Counter-History of the Present: Untimely Interrogations into Globalization, Technology, Democracy*. Duke University Press.
Rodney, W. (2018). *How Europe Underdeveloped Africa*. Verso.
Rosa, H. (2013). *Social Acceleration: A New Theory of Modernity*. Columbia University Press.
Rosenberg, N. (1982). *Inside the Black Box: Technology and Economics*. Cambridge University Press.
Saunders, F. S. (2013). *The Cultural Cold War: The CIA and The World of Arts and Letters*. The New Press.
Shakespeare, W. (2004). *Timon of Athens* (J. Jowett, Ed.). Oxford University Press.

Shakespeare, W. (2016). *Die Fremden: Für mehr Mitgefühl*. dtv.
Shiva, V. (2016). *Biopiracy: The Plunder of Nature and Knowledge*. North Atlantic Books.
Smythe, D. W. (1977). Communications: Blindspot of Western Marxism. *Canadian Journal of Political and Social Theory, 1*(3), 1–27. https://journals.uvic.ca/index.php/ctheory/article/view/13715
Sum, N.-L., & Jessop, B. (2013). *Towards a Cultural Political Economy: Putting Culture in Its Place in Political Economy*. Edward Elgar Publishing.
Szepanski, A. (2014). *Kapitalisierung Band 2: Non-Ökonomie des gegenwärtigen Kapitalismus*. LAIKA Verlag.
Szepanski, A. (2018). *Imperialismus, Staatsfaschisierung und die Kriegsmaschinen des Kapitals: Drei Essays*. LAIKA Verlag.
Szepanski, A. (2022). *Financial Capital in the 21st Century: A New Theory of Speculative Capital*. Palgrave Macmillan. https://doi.org/10.1007/978-3-030-93151-3
Taibbi, M. (2023, April 13). Meet the Censored: Me? *Racket News*. https://www.racket.news/p/meet-the-censored-me
Terranova, T. (2000). Free Labor: Producing Culture for the Digital Economy. *Social Text, 18*(2), 33–58. http://muse.jhu.edu/article/31873
Varoufakis, Y. (2020). *Another Now: Dispatches from an Alternative Present*. Random House, Inc.
Vault 7: CIA Hacking Tools Revealed. (2017, March 7). WikiLeaks. https://wikileaks.org/ciav7p1/
Vitali, S., Glattfelder, J. B., & Battiston, S. (2011). The Network of Global Corporate Control. *PLoS One, 6*(10), 1–6. https://doi.org/10.1371/journal.pone.0025995
von Hayek, F. A. (1948). *Individualism and Economic Order*. The University of Chicago Press.
Walpen, B. (2004). Die offenen Feinde und ihre Gesellschaft: Eine hegemonietheoretische Studie zur Mont Pèlerin Society. *Angewandte Chemie International Edition, 6*(11), 951–952.
Wittel, A. (2017). Digital Marx: Toward a Political Economy of Distributed Media. In C. Fuchs & V. Mosco (Eds.), *Marx in the Age of Digital Capitalism* (pp. 68–104). Haymarket Books.
Wood, E. M. (2017). *The Origin of Capitalism: A Longer View*. Verso.
Wood, E. M. (2022). Citizens to Lords: Antiquity to the Middle Ages. In *A Social History of Western Political Thought*. Verso.

Zarko Dimitrioski. (2019, February 13). How Much Money is in the Global Marketing Industry—More than We Believed. *Forbes*. https://www.forbes.com/sites/zarkodimitrioski/2019/02/13/how-much-money-is-in-the-global-marketing-industry-more-than-we-believed/

Zuboff, S. (2019). *The Age of Surveillance Capitalism: The Fight for a Human Future at the New Frontier of Power*. Profile Books.

5

Conclusion: Social Disintegration and the Privatisation of Knowledge

Under capitalism, it has become impossible to discuss knowledge appropriation if, first, the question of intellectual appropriation being increasingly subsumed by capitalist private relations is not addressed and, second, if knowledge production, appropriation, and reproduction are not related to the sphere of social power since the latter cannot per excellence be extricated from the former and vice versa.

Nonetheless, the leap towards dealing with intellectual property cannot be uncritical. In virtually all analyses, intellectual appropriation and intellectual private appropriation remain undifferentiated; instead, two generic terms are used, namely, intellectual commons and intellectual property, assuming what needs to be explained. The category commons is simply postulated without further explanation, and the concrete identity between property and appropriation disappears. Instead, property is not only mostly conflated with private property but also private property with personal property. In this sense, intellectual appropriation is deprived of its general ontological condition; at the same time, capitalism's crucial peculiarity emerging from particular social property relations is uncritically brushed aside, as if it were irrelevant to the very analyses dealing with social relations under the capitalist mode of production. [Exclusive] Private property of the means of production, marking the

J. Romeiro Hermeto, *The Paradox of Intellectual Property in Capitalism*,
https://doi.org/10.1007/978-3-031-49967-8_5

beginning of capitalism, imparted on social relations a completely new quality, as the economy ceased to be a locus which enabled the unfolding of the various social arrangements to become an imperative and constraint.

This book acknowledges the value of the contemporary intellectual property discourse and theories but aims to bring a fresh perspective to the ongoing discussions by utilising the method of immanent critique. This approach allows for a more critical analysis of the social conditions of intellectual property and, correspondingly, existing theories. Each of the three main chapters of this book is preceded by a brief summary of the corresponding chapter in a still unpublished manuscript, and although they are standalone endeavours, this abridgement helps to unify the ideas present in them both. It goes without saying that this investigation can neither exhaust the topic nor does it have this pretension. On the one hand, there were sections in this book which were consciously left out due to restrictions of time and space; on the other, there must be many other aspects of which I must have remained hitherto ignorant.

This last brief section does not seek to produce a faithful summary of the whole book. Instead, it intends to connect some fundamental elements and demonstrate the importance of portraying them not in isolation but as parts of a whole.

What is the condition for human existence? Production of human existence. What is the condition for the production of human existence? The human activity of production. What is the human activity of production? Labour. What is the condition of labour? Appropriation and transformation of nature. What is the condition of human appropriation and transformation? The teleological setting—or simply the concrete actualisation of the imagined intentionality. What is the condition of the teleological setting? Intellectual appropriation. What is the condition for intellectual appropriation (property)? The existence of knowledge. What is the condition for the existence of knowledge? Production and reproduction (transmission) of knowledge. What is the condition for the production and transmission of knowledge? An objective reality, existing subjective living beings, and existing knowledge. What is the condition for creating new knowledge and reproducing existing knowledge? Non-private knowledge. Moreover, why do subjective living beings create and foster non-private knowledge from an objective reality? Because of their concrete natural and social needs to produce their human existence.

This reasoning could give the impression of linearity or even of an abstract knowledge in-itself. Needless to say, this process occurs through interdependent practices, and the production of knowledge necessarily means its embeddedness in a material reality. The metaphysical notion of abstract, unrestricted, incorporeal knowledge must consequently necessarily hypostasise the ontological condition of knowledge. Intellectual creation, appropriation, and reproduction can only occur within material-historical dimensions. They are contingent on each society's historical stage and the level of material development. Primitive societies deprived of means of storing knowledge had (and some still have) in their singular individuals the necessary means which embody, objectify, and concretise knowledge production and reproduction. In such a setting, it is obvious the absurdity of conceiving appropriation of knowledge as something private and isolated, monopolised by a singular actor. While the basis of singular knowledge necessarily connects to the social body, improvements developed by isolated individuals can only be actualised when it falls back to the same social body, gaining a dimension that does not exclude the singular actor but which necessarily relates to his social reality.

The history of *intellectual property*$_{(private)}$ is non-linear and often contradictory. For instance, while the book trade in *Venezia* became an enormous enterprise, its spark was the patent of Johannes Gutenberg's invention granted to von Speyer, who merely privately appropriated elsewhere an already existing invention and social practice; furthermore, the book trade then upsurged not because of the patent but because of its absence brought about with von Speyer's death (Schippel, 1989; Squassina, 2019). In England, the system of the Stationers had created a proto-copyright which was neither based on the law nor state power but operated among book traders. The British crown created a system of patents (privileges) which competed with the ongoing practice, benefiting authors (Johns, 2009).

Therefore, common notions claiming that this system enables knowledge promotion and welfare fail from the outset to stand historical scrutiny. Moreover, when considering the characteristics of knowledge production and reproduction, it becomes even more evident that privatisation also fails the test of efficient allocation. Nonetheless, there is a difference between rhetoric and reality. While the former asserts an image of itself, that is, an imaginary hypostasised reality, the latter, as the ultimate criterion of truth, reveals the concealed bowels of these relations.

With the end of the so-called Golden Age, an extraordinary phase of capitalist structural crisis began (Castro, 1979). The Fordist-Keynesian model, which after the Second World War had been remarkably successful in enabling European and Japanese societies to build a sizeable capitalist capacity and accumulate capital, was coming to an end due to multiple factors. Here is not the place to analyse this, but some factors are briefly described next. Bretton Woods collapsed with the US-American unilateral withdrawal; energy prices skyrocketed; the cost of labour rose as well; the growth of the mass of capital imposed more difficulty in sustaining profit rates; colonial liberation struggles promoted worldwide by the Soviet Union rendered access to cheap resources less accessible; developing countries pressured international competition; etc. In short, the conditions which had permitted the hitherto post-war re-emergence of Europe and Japan, both sponsored mainly by the United States, were now virtually absent.

The politically driven neoliberal ideology, which started to be already formed before World War II, was, with the debacle of the Fordist-Keynesian model, finally taking off to become a significant influence over worldwide politics, economy, and culture. While neoliberal therapy shock was being imposed upon third world countries since the 1960s (Bevins, 2020), and even with greater impetus during the 1970s (Klein, 2008), it finally culminated in no longer being relegated to the capitalist peripheries to invade the capitalist core—the most evident and relevant examples are of course Ronald Reagan in the United States and Margaret Thatcher in England (needless to say, it also invaded the whole Western capitalist block of the G7 and beyond) (Loewenstein, 2017). Nevertheless, during the 1980s, a second phenomenon started to take shape. As the Soviet Union imploded due to internal and external forces, the multipolar world (dominated by a bipolar world of capitalist and socialist blocks) shifted towards a US-American hegemony. The beginning of the 1990s witnessed its consolidation. Based on this unique and privileged position, blocks of capital based in the United States used this leverage to their own advantage.

In this context, *intellectual property$_{(private)}$* suffered an unparalleled metamorphosis from its hitherto existence to its present dominating form. Until that moment, *intellectual property$_{(private)}$* had a relatively limited existence, for each nation had its own intellectual property system or even none whatsoever, causing an immense problem in enforcing international legal charges against infringement claims. Unipolarity enabled US-American capital headed by Pfizer to develop and implement a groundbreaking strategy. As a crucial trade partner of virtually every nation on the planet, the United States imposed a novel condition upon other nations which subordinated intellectual property regimes to trade (Drahos & Braithwaite, 2002). The practical consequence was as powerful as it was simple. Trade became an economic weapon pointed against other countries' "heads", whose choices were either to surrender to the US-American intellectual property system or to be excluded from world trade. Any country trading with a non-aligned country would be likewise excluded. This forced countries not only to subordinate themselves to the US-American system but also to preemptively exclude those that would not; this, in turn, created the necessary feedback loop to make the United States imposition actual and universal. TRIPS emerged as the consolidation of an international homogenised system of private appropriation and control of intellectual property. Despite standard claims that confer the abstract right or actual concrete laws as elements of neutral mediation, organisation, regulation, etc., it represents instead—by definition—an arbitrary imposition. Embedded in particular power relations, it can attain the necessary condition to render itself a coercive power. A norm, a right, a law which cannot be enforced is void. Therefore, when such arbitrary power is enforced, it also commands certain behaviours. The scope of action becomes not only limited *a priori* but also the very action is shaped by the notions legitimated and rooted within the normative power. It is thus absurd to conceive any legal system as a realm of emancipatory possibilities. In reality, normative systems and precepts are negative per excellence. The so-called freedom transpired by it is henceforth a form of negative freedom. In this sense, intellectual property systems—instead of fostering, as they are commonly regarded—hinder the development and limit the scope of knowledge production and reproduction. This intellectual private system is itself a means of legitimation and normalisation of determined power relations. As shown, it is an illusion to regard legal arrangement as the locus of the genesis of property when, in reality, it merely attests to and confirms ongoing social relations, providing the private property of the means of production with a crucial ideological veil of social validity.

Consequently, it is also an illusion to conceive the so-called primitive accumulation as two original moments of appropriation, the first referring to the English enclosure of land and the second to the contemporary enclosure of the mind, especially by the *Digital*. Primitive accumulation by no means represents isolated moments; it is a crucial feature of capital formation and accumulation. Economic power historically and continuously bases its power on extra-economic factors. Both intellectual and non-intellectual private property require governmental, juridical, military, social-ideological, and mediatic-propagandistic powers to be sustained. Their emergences are products of specific historical conditions and social arrangements, thus products of socio-historical causal relations, and by no means aprioristic teleological imposition by some arbitrary will and higher intelligence—reinforcing again, as is commonly regarded, that private property would be the product of legal doctrines. While during the most significant portion of human history, multiple forms of common property of the means of production dominated social relations, the emergence of exclusive private property only arose by means of violence, plunder, control and subjugation; the fact that personal property, often called private property, has a millennial existence often obscures these historical facts. The constant accumulation of property employing extra-economic powers is often concealed behind a speculative form of jurisprudence and mythological history expressed by the hypostasis of a dual-enclosure movement.

With the emergence of the Digital, the social objective and subjective conditions for knowledge production and reproduction have been transformed. The Internet appeared to have brought about the utopic locus for a gift economy. Insofar as knowledge is regarded as something abstract and the Internet a venue of free social exchange, illusions veiling the Internet's appropriation and control by capitalist power obfuscate critical perceptions. The notion of the thing in-itself seems to overcome the concrete practice of particular social relations. The fact that five capitalist companies virtually owned all Internet data is disguised behind the appearance that each individual can autonomously create her own website. The relationship between quantity and quality is superseded by the idealisation of subjective apprehension of reality; that is, while monopoly power has immense power in this so-called digital gift economy, the individual perception of self-assertion because of how one perceives the digital or how one can imprint her wants and views in social media seems to overshadow the reality in which the Internet has been captured and subjected to the constant capitalist appropriation, accumulation, and control.

Banishing the vulgarised notion of rigidity or, conversely, absolutisation (total abstraction) of what represents the beginning and the end, the premise and the result, the condition and the product, is absolutely imperative and must be emphasised. In both Hegel and Marx, this problem is not an isolated methodological question but instead becomes entrenched within each category (Hegel) and relation (Marx). Both poles exist as separate entities only on an analytical level. In reality, they are both the same, two elements of a totality, representing two different perspectives towards the same unity. It goes without saying that this does not impose a rigid existence, for each moment (re)presents a difference in the form-content duality. What is vital to grasp is that what appears as the premise is the result of something, and what results from one thing becomes the premise for something else. This is an absolute imperative to the understanding of the development of knowledge and the relationship between property and intellectual property.

Knowledge (re)production thus has two realities. It entails a general and a particular condition of existence. Before differentiating between them, it is critical to understand the conditions that shape the particular form.

The capitalist mode of production entails two dimensions of dominance over, first, concurrent modes of production and, second, social relations in general. These two dimensions are also products of two modes of exploitation which derive from the particularity of capitalist property relations. The historical private appropriation of land, conferring the English aristocracy monopoly over land, imposed upon agriculture an economic imperative previously unknown. The dispossession, on the one hand, and the concentration by appropriation of the means of survival, on the other, created a twofold economic pressure. The fact that producers now did not own the means of production yielded a condition of competition among them. Owners, removing themselves from feudal social compulsion, subjected their dominant condition not to tradition, religion, or military might but to economic power. Therefore, also owners were exposed to the new economic imperative. These pressures concomitantly generated pressure to increase the rate of production output per unit of land. British capitalism was born. Meeting the demands of this sort of compulsion involves two modes of exploitation. The first is to remove each and every limit possible that could restrain labour from performing its productive activities, that is, not only extending the natural working day and its intensity towards the barriers of human natural limits but also removing the social barriers of tradition, religion, moral norms, etc. This mode of exploitation relates to the absolute surplus-value. And when capitalism starts expanding its logic elsewhere, it first subjugates other modes of production to this quantitative imperative, formally subsuming them. The second mode of exploitation occurs when capitalist relations manage to expand further, but this time at a qualitative level. Therefore, improvements in the production process itself, rendering greater output per unit of time, impose the condition of efficiency. It is only when this logic is imposed over other modes of production, that is, they metamorphose themselves into the capitalist mode of production, that the real subsumption of labour under capitalism takes place.

Ignoring these crucial relations of exploitation, in which knowledge production, reproduction and utilisation are pivotal for the real subsumption process, most contemporary intellectual property theories provide uncritical justifications instead of exposing the limits of these relations, thus fostering a fetishised apprehension and existence of *intellectual property$_{(private)}$*. Recognising these theoretical shortcomings indicates neither the imposition of a homogenous analytical framework upon them nor the complete rejection of many important theoretical insights. Alexandra George's *Constructing Intellectual Property* provides an essential basis for any discussion of *intellectual property$_{(private)}$*. Peter Drahos' philosophical work discusses crucial aspects of intellectual property and relates some philosophical teachings of great Western philosophers. Adrian Johns' analysis of piracy teaches how *intellectual property$_{(private)}$* relates to piracy and its history in a comprehensive fashion. On the other hand, John Braithwaite and Peter Drahos also draw on historical aspects of intellectual property but, most importantly, give a brilliant overview of the transformative process of intellectual property's modern form culminating in TRIPS (Drahos & Braithwaite, 2002). It goes without saying that the list of authors and works which enriches the intellectual property debate is vast and cannot be summarised within these few lines. What is important to emphasise, however, is the constant separation of social relations into pure categories deprived of ontological bearings. Creativity is expurgated and purified from estranged and alienated labour; intellectual property is elevated beyond and above the physical world to attain a metaphysical reality (in-itself); indigenous knowledge is determined to belong within *intellectual property*$_{(common)}$, whereas Western knowledge is placed within a system of protection under the banner of *intellectual property*$_{(private)}$; etc. The consequence is the fetishisation of human thinking and its transformation into an arbitrary category instead of framing it within its historical-ontological dimensions.

Despite relatively recent discoveries that indicate that great apes possess extraordinary cognitive capacity and abilities, a not unimportant gap between their and human cognition nonetheless remains. Under different banners, research on cognition has confirmed what Marx and Marxism have long emphasised, basing their critical analytical framework on an ontology of the social-being. While great apes produce their lives mediated by egoistic "social" relations, similar to how thus far liberal ideology has (wrongly) conceived human relations, the existence of the latter entails a truly social character in which intentionality gains a much broader and more complex scope of collective dimension. While cognitive research underlines the significance of the activities which account for the production and reproduction of the life of both the species and singular beings, it fails to give a proper accent to the peculiarity of the human mode of doing. It is precisely the mediation by social intentionality what is known as labour. Therefore, human cognition is forged throughout a historical-ontological process in which labour activities have played a fundamental role. It goes without saying that labour and human cognition cannot be separated from one another; they are two dimensions of the same totality and, thus, develop together.

The cooperation process, namely, human collective doing, imposes new conditions and the need to meet them. Normative behaviour arises from labour relations because collective actions require the capacity of appraising. Acts of evaluation are neither unidirectional nor bidirectional but rather entail a greater complexity in which assessment also determines and shapes the behaviour of the self. It is not enough to estimate the capacity of singular beings or even certain group formations which could enhance the capabilities of the self nor to be evaluated by others in the same manner; it is pivotal that the self posits herself from the perspective of the other, thus performing her own self-appraisal. Therefore, conceiving normative categories, behaviours, and so on deprived of socio-ontological dimensions based on labour relations must remain a metaphysical, moral and superficial postulation. This sort of normative determination represents the very denial of normative relations. Human assessment must depart not from an abstract normative postulation in-itself, as one-dimensional and abstract, but rather from interdependent assessments occurring within concrete context-based labour relations. Only by understanding the contemporary ontological conditions of capitalist relations can the regulations involving intellectual appropriation be critically and (tendentiously) correctly apprehended.

While metaphysics imposes intentionality (telos) as destinies to be realised, understanding the relationship between teleology and labour provides a more nuanced and complex perspective of reality. Both intention and the act of doing are in-themselves void. It is undisputable that intention in-itself is abstract content without movement, whereas a concrete act without intention is a movement without content. With labour, human beings reveal the capability not to impose a teleological reality—namely, the idea as an authentic movement—but rather to give causal relations a new qualitative inflexion. Collective action thus presupposed common understandings and shared goals. If appropriation of reality occurs by means of labour, labour as the act which actualises intentionality presupposes an apprehension of reality and its preconception on an imaginary level. In this sense, it becomes evident that appropriation presupposes intellectual appropriation. At the same time, the actualisation of the latter presupposes the former as its concretisation and real movement. Consequently, property relations cannot be an isolated normative postulation, nor do they entail a one-sided reality. Property must be regarded as a totality which necessarily consists of a dialectical relationship of mutual determination of property and intellectual property. Collapsing its specific historical forms found in capitalism, namely, private property and *intellectual property*$_{(private)}$, together with its universal dimensions, must thus eradicate humans' ontological condition of labour and eternalised capitalist relations.

However, intellectual appropriation is not an *ad hoc* condition, and its refinement culminating in science does not characterise a *creatio ex nihilo*. Despite its unmistakable transformative potential, thus representing a crucial premise for altering the acts of doing, science first emerged as a product. As Lukács shows, labour contains an essential dimension of choices in which different alternatives (co-)exist. When one recognises two stones as being different and, as such, enabling different potentials to be developed, one starts to differentiate, select, categorise, etc. Each moment of choice first appears out of the constraint of objective necessities. Finding solutions to solve given problems further furnishes the capacities of apprehension and differentiation. A process of intellectual appropriation is therefore inseparable from the process of transformation. As shown by Clifford D. Conner, the solutions found and (or) created thus represent technological advancements. Consequently, the repetition and generalisation of these achievements form a body of knowledge. Science does not emerge from a body of pure theory; instead, theory merely provides real science with a qualitative means for scientific development.

With the historical developments which culminated in the Digital, knowledge production suffered a tremendous blow. Because use-value is often mixed with value (that is, exchange-value), the broadening of the notion of knowledge production has carried with itself a misrepresentation of the value of knowledge as if it were augmenting. Even if one assumes that knowledge has become ubiquitous—for, in reality, it has always been present and a necessary condition of human ontological production—this does not aprioristically reveal the trend of its value. In fact, as the Digital developed to the point of computers ceasing to be enormous and highly expensive machines, of data storage and transfer becoming cheap and fast, to the point of computers, smartphones, etc., becoming so symbiotically merged in daily life that the true representation of the value of knowledge can be apprehended. Knowledge and information production, accumulation, transformation, and transmission/reproduction always depend on material means. It is thus an illusion to conceive knowledge and the means of knowledge as two separate things. As the value of the means of knowledge collapsed, so did the value of knowledge production. Building upon existing knowledge or simply copying it has become relatively easy precisely because its means have become highly accessible. This has posed a qualitative new conflict in a system based on social production and private appropriation. Control over non-intellectual property was suddenly not enough to secure its intellectual basis. If earlier the difficulty of accessing the means of knowledge production has maintained property as a totality protected, now the availability of the previously unattainable means has distressed the monopolistic power over property's totality. Private property of the means of production ceased to represent the necessary guarantee to capitalist power. The contradiction between social production and private appropriation had reached such a height that control over intellectual appropriation also had to become ubiquitous. The already ongoing separation of property and intellectual property epitomised its exclusionary potential when TRIPS came into being, providing virtually global control over intellectual appropriation.

If, on the one hand, the value of knowledge production has plummeted, on the other, the creation of new knowledge not only remains an unpredictable endeavour but also becomes more complex since each new discovery is built upon a combination of a vast array of existing knowledge. This sort of complexity imposes temporal-economic limits on the capacity of private capital. To invest research funds, not knowing how much it will cost and how long it will take to yield profits, if any, becomes much more challenging and riskier, depending on how unforeseeable the undertaking is. In this context, the capitalist state takes over the responsibility, organising the labour-force, redirecting social resources to knowledge production, imposing and creating the necessary material and subjective conditions, socialising the costs, and assuming virtually all the risks. Moreover, after the state has yielded positive results, despite the common-sense rhetoric about private investments and risky endeavours, historically, private capital gladly appropriates with little risk all these social activities of research and development and builds on a base of products to commercialise and privately appropriate such collective effort. This practice has remained an important method to protect and foster the capitalist mode of production, especially since the end of World War II, thus incubating all modern technology often associated with private capital, including big tech, big pharma, spatial, military, or even the financial sector.

Intellectual property theories often recognise this tension between the social production of knowledge and its private appropriation by the capitalist class. It is an ontological condition of knowledge to be socially conceived, used, and transformed; this must remain at odds with capitalist private appropriation. This inherent tension is what I call the first paradox of intellectual property. Theorists have hitherto struggled to determine how to maintain a relevant pool of informational resources fostering basic research while sustaining the process of capitalist privatisation. It is a contradictory situation in which an artificial limit cannot be set. While theory may establish neat haircuts[1] and thresholds, reality is not determined by intellectual postulations but rather by social relations. As capitalist relations impose enormous power upon politics, the judiciary, discourse (academia and media), etc., the limits of intellectual appropriation will be mainly determined by the extension of this very capitalist power and not by its subjugated instances struggling to impose some barriers. Of course, counterforces may hinder capitalist expansionary rule to some extent, but only to the degree that it fosters sustaining capital as dominant relations—analogous to laws limiting labour hours because the labour class was not being able to reproduce itself, thus hurting the very powers which exploited them (Marx, 1962).

This apprehension overlooks a pivotal condition of knowledge production. As labour power is exploited by capital, the labourer must knowingly subject himself to capital to secure his existence. This subservient behaviour is not an act of will since not owning the means of production

[1] Term used in finance, which refers to the difference between the market value of an asset and the underestimated value set as collateral; thus, it expresses the perceived risk of certain financial operations as if it could be aprioristically attained; it is consequently a hypostasis.

leaves him no choice but to subject himself to the economic imperatives of capitalism, however impersonal. Labour, as the confirmation of his life, simultaneously represents its denial. This relation enables an estranged and paradoxical reproduction of labour. From the perspective of intellectual production, despite being necessarily a social feat at the level of general ontology, when subsumed under the capitalist mode of production, knowledge must be privatised to attain social existence. From being social in its conception, it has to become privatised through the process of actualisation to reveal its social existence. Therefore, its actualised social dimension is private and must remain at odds with its own seminal existence. Its social actualisation thus represents the demised of its social reproduction because instead of being part of a social movement of apprehension and transformation of reality, it becomes epitomised in an isolated anti-social form. This anti-social existence of knowledge production itself represents what I call the second paradox of intellectual property. That is, not only do capital and knowledge retain a paradoxical existence in relation to one another, but intellectual production itself is paradoxically separated into, on the one hand, in-itself and, on the other, for-itself. The separation, which splits the totality of property into property and intellectual property, simultaneously represents the separation of intellectual appropriation in-itself and for-itself.

The separation of intellectual property in a double existence is the expression of a social power that controls the means of its actualisation and hence intellectual appropriation itself. Monopoly not only cannot be regarded as belonging to only some isolated practices—for instance, when a company virtually exclusively controls a particular activity—or the necessity of innate control of specific sectors—the so-called natural monopolies. Additionally, control over knowledge corresponds to monopolistic practices. In-itself, *intellectual property*$_{(private)}$, regardless of copyright, trademark, or patent, is a form of monopoly power. It consolidates exclusive control over certain intellectual practices. The more socially relevant a certain knowledge is, the more power its private controller can yield under his restricted dominium. For instance, Bill Gates' strategy of pushing DOS to power computers, as described by Peter Drahos and John Braithwaite, is an excellent example in which a colossal dependency on Gates' proprietary position was created regardless of the computer manufacturer (Drahos & Braithwaite, 2002). Today, even though Microsoft servers Azure are often powered by Linux, for the consumers of personal computers, buying Gates' Microsoft OS (Windows) is (virtually) compulsory when purchasing a new computer, whether or not one wishes to. The other go-to alternative is Apple's proprietary MacOS system, which runs its own computers. Accordingly, such a binary dominant division can also be found within smartphones, which are powered by pre-installed proprietary closed-source software. While Apple runs its proprietary iOS, virtually all other phones run an Android version, which is then owned by Google, despite Android Open Source Project (AOSP) being a free and open source software based on Linux—an open, freely and collectively created kernel, often mistaken for an OS (Amadeo, 2018). There are several types of Linux-based OSs that most users do not know how to access or use. In addition, recently Huawei, after being cornered by the US-American economic war, has developed its own OS (Harmony) to run its devices independently from Microsoft (for computers) and Google (for Smartwatches, Smartphones, and Tablets).[2]

In this sense, it is essential to highlight that property is not an eternal static condition but a historically ever-changing social relation. Consequently, it is clear that despite the contemporary dominance of intellectual property relations by few influential capitalist players, antagonistic movements and processes continue to occur, hence creating latent possibilities for change as concomitantly social conditions mutate—as seen with the just mentioned Linux-based OS examples and Huawei's Harmony.

Nevertheless, the changes in property relations do not simply mean the possibility for the obstruction, supersession, or ostracisation of private property. Likewise, its metamorphosis into more multifaceted relations—such as Creative Commons or the BRR—reaffirms existing social property relations, prologuing private property relations. Further unfolding of the totality of property, now broken in two, is thus not only propelled by the necessity to sustain private power utilising the rigid protection of non-intellectual property to secure machines, hardware, buildings, etc., but of *intellectual property*$_{(private)}$, amalgamating in-itself various spheres of

[2] Additionally, Kylinsoft, a subsidiary of state-owned China Electronics Corporation, launched in July 2023 "the country's first open-source desktop operating system (OS) named OpenKylin 1.0" (Hongpei, 2023).

capitalist power. From financial capital to the propaganda apparatus, from digital participation to digital mass surveillance, the mechanisms of intellectual property systems act as crucial propelling elements for their functioning.

The power conveyed by *intellectual property$_{(private)}$* involves another dimension of capitalist power. Capitalisation, or the formation of fictitious capital, possesses similar features of *intellectual property$_{(private)}$* not only because it endows an artificial independent existence from the totality of property. Whereas the latter represents the separation of teleology from the setting, the former confers social reality to a future idealised existence. Furthermore, as fictitious capital moved away from those more straightforward formations already characterised by Marx into more complex bonds, securities and derivatives contracts, *intellectual property$_{(private)}$* becomes pivotal to safeguarding proprietary intellectual tools such as algorithms and software (for instance, trading, risking, and pricing systems).

The prerogative of these instruments is not a monopoly of the banking system. Instead, they are widely entrenched in industrial multinationals as well as governments. In the 1990s, it gained a qualitatively new dimension when restrictions on the financial system were suppressed. Outstretching national borders, foreign capital started to flood national economies and supply chains, thus becoming much more interconnected and interdependent. This transnational mechanism provided leading capitalist players with significant leeway and power. Investing more in the financial sector and withdrawing from production, the dependency on financial gains, marketing activities and outsourced production grew accordingly. All of these invariably solidify and further concentrate the separation of property and intellectual property. Without the fortification of the latter, these spheres of power could not be properly enforced. *Intellectual property$_{(private)}$* had become part of an economic weapon arsenal.

Although marketing, which heavily relies on *intellectual property$_{(private)}$*, has relatively been universally internalised as the new normal, it entails two crucial dimensions that must be denaturalised. First, ruling-class propaganda appears to many as nothing more than communicative information. Consequently, both the apologetic and critical teachings of, respectively, Gustave Le Bon and Edward Bernays, on the one hand, and Edward S. Herman and Noam Chomsky, on the other, seem broadly forgotten. The character of not only controlling but, most importantly, shaping behaviour is paramount to propagandistic activities, often concealed by the taxonomy of marketing and advertisement. Nevertheless, marketing-propagandistic functions do not end there. In addition to its role in legitimating the *status quo*, the whole advertisement apparatus also performs a significant function in the process of extraction of surplus-value. Now, each moment of consumption constitutes a moment of surplus-value extraction by marketing. In the price of each commodity, a not irrelevant portion is destined to cover marketing costs, which correspondingly provides a portion of surplus-value that yields profit for this branch of capitalist activity. Needless to say that in-itself marketing cannot create surplus-value; however, being embedded within the process of commodity production and surplus-value extraction, its surplus-value does not represent a simple gratuity from marketing buyers. It has itself become a crucial element in the valorisation process of capitalist production and accumulation.

In the so-called Digital Age, the marketing apparatus has become even more ubiquitous. Moreover, as industrial and banking capital had already merged at the beginning of the twentieth century to form financial capital and financial capital with the capitalist state forming capitalist imperialism, in the twenty-first century, a new merger occurred; capitalist imperialism also fused with advertisement, epitomising a total control system. Surveillance is perpetrated by the capitalist state as well as capitalist corporations. Nonetheless, they are not competing to impose unilateral control but rather work hand-in-hand to impose total control. Controlling and shaping behaviour is not enough. Every action is now being monitored for the dual purpose of manufacturing obedient consent and surplus-value extraction. With the tools designed along and around *intellectual property* $_{(private)}$, exploitation gains a new dimension because it becomes totalising not only in the scope of action but also outstretches its full potential. The very consumer of the Digital performs labour both actively and passively and provides this totalising capitalist system with the raw material and the necessary labour for a constant and universal extraction of surplus-value.

The privatised control of information has fostered an apparently indefinite means of dehumanisation, estrangement, alienation, anomie, and despair. Compared to the beginning of capitalism, material conditions have improved immensely; on the other hand, its contradictory character of social production and private appropriation not only destroys a significant amount of social and material wealth during its various crises but also has become an impediment to further developments. This anachronic existence gained great accent during the period of 1914 to 1945 with the two World Wars, or the Great World War, as some would call it, and after the 1970s with the still ongoing structural crisis of capitalism. Other than some exceptions in the Global South, striving for social relations beyond the immediate dominium of capitalism, the conditions of social life are becoming increasingly more disastrous. Nonetheless, the means to recognise the existing problem and simultaneously create feasible solutions are being removed from the general social domain. The very capitalist elites no longer appear to simply cynically impose their narrative to forge and sustain their own gains; instead, their pervasive propagandistic apparatus appears to have propagandised themselves to the point that they cannot recognise reality and instead live in their own cloud-cuckoo-land, deprived of any historicity, rationality, and sense of reality. Therefore, the privatisation of knowledge fosters a novel and unprecedented degree of irrationalism to the point that social collapse seems an ever more significant possibility, if not worldwide, at least in the West. The amount of information and knowledge available does not compose in-themselves the necessary means for concrete solutions because real knowledge is only actualised as social relations through a process of social knowledge appropriation. Instead, a seemingly universal paralysis renders most people apathetic, apolitical, incapable of acting, seeking miraculous and mystical solutions, powerless to counter ongoing tendencies, regardless of never-ending imperialist wars, worldwide hunger, malnutrition, diseases, environmental destruction, their conditions of being incessantly exploited, or merely to create social bonds to reconnect to social reality and initiate an arduous process of necessary transformation. The social reappropriation of knowledge is a fundamental necessity in the struggle against barbarism. Can we still succeed?

References

Amadeo, R. (2018, July 21). Google's Iron Grip on Android: Controlling Open Source by Any Means Necessary. *Ars Technica*. https://arstechnica.com/gadgets/2018/07/googles-iron-grip-on-android-controlling-open-source-by-any-means-necessary/

Bevins, V. (2020). *The Jakarta Method: Washington's Anticommunist Crusade & The Mass Murder Program That Shaped Our World*. PublicAffairs.

Castro, A. B. de. (1979). *O Capitalismo Ainda É Aquele*. Forense-Universitária.

Drahos, P., & Braithwaite, J. (2002). *Information Feudalism: Who Owns the Knowledge Economy*. Earthscan Publications Ltd. https://doi.org/10.4324/9781315092683

Hongpei, Z. (2023, July 6). China Launches First Open-source Desktop Computer Operating System OpenKylin 1.0. *Global Times*. https://www.globaltimes.cn/page/202307/1293846.shtml

Johns, A. (2009). *Piracy: The Intellectual Property Wars from Gutenberg to Gates*. The University of Chicago Press.

Klein, N. (2008). *The Shock Doctrine: The Rise of Disaster Capitalism*. Penguin Books.

Loewenstein, A. (2017). *Disaster Capitalism: Making a killing out of Catastrophe*. Verso.

Marx, K. (1962). Das Kapital: Kritik der politischen Ökonomie: Erster Band: Buch I: Der Produktionsprozeß des Kapitals. In *MEW Band 23*. Dietz Verlag Berlin.

Schippel, H. (1989). *La Storia delle privative industriali nella Venezia del '400*. Centro Tedesco di Studi Veneziani.

Squassina, E. (2019). I privilegi librari a Venezia (1469–1545). In *Privilegi librari nell'Italia del Rinascimento*. FrancoAngeli.

Index[1]

[1] Note: Page numbers followed by 'n' refer to notes.

J. Romeiro Hermeto, *The Paradox of Intellectual Property in Capitalism*,
https://doi.org/10.1007/978-3-031-49967-8

SPRINGER NATURE

GPSR Compliance

The European Union's (EU) General Product Safety Regulation (GPSR) is a set of rules that requires consumer products to be safe and our obligations to ensure this.

If you have any concerns about our products, you can contact us on ProductSafety@springernature.com

In case Publisher is established outside the EU, the EU authorized representative is:

Springer Nature Customer Service Center GmbH
Europaplatz 3
69115 Heidelberg, Germany

FSC
www.fsc.org
MIX
Papier | Fördert
gute Waldnutzung
FSC® C083411

Kolibri 360 GmbH
Ferdinand-Jühlke-Straße 7
99095 Erfurt, Deutschland
produktsicherheit@kolibri360.de